THE NAVARRE BIBLE: STANDARD EDITION

THE CATHOLIC LETTERS

VOLUMES IN THIS SERIES
Standard Edition
NEW TESTAMENT
St Matthew's Gospel
St Mark's Gospel
St Luke's Gospel
St John's Gospel
Acts of the Apostles
Romans and Galatians
Corinthians
Captivity Letters
Thessalonians and Pastoral Letters
Hebrews
Catholic Letters
Revelation

OLD TESTAMENT
The Pentateuch
Joshua–Kings [Historical Books 1]
Chronicles–Maccabees [Historical Books 2]
The Psalms and the Song of Solomon
Wisdom Books
Major Prophets
Minor Prophets

Reader's (Omnibus) Edition
The Gospels and Acts
The Letters of St Paul
Revelation, Hebrews and Catholic Letters

Single-volume, large-format New Testament

THE NAVARRE BIBLE

The Catholic Letters

James, Peter, John, Jude

in the Revised Standard Version and New Vulgate
with a commentary by members of the
Faculty of Theology of the University of Navarre

FOUR COURTS PRESS • DUBLIN
SCEPTER PUBLISHERS • NEW YORK

Typeset by Carrigboy Typesetting Services for
FOUR COURTS PRESS LTD
7 Malpas Street, Dublin 8, Ireland
www.fourcourtspress.ie
Distributed in North America by
SCEPTER PUBLISHERS, INC.
P.O. Box 211, New York, NY 10018–0004
www.scepterpublishers.org

The translation of introductions and commentary was made by Michael Adams.

Nihil obstat: Stephen J. Greene, *censor deputatus*
Imprimi potest: Desmond, Archbishop of Dublin, 4 February 1992

A catalogue record for this title is available from the British Library.
First edition 1992; reprinted many times
Second edition (reset and repaged) 2005; reprinted 2010, 2017, 2023.

ISBN 978–1–85182–910–1

Library of Congress Cataloging-in-Publication Data [for first volume in this series]

Bible. O.T. English. Revised Standard. 1999.
    The Navarre Bible. – North American ed.
        p.   cm
    "The Books of Genesis, Exodus, Leviticus, Numbers, Deuteronomy in the Revised
        Standard Version and New Vulgate with a commentary by members of the
        Faculty of Theology of the University of Navarre."
    Includes bibliographical references.
    Contents: [1] The Pentateuch.
    ISBN 1–889334–21–9 (hardback: alk. paper)
I. Title.
    BS891.A1   1999.P75   99–23033
    221.7'7—dc21   CIP

The title "Navarre Bible" is © Four Courts Press 2003.

ACKNOWLEDGMENTS
Quotations from Vatican II documents are based on the translation in *Vatican Council II: The Conciliar and Post Conciliar Documents*, ed. A. Flannery, OP (Dublin 1981).

The New Vulgate text of the Bible can be accessed via
http://www.vatican.va.archive/bible/index.htm

Printed and bound by CPI Group (UK) Ltd, Croydon, CR0 4YY

Contents

Preface and Preliminary Notes   7

Abbreviations   9

General Introduction to the Catholic Letters   11
    Canonicity   11
    Common features   12

Introduction to the Letter of St James   13
    The author   13
    Canonicity   14
    Date of composition   15
    Immediate readership   15
    Content   16
    Doctrinal and moral questions   18

The Letter of James: English version, with notes   21

Introduction to the First Letter of St Peter   55
    St Peter the Apostle   55
    The author   57
    Immediate readership and date of composition   59
    Content   59
    Trials   60
    Baptism   61
    Other doctrinal aspects   63

The First Letter of Peter: English version, with notes   65

Introduction to the Second Letter of St Peter   93
    The author   93
    Immediate readership   94
    Links between 2 Peter and the Letter of St Jude   95
    Content   95
    The final coming of the Lord   96
    The false teachers   96
    Moral conduct   97

Contents

The Second Letter of Peter: English version, with notes   99

Introduction to the First Letter of St John   119
    Immediate readership   120
    Date of composition   121
    The reason for the letter   121
    Content   122
    Teaching   123

The First Letter of John: English version, with notes   129

Introduction to the Second and Third Letters of St John   165
    The author   165
    Special introduction to 2 John   168

The Second Letter of John: English version, with notes   169

    Special introduction to 3 John   175

The Third Letter of John: English version, with notes   177

Introduction to the Letter of St Jude   183
    The author   183
    Authenticity   184
    Canonicity   184
    Immediate readership   185
    Background and purpose   185
    Plan and content   186

The Letter of Jude: English version, with notes   187

New Vulgate Text   199

Explanatory Notes   209

Headings added to the Biblical Text   211

Sources quoted in the Commentary   213

Preface and Preliminary Notes

The Commentary

The distinguishing feature of the *Navarre Bible* is its commentary on the biblical text. Compiled by members of the Theology faculty of the University of Navarre, Pamplona, Spain, this commentary draws on writings of the Fathers, texts of the Magisterium of the Church, and works of spiritual writers, including St Josemaría Escrivá, the founder of Opus Dei; it was he who in the late 1960s entrusted the faculty at Navarre with the project of making a translation of the Bible and adding to it a commentary of the type found here.

The commentary, which is not particularly technical, is designed to explain the biblical text and to identify its main points, the message God wants to get across through the sacred writers. It also deals with doctrinal and practical matters connected with the text.

The first volume of the *Navarre Bible* (the English edition) came out in 1985—first, twelve volumes covering the New Testament; then seven volumes covering the Old Testament. Many reprints and revised editions have appeared over the past twenty years. All the various volumes are currently in print.

The Revised Standard Version

The English translation of the Bible used in the *Navarre Bible* is the Revised Standard Version (RSV) which is, as its preface states, "an authorized revision of the American Standard Version, published in 1901, which was a revision of the King James Version [the "Authorized Version"], published in 1611".

The RSV of the entire Bible was published in 1952; its Catholic edition (RSVCE) appeared in 1966. The differences between the RSV and the RSVCE New Testament texts are listed in the "Explanatory Notes" in the end-matter of this volume. Whereas the Spanish editors of what is called in English the "Navarrre Bible" made a new translation of the Bible, for the English edition the RSV has proved to be a very appropriate choice of translation. The publishers of the *Navarre Bible* wish to thank the Division of Christian Education of the National Council of the Churches of Christ in the USA for permission to use that text.

The Latin Text

This volume also carries the official Latin version of the New Testament in the *editio typica altera* of the New Vulgate (Vatican City, 1986).

Preface

The headings within the biblical text have been provided by the editors (they are not taken from the RSV). A full list of these headings, giving an overview of the New Testament, can be found at the back of the volume.

An asterisk *inside the biblical text* signals an RSVCE "Explanatory Note" at the end of the volume.

References in the biblical text indicate parallel texts in other biblical books. All these marginal references come from the *Navarre Bible* editors, not the RSV.

Abbreviations

1. BOOKS OF HOLY SCRIPTURE

Acts	Acts of the Apostles	1 Kings	1 Kings
Amos	Amos	2 Kings	2 Kings
Bar	Baruch	Lam	Lamentations
1 Chron	1 Chronicles	Lev	Leviticus
2 Chron	2 Chronicles	Lk	Luke
Col	Colossians	1 Mac	1 Maccabees
1 Cor	1 Corinthians	2 Mac	2 Maccabees
2 Cor	2 Corinthians	Mal	Malachi
Dan	Daniel	Mic	Micah
Deut	Deuteronomy	Mk	Mark
Eccles	Ecclesiastes (Qoheleth)	Mt	Matthew
Esther	Esther	Nah	Nahum
Eph	Ephesians	Neh	Nehemiah
Ex	Exodus	Num	Numbers
Ezek	Ezekiel	Obad	Obadiah
Ezra	Ezra	1 Pet	1 Peter
Gal	Galatians	2 Pet	2 Peter
Gen	Genesis	Phil	Philippians
Hab	Habakkuk	Philem	Philemon
Hag	Haggai	Ps	Psalms
Heb	Hebrews	Prov	Proverbs
Hos	Hosea	Rev	Revelation (Apocalypse)
Is	Isaiah	Rom	Romans
Jas	James	Ruth	Ruth
Jer	Jeremiah	1 Sam	1 Samuel
Jn	John	2 Sam	2 Samuel
1 Jn	1 John	Sir	Sirach (Ecclesiasticus)
2 Jn	2 John	Song	Song of Solomon
3 Jn	3 John	1 Thess	1 Thessalonians
Job	Job	2 Thess	2 Thessalonians
Joel	Joel	1 Tim	1 Timothy
Jon	Jonah	2 Tim	2 Timothy
Josh	Joshua	Tit	Titus
Jud	Judith	Wis	Wisdom
Jude	Jude	Zech	Zechariah
Judg	Judges	Zeph	Zephaniah

2. OTHER ABBREVIATIONS

ad loc.	*ad locum*, commentary on this passage	f	and following (*pl.* ff)
		ibid.	*ibidem*, in the same place
AAS	*Acta Apostolicae Sedis*	in loc.	*in locum*, commentary on this passage
Apost.	Apostolic		
can.	canon	loc.	*locum*, place or passage
chap.	chapter	par.	parallel passages
cf.	*confer*, compare	Past.	Pastoral
Const.	Constitution	RSV	Revised Standard Version
Decl.	Declaration	RSVCE	Revised Standard Version, Catholic Edition
Dz-Sch	Denzinger-Schönmetzer, *Enchiridion Biblicum* (4th edition, Naples & Rome, 1961)	SCDF	Sacred Congregation for the Doctrine of the Faith
		sess.	session
Enc.	Encyclical	v.	verse (*pl.* vv.)
Exhort.	Exhortation		

"Sources quoted in the Commentary", which appears at the end of this book, explains other abbreviations used.

General Introduction to the Catholic Letters

The canon of the books of the New Testament includes, along with the Pauline corpus (thirteen letters plus Hebrews), a group of seven letters described as the "Catholic Letters"—James; 1 and 2 Peter; 2 and 3 John; and Jude.

Apparently the reason why they are grouped like this is not because of similarities of style or doctrine, but simply to distinguish them from the Pauline corpus. The grouping is found as early as the fourth century AD[1] but they were not always put in the same place in the canon: the great early codexes—the Codex Vaticanus and the Codex Sinaiticus—put them after the Acts of the Apostles; from St Jerome onwards, they always appear in bibles just after the writings of St Paul, before the book of Revelation. Nor do they always occur in the same order within the group; often the two letters of St Peter come first,[2] although from St Jerome onwards they are usually positioned in manuscripts in the order familiar to us.

The name "catholic" was given by Origen to 1 Peter, 1 John, and Jude.[3] Later Eusebius and St Jerome extended the title to all seven. It would seem that they were described in this way because they were letters addressed to the whole Church and not just to specific churches or individuals, as in the case of St Paul's letters. The Second and Third Letters of St John do have particular addressees but they are put into the "catholic" category for the sake of convenience.[4]

CANONICITY

Some early commentators explained the title "catholic" as meaning "canonical", indicating that everyone regarded these as inspired books.[5] However, this explanation is not very convincing. Five of seven were slow to receive unanimous acceptance as canonical (this is dealt with in the introductions to the particular letters); these five are the so-called "deuterocanonical" letters—James, 2 Peter, 2 and 3 John and Jude. In his famous canon Eusebius locates all five among the disputed books (*antilegómena*) but acknowledges that most people accepted them as inspired.[6]

---

1. Cf. Eusebius of Caesarea, *Ecclesiastical History*, 3, 25, 2–3. 2. This is the case in the list of canonical books issued by the Council of Trent. 3. Cf. Eusebius, *Ecclesiastical History*, 6, 25,8. 4. Cf. ibid., 2, 23, 25; St Jerome, *On Famous Men*, 2, 4. 5. Cf. St Isidore of Seville, *Eytmology*, 6, 24. 6. Cf. *Ecclesiastical History*, 3, 25, 3.

In the West they were unanimously accepted as canonical from the fourth century onwards (this is confirmed by the provincial council of Hippo, 393, and the third and fourth councils of Carthage, 397 and 419). The Syrian Church gradually came round to accepting them and by the end of the seventh century, it is fair to say, the entire Church accepted them.

In the sixteenth century, the Protestants began to resurrect the old doubts about the canonicity of some of these letters—but for new reasons, as shall be explained in the particular introductions. This led the Council of Trent solemnly to define the witness of Tradition—that all these books have to be received "as sacred and canonical in their entirety, with all their parts, according to the text usually read in the Catholic Church".[7]

COMMON FEATURES

Each letter has a specific purpose and content of its own, and they have very few features in common. St Augustine says that they all have to do with refuting errors which were beginning to appear.[8] And all of them evidence the teaching and catechesis given to the early Christians communities. For the most part the tone is pastoral and the letters contain religious instruction and moral teaching encouraging people to lead deeply Christian lives.

---

7. Council of Trent, *De libris sacris.*   **8.** Cf. *De fide et operibus*, 14, 21.

Introduction to the Letter of St James

The Letter of St James heads up the list of "Catholic Letters". Over the course of the centuries it has not been commented on to any great extent, probably because it has to do with moral as distinct from doctrinal matters; from the sixteenth century onwards commentators focused mostly on the subject of faith and works (cf. 2:14–26). Because of the paucity of commentaries and the complexity of the letter's language (it is written in very sophisticated Greek, and the background of the language is clearly Semitic), scholars even nowadays raise questions about its authorship, date of composition, etc. However, in recent decades this letter has attracted a lot of attention due to the fact that it is a very faithful reflection of the very vital, spontaneous exposition given to the Christian message in the first communities, and because it very clearly points up the unity between the Old and New Testaments.

THE AUTHOR

At the beginning of the letter the writer introduces himself simply as "James, a servant of God and of the Lord Jesus Christ" (1:1). In the Old Testament the expression "servant of God" is applied to people like Abraham (Ps 105:42), Moses (Josh 14:7), David (Ps 89:3) or the prophets (Amos 3:7) who had a prominent mission; in the New Testament St Paul describes himself as "a servant of Jesus Christ" (cf., e.g., Rom 1:1; Phil 1:1). The rest of the letter hardly gives us any further information about the writer except that he includes himself among the teachers (3:1); that, as such, he teaches with authority (1:13ff; 3:13ff), he reproaches his readers (1:21ff; 4:13ff) and takes them to task (4:1ff) and even threatens them (5:1ff). The author of the letter then, is someone called James who is well-known to the early Christians, someone held in high regard.

The name James—*Iaaqob* in Hebrew—was very common, so it is not surprising that up to five men called James appear in the New Testament— James, the son of Zebedee, called the Greater (Mt 10:2; Lk 8:51; Acts 1:13; 12:2); James, the son of Alphaeus, also an Apostle, called the Less (Mt 10:3; Mk 3:18; Lk 6:15; Acts 1:13); James, "the Lord's brother" (Gal 1:19; cf. Mt 13:55; Mk 6:3); James, bishop of Jerusalem (Acts 12:17; 15:13; 21:18; Gal 1:19); and James, to whom the risen Jesus appeared (1 Cor 15:17). Scholars are generally agreed that the "brother of the Lord" (that is, his cousin or relative: cf. note on Mt 6:1–3) is the bishop of Jerusalem, to whom the risen Lord appeared; this reduces the number of possible Jameses to three—James the Greater, James the Less, and James, the Lord's brother and bishop of Jerusalem. The first-mentioned was martyred by Herod Agrippa around AD 44 (Acts 12:12) and it is unlikely that he could have been the author of the letter. As regards the two remaining Jameses, we cannot be sure that they were one and the same person but the likelihood is that they were: in fact, St Luke and St Paul, after the death of James the Greater, make reference only to one James, the bishop of Jerusalem and brother of the Lord (Acts 12:17; Gal 2:9, 12).

This James was a relative of Jesus, the son of one of the Marys who kept our Lady company at the foot of the cross (Mt 25:56; Jn 19:25). After St Peter went to Rome, this James stayed behind as head of the Jerusalem community (cf. Acts 12:17; 21:18ff) and as such was visited by St Paul after his conversion (cf. Gal 1:19). He was martyred around the year 62 at the instigation of the high priest Annas II.[1]

Summing up, it is fairly clear that the letter was written by James, "the Lord's brother" and bishop of Jerusalem, who was probably the same person as the James, son of Alphaeus, listed in the Gospel as an apostle (cf. Mt 10:3; Mk 3:18).

The text of the letter confirms this attribution; on the one hand, the background to the language is Semitic, the Old Testament is frequently quoted, and the Aramaic turns of phrase indicate an author of Jewish background; on the other hand, a Christian spirit clearly imbues the entire letter. Its eminently pastoral character suggests that it was written by someone who was responsible for a Christian community (as the bishop of Jerusalem was). The objection often raised that the letter is written in very good Greek (such as one would not expect someone from Palestine to use) can be explained by James' employing a secretary or amanuensis (common at the time) who had a good knowledge of Greek.

Some non-Catholic commentators assign the letter to an anonymous pre-Christian Jew of the first century BC, arguing that it was later touched up to "christianize" it; but this theory does not hold up in the light of the arguments outlined above. Nor is there any basis for the "pseudo-epigraphic theory", which argues that the letter was written around the end of the first century or beginning of the second century AD by an unknown author who credited it to James in order to reinforce its authority.

CANONICITY

Explicit references in the Fathers to the Letter of St James are to be found from the third century. However, there are earlier allusions to it, even in letters

---

1. Cf. Flavius Josephus, *Jewish Antiquites*, 20, 9, 1; Eusebius of Caesarea, *Ecclesiastical History*, 2, 23, 19–23.

of St Paul and in St Jude.[2] There are also references in writers as early as St
Clement of Rome (end of first century), St Justin (mid second century) and St
Irenaeus (second half of the second century).

The first explicit acknowledgment comes from Origen (185–255),[3] who
echoes a second-century Egyptian tradition that the letter was inspired. From
the time of Origen onwards the church of Alexandria was in no doubt about
the letter's canonicity. Eusebius of Caesarea lists it among the "disputed"
books, even though he admits that most people accepted it,[4] and he himself,
bearing witness to the Palestinian tradition, considers it canonical.

From the time of the provincial Council of Laodicea (c.360) the letter
appears in all lists of inspired books. No doubts were raised about its canonicity from then until the sixteenth century, when Luther rejected it for the
simple reason that he found its teaching at odds with his doctrine of justification. The Council of Trent, basing itself on the centuries-old tradition of
the Church, solemnly defined it to be canonical.

DATE OF COMPOSITION

There are two possible dates, depending on the relationship between St James
and St Paul in their treatment of the topic of faith and good works and who
depends on whom. Given that, in treating of this subject, the same biblical
texts are used here and in Romans and Galatians, some scholars have argued
that St James was the first to speak about it, and did so prior to the problems
solved by the Council of Jerusalem (49/50) raised their head. According to this
view, the Letter of St James is the earliest New Testament text.

However, we cannot rule out the possibility that St James was acquainted
with St Paul's Letters to the Galatians and Romans (written in 54 and 58
respectively) and that, without making mention of them, he wrote his letter to
counter mistaken conclusions some people were trying to draw from what St
Paul had said. In this case the date of composition would be around AD 60,
shortly before the author died a martyr's death.

As we have indicated, there is no sound basis for the theory that the letter
was written by a pre-Christian author, nor for the suggestion that it was written
in the second century AD, by which time all the apostles were dead.

IMMEDIATE READERSHIP

The letter is addressed to "the twelve tribes in the Dispersion" (1:1), that is,
the Jews who lived outside Palestine, among the Gentiles. Those who say that

---

2. Cf., e.g., Jas 1:1 with 1 Pet 1:1 and Jude 1; Jas 1:18 with 1 Pet 1:23; Jas 1:2–3 with 1 Pet 1:6; Jas 4:6–20
with Pet 5:5–9. **3.** Cf. *In Iesu Nave*, 7; *In Ioann. Comm.*, 19, 6. **4.** *Ecclesiastical History*, 3, 25, 3.

the letter is pre-Christian Jewish base their argument mainly on these few words; yet there are many pointers to its Christian origin, for example, the explicit references to Jesus Christ (1:1; 2:1), the allusion to the "honourable name" (2:7) and to the second coming of the Lord (5:7–8). Moreover, the letter's moral exhortations are very akin to the sayings of Jesus, particularly the Sermon on the Mount as reported by Matthew (Mt 5–7)—for example, joy in suffering (cf. 1:2, 12 and Mt 5:11ff); the poor will inherit the Kingdom (cf. 2:5 with Mt 5:3); the merciful will obtain mercy (cf. 2:13 with Mt 5:7); prohibition of oaths (cf. 5:12 with Mt 5:37); etc.

Besides, Christians also can be described as "the tribes in the Dispersion", for they are the heirs of the promises made to the Patriarchs and are pilgrims in alien lands in this life (cf. 1 Pet 1:1; 2:11; Heb 11:13); and there was even more justification for describing in this way Christians of Jewish background living outside Jerusalem.

Given that the letter was addressed originally to Jewish converts, it is easy to see why James uses expressions familiar to people of Hebrew origin—for example, "hearers of the word" (cf. 1:22–25); "assembly" (synagogue, in the Greek text: 2:2); the mention of Old Testament characters (Abraham, Rahab, Job, Elijah); the use of the title "Lord of hosts" (5:4); etc. On the other hand sins more frequent among pagans, such as idolatry, dissolute lifestyles, drunkenness, etc., are not mentioned, whereas these sins are referred to by St Paul when he addresses Christians of Gentile background (cf. 1 Cor 6:9–11; Gal 5:19–21; etc.). But, as we have already pointed out, the entire letter is imbued with Christian thinking.

As regards the circumstances which led James to write the letter, we know little other than what it tells us itself, that is, that various defects were threatening the progress of these Christian communities. Almost all the disorders denounced in the letter have to do with behaviour towards one's neighbour—grumbling (5:9), jealousy and covetousness (3:13–16; 4:1–3); evil speech (4:11f), etc., and particularly discord between rich and poor: he has some very harsh things to say on this score (cf. 2:1–13; 5:1–6), making it very clear that people must not selfishly turn their back on the disadvantaged.

CONTENT

Running right through the letter is an emphasis on the need for consistency between a Christian's faith and actions: everything a Christian does should reflect the faith he or she professes.

Naturally enough, the letter is not structured like a systematic treatise. As in the case of Jewish wisdom writing (Proverbs, Ecclesiastes and Wisdom are good examples), the letter is structured in what we might call a psychological and pedagogical manner: one thought leads off to another, using similar-sounding words, repeating the same idea more than once (as in a series of concentric circles), pressing short maxims into service, etc. This type of writing makes it easier for the listener or reader to commit its message to memory. All this undermines the theory that the letter is a composite of homilies delivered on different occasions and copied down much later. Clearly there is an underlying unity to the various counsels contained in the letter.

Accepting that the letter does not have any rigid structure, we can divide it into three sections, the second of which deals specifically with the basic teaching about consistency between the faith one professes and the works one does. The first section contains preparatory instructions and the third a series of applications of the basic principle.

1. The *first section* (1:1—2:13), which begins after the short heading and greeting (1:1), consists of a series of instructions so interlinked that it is difficult to say where one ends and the next begins: it teaches the value of suffering (1:2–12); it emphasizes that only good can come from God and therefore God never tempts man or seeks to harm him (1:13–18); accepting what comes from God means doing what he says (1:19–27) and not being a respecter of persons (2:1–13). All these teachings point to the need for there to be no discrepancy between what one receives from God and the way one puts it into practice.

2. The *second section* (2:14–26) develops the central idea: a faith which does not translate into good works is a dead faith (2:14–19). This point is made again and again, like a refrain running right through the passage; the argumentation is based mainly on the example of well-known biblical personalities (2:20–26).

3. In the *third section* (3:1—5:6) practical applications of this teaching are piled one on another and woven together. Christians are exhorted to control the tongue (3:1–12), to seek true wisdom and reject false wisdom (3:13–18), to recognize the source of disagreement (4:1–12), and to put all their trust in divine providence and not be preoccupied by their private affairs (4:13–17) or riches, for that only leads to flagrant injustice (5:1–6). In this part of the letter the sacred writer speaks with greater severity, not mincing his words, in order to make people see that actions of the kind he condemns are incompatible with the profession of the Christian faith.

4. The letter concludes with a series of pithy counsels (5:7–20): it insists on the need to keep true to the faith with patience and constancy (5:7–11); it teaches the value of prayer (5:13–18), encouraging prayer at all times; it speaks about the sacrament of the Anointing of the Sick (5:14–15); and finally it encourages Christians to have concern for one another (5:19–20).

Introduction to the Letter of St James

DOCTRINAL AND MORAL QUESTIONS

The main purpose of the epistle is a moral and ascetical one, hence the predominance of exhortations and warnings about how to cope with difficulties and temptations, about the need to be objective in one's judgment of others and to avoid backbiting etc.; about detachment from material things, and the need to be concerned about the poor and needy; the practice of prayer; the correction of those who go astray. These are the main themes of the letter.

Although it does not overtly deal with doctrinal matters, these underlie the whole letter. There are many references to God's attributes and actions: he is the Creator (1:17; 5:4; 3:9), Father (1:27; 3:10), Rewarder and Judge (4:12), merciful Saviour (2:13). Except for 1:1 and 2:1 there is no explicit mention of Jesus Christ but he is portrayed as Lord and Saviour; his second coming is alluded to (5:8) and the fact that he is Judge (5:9), and his teachings echo throughout the epistle. The Church is spoken of as a community of believers (2:2), in which teachers (3:1) and elders (5:14) have specific functions of government and of administration of the sacraments (1:18; 2:7; 5:14).

1. *The sacrament of the Anointing of the Sick*

Apart from the allusion to this sacrament in Mark 6:13, this letter is the only place in the New Testament where there is explicit mention of the Anointing of the Sick: "Is any among you sick? Let him call the elders of the church, and let them pray over him, anointing him with oil in the name of the Lord; and the prayer of faith will save the sick man, and the Lord will raise him up; and if he has committed sins, he will be forgiven" (5:14–15). As explained in the notes on this passage, these words of St James identify the elements of this sacrament: it is a sensible sign with remote matter (oil), proximate matter (anointing), form (liturgical prayer), minister (elders, that is, priests), subject (the sick Christian) and effects (curing and salvation). The Church has solemnly defined that this sacrament was instituted by Christ; and this passage of St James is referred to in Vatican II's recommendation of the sacrament: "By the sacred anointing of the sick and the prayer of the priests the whole Church commends those who are ill to the suffering and glorified Lord that he may raise them up and save them (cf. Jas 5:14–16). And indeed she exhorts them to contribute to the good of the people of God by freely uniting themselves to the passion and death of Christ (cf. Rom 8:17; Col 1:24; 2 Tim 2:11–12; 1 Pet 4:13)."[5]

2. *Faith and works*

The central teaching of the letter has to do with consistency between faith and works. In a simple and lively way, the sacred author outlines this teaching particularly in 2:14–26, a passage whose tone is reminiscent of the wisdom

---

5. Vatican II, *Lumen gentium*, 11.

books of the Old Testament, and which may well be an example of the formal religious instruction imparted to those first Christian communities. The passage begins by pointing to the absurdity of the behaviour of a person who, finding someone in need, instead of coming to his aid is content simply with giving him good advice (vv. 14–16); these lives are followed by the enunciation of a key moral principle: "So faith by itself, if it has no works, is dead" (v. 17). This teaching is supported by well chosen examples: the demons have faith but it does them no good (v. 19), whereas Abraham and Rahab, whose faith expressed itself in actions, were thereby justified (vv. 20–26).

This Catholic teaching was accepted unquestionably up to the time of the Reformation, when this text was seen as an unsurmountable obstacle for the theory of justification by faith alone; Luther was the most outspoken enemy of this letter, which he described as "an epistle of straw".

From that point onwards, in Protestant circles, the claim is made that this text was written as a correction to what St Paul says in Romans 3:20–31 and Galatians 2:16; 3:2, 5, 11. There is undoubtedly a parallel between James and those two passages: the argumentation is along the same lines, as is even the wording: both make reference to Abraham as a model of how a man is justified (Jas 2:21–25 and Rom 4:1–3), and both speak of faith, works, and justification. The following two verses show the similarly in language and apparent contradiction.

> Jas 2:24   "You see that a man is justified by works and not by faith alone."

> Rom 3:28   "We hold that a man is justified by faith apart from works of the law" (cf. Gal 2:16).

However, although the terms used are identical, the perspective is different and there is no contradiction: St Paul says that faith works through love (Gal 5:6); but in his argument with the Judaizers he denies that the works of the Old Law are necessary: it is faith that is important. St James is emphasizing above all that faith must be reflected in one's behaviour. Arguably St James is interpreting St Paul and correcting erroneous conclusions which might be drawn from a misreading of Paul.

For St James, "works" are morally correct behaviour, which must be in line with the religious faith one professes. For St Paul "works" are the legal rules of the Old Law, which no longer have validity, now that Christ has promulgated the New Law.

In this letter "justification" means moral perfection, which is attained, once grace has been conferred, by the practice of virtue, by upright conduct; it is for St Paul what is usually termed "first justification", that is, the union with God that comes with initial grace.

Clearly the two inspired authors are not contradicting one another: in both instances one needs to adhere to God ("faith" in St Paul), which includes assenting to revealed truths ("faith" in St James), which has to find expression in a coherent Christian life ("works" in St James). This consistency between faith and works is something St Paul calls for when he says that faith "works through love" (Gal 5:6; cf. 1 Thess 1:3; 2 Thess 1:11), or "he who loves his neighbour has fulfilled the law" (Rom 13:8) or when he says in connexion with the just judgment of God that "he will render to every man according to his works" (Rom 2:6).

THE LETTER OF JAMES

The Revised Standard Version, with notes

Greeting

1 Pet 1:1
Acts 12:17
Jn 7:35

1 ¹James, a servant of God and of the Lord Jesus Christ,
To the twelve tribes* in the Dispersion:
Greeting.

1. OPENING INSTRUCTIONS

The value of suffering

²Count it all joy, my brethren, when you meet various trials, ³for
you know that the testing of your faith produces steadfastness.

1 Pet 1:6

1 Pet 1:7

1:1. The author of the letter is St James, who was in charge of the Christian community of Jerusalem for a number of years (cf. Acts 12:17; 15:13; 21:19), a close relative of our Lord. As to the author being the apostle St James the Less, the son of Alphaeus, cf. the Introduction to this letter, pp. 13–14.

James introduces himself as "a servant of God and of the Lord Jesus Christ". The title of "servant of God" was given to people in the Old Testament who were outstandingly faithful to the Lord (cf. Ps 34:22), such as Moses, David, the prophets; the title applies in a special way to the Messiah, the "Servant of Yahweh" (cf. Is 42–53). In the New Testament it is applied to all Christians, particularly the apostles (cf. Acts 4:29; 16:17; Rev 1:1). At the start of their letters, St Peter, St Paul and St Jude sometimes describe themselves in this way to make the point that they are mere messengers of divine truth.

The term "Lord"—*Kyrios* in Greek—which is applied to Jesus Christ is used in the second-century BC Septuagint Greek version of the Old Testament to translate the name of Yahweh. St Paul also uses it frequently. It is an explicit profession of faith in the divinity of Jesus Christ, part of the Christian creed from the very beginning.

The letter is addressed "to the twelve tribes in the Dispersion" or Diaspora. The term *diaspora* originally meant Jews domiciled outside Palestine. Here it refers to Christians—the twelve tribes of the new, true Israel—who were to be found all over the Greco-Roman world. It is very likely that it refers particularly to Jewish converts to Christianity.

The salutation used by James—which the New Vulgate translates as "health" and the RSV gives as "greeting"—literally means "rejoice". It was the customary form of greeting in the Greek of the time. The same word is used in v. 2, perhaps to make it quite clear what kind of joy he means.

1:2–12. In these opening verses, St James points out how Christians should behave in the face of trials: they should accept them with joy (vv. 2–4); if they find it difficult to see why they are experiencing difficulties, they should ask God to give them the necessary wisdom (vv. 5–8); the poor and well-to-do should have the same attitude to things (vv. 9–11); finally, he reminds them that the reward God promises to those who endure trials is blessedness (v. 12). The whole passage clearly reflects the Beatitudes of the Sermon on the Mount (cf. Mt 5:1–12).

The problem of the suffering experienced by the righteous in contrast with the prosperity of the impious in this life is one often dealt with in the Old

Mt 5:48
Rom 5:3

Prov 2:3–6
Mt 7:7

Mt 21:21

⁴And let steadfastness have its full effect, that you may be perfect and complete, lacking in nothing.

⁵If any of you lacks wisdom, let him ask God, who gives to all men generously and without reproaching, and it will be given him. ⁶But let him ask in faith, with no doubting, for he who doubts is like

---

Testament, particularly in the Psalms and in the book of Job. But it was not fully and finally solved until the coming of Jesus Christ, who by his teaching and his life revealed the redemptive value of suffering, and the great reward which heaven holds. "It is through Christ and in Christ that light is thrown on the riddle of suffering and death which, apart from his Gospel, overwhelms us" (Vatican II, *Gaudium et spes*, 22).

Human suffering has a redemptive value when borne in union with Christ: "The Gospel of suffering", Pope John Paul II says, "is being written unceasingly, and it speaks unceasingly with the words of this strange paradox: the springs of divine power gush forth precisely in the midst of human weakness. Those who share in the sufferings of Christ preserve in their own sufferings a very special *particle of the infinite treasure* of the world's Redemption, and can share this treasure with others" (*Salvifici doloris*, 27).

1:2–4. The "trials" referred to here do not seem to be persecutions, but rather everyday adversity—perhaps poverty especially (cf. 1:9; 2:5–7)—which tests the Christian's faith: for this reason the word is sometimes translated as "temptations". These trials act as a test of perseverance in the pursuit of good, and help the soul to grow in patience, a much needed virtue: "There is nothing more pleasing to God", St Alphonsus comments, "than to see a soul who patiently and serenely bears whatever crosses it is sent; this is how love is made, by putting

lover and loved one on the same level [...]. A soul who loves Jesus Christ desires to be treated the way Christ was treated—desires to be poor, despised and humiliated" (*The Love of Jesus Christ*, chap. 5).

Patience, steadfastness, is quite different from mere passive endurance of suffering; it comes from the virtue of fortitude and leads one to accept suffering as something sent by God. It is grounded on hope (cf. 1 Thess 1:3) and on faith put to the test (Jas 1:3); it is very fruitful (cf. Lk 8:15), particularly in terms of Christian joy (cf. Acts 5:41), and implies sustained effort to the point of perfection.

1:5–8. The wisdom that St James refers to views everything in the light of Christ crucified—the wisdom of the cross in the phrase of St Paul (cf. 1 Cor 1:18ff), which is the only type of insight that enables one to be joyful in the midst of adversity and suffering, because it allows one to see these things as an opportunity to share in our Lord's suffering. When we find it difficult to view things in this light, we need to ask God to give us wisdom.

Our prayer for wisdom should be a prayer full of faith: "Whatever you ask for in prayer, you will receive, if you have faith" (Mt 21:22). The *St Pius V Catechism* (4, 7, 3) reminds us that "believe, we must, both in order to pray, and that we be not wanting in that faith which renders prayer fruitful. For it is faith that leads to prayer, and it is prayer that, by removing all doubts, gives strength and firmness to faith. This is the

a wave of the sea that is driven and tossed by the wind. [7,8]For that person must not suppose that a double-minded man, unstable in all his ways, will receive anything from the Lord.

[9]Let the lowly brother boast in his exaltation, [10]and the rich in his humiliation, because like the flower of the grass he will pass away. [11]For the sun rises with its scorching heat and withers the grass; its flower falls, and its beauty perishes. So will the rich man fade away in the midst of his pursuits.

Jas 2:5
Is 40:6
1 Tim 6:17
Is 40:7

---

meaning of the exhortation of St Ignatius to those who approach God in prayer: 'Be not of doubtful mind in prayer; blessed is he who hath not doubted' (*Ep. X ad Heronem*). Therefore, to obtain from God what we ask, faith and an assured confidence are of first importance, according to the admonition of St James: 'Let him ask in faith, with no doubting' (Jas 1:6)."

1:5. "Who gives to all men generously and without reproaching": God always listens to our requests, and he answers them without humiliating us, without reminding us of our unworthiness. This should help us address the Lord with complete confidence, not being inhibited by our shortcomings and sins. "You are so conscious of your misery", St Josemaría Escrivá says, "that you acknowledge yourself unworthy to be heard by God. But, what about the merits of Mary? And the wounds of your Lord? And ... are you not a son of God? Besides, he listens to you '*quoniam bonus ..., quoniam in saeculum misericordia ejus*: because he is good, because his mercy endures for ever'" (*The Way*, 93).

1:7–8. "A double-minded man": an indecisive soul who is unsure whether to trust in the efficacy of prayer or not. St Bede comments: "A double-minded person is one who kneels down to ask God for things and beseeches him to grant them, and yet feels so accused by his con-

science that he distrusts his ability to pray. A double-minded person is also one who, when he does good deeds, looks for external approval rather than interior reward. The wise man is right when he says, 'Woe to the sinner who walks along two ways!' (Sir 2:12) [...] People of this type are inconstant in all their ways, for they are very easily overpowered by adverse circumstances and entrapped by favourable ones, with the result that they stray from the true path" (*Super Iac. expositio*, ad loc.).

1:9–11. Apparently poverty was one of the hardest trials these Christians were experiencing. The Semitic mind was fond of expressing itself in terms of contrasts, and this may make it difficult for us to grasp the full thrust of St James' maxims; to do so we need to draw on our general knowledge of Christian doctrine. God and the Church have a predilection for the poor, and Christ describes the poor as blessed (cf. Mt 5:3 and par.): this teaching applies in the first instance to those who experience material need, but material need is a symbol of the truly poor, that is, those who, independently of whether they have many or few material possessions, realize that they are in dire need of God (cf. note on Lk 6:24). In principle, it may be easier for a materially poor person to feel in need of God, whereas someone who is well off needs to be detached from possessions in order to trust fully in God.

Dan 12:2
1 Cor 9:25
1 Pet 5:4
¹²Blessed is the man who endures trial, for when he has stood the test he will receive the crown of life which God has promised to those who love him.

The source of temptation

Sir 15:11–20
¹³Let no one say when he is tempted, "I am tempted by God"; for God cannot be tempted with evil and he himself tempts no one; ¹⁴but

The sacred writer does not require people who have possessions to give them up: what they have to do is to realize that material possessions are transitory, impermanent things to be used in the service of others and of society, and not just for oneself.

The impermanence of earthly possessions—indicated here by the simile of the flower of the grass (cf. Is 40:6–8)—is an idea which occurs frequently in Holy Scripture (cf., e.g., Job 27:13–23; Ps 49:17–20; Mt 6:19f; Lk 12:16–21).

1:12. These words, which expand on the idea contained in vv. 2–4, echo our Lord's own words: "Blessed are you when men revile you and persecute you and utter all kinds of evil against you falsely on my account. Rejoice and be glad, for your reward is great in heaven" (Mt 5:11–12). The simile of the crown— a mark of victory and kingship—is used to convey the idea of definitive triumph with Christ: the Lord will appear crowned in glory (Rev 14:14); the Woman of the Apocalypse, symbolizing the Church and the Blessed Virgin, is also described as crowned (cf. Rev 12:1); and this reward is promised to those who stay true to God in this life (cf. Rev 2:10; 3:11). It is also to be found in other New Testament passages to convey the idea of the ultimate reward of heaven (cf. 1 Cor 9:25; 2 Tim 4:8; 1 Pet 5:4).

This means that Christians should not be depressed or cowed by the difficulties which God permits them to experience;

on the contrary, they should see them as a series of tests which with God's help they should surmount in order to receive the reward of heaven. "The Lord does not allow his followers to experience these trials and temptations unless it be for their greater good," St John of Avila comments. "[…] He disposed things in this way: endurance in adversity and struggle against temptation prove who his friends are. For the mark of a true friend is not that he keeps you company when times are good, but that he stands by you in times of trial […]. Companions in adversity and later in the Kingdom, you should strive to fight manfully when you meet opposition that would separate you from God, for He is your help here on earth and your reward in heaven" (*Audi, filia*, 29).

1:13–18. These verses identify the source of the temptations man experiences: they cannot come from God but are, rather, the effect of human concupiscence (vv. 16–18).

Sometimes temptation means putting a person's faithfulness to the test; in this sense it can be said that God "tempts" certain people, as happened in the case of Abraham (cf. Gen 22:1ff). However, here the reference is to temptation in the strict sense of incitement to sin: God never tempts anyone in this way, he never encourages a person to do evil (cf. Sir 15:11–20). Therefore, we cannot attribute to God our inclination to sin, nor can it be argued that by endowing us with

each person is tempted when he is lured and enticed by his own desire. ¹⁵Then desire when it has conceived gives birth to sin; and sin when it is full-grown brings forth death.

¹⁶Do not be deceived, my beloved brethren. ¹⁷Every good endowment and every perfect gift is from above, coming down from the Father of lights with whom there is no variation or shadow due to change.^a ¹⁸Of his own will he brought us forth by the word of truth that we should be a kind of first fruits of his creatures.

> Rom 7:7–8
> Rom 7:10
> Mt 7:11
> Jn 3:3
> Jas 3:15–17
> 1 Jn 1:5
> Jn 1:13
> 1 Pet 1:23
> Rev 14:4

freedom he is the cause of our sin. On the contrary, the natural and supernatural gifts we have received are resources which help us act in a morally good way.

1:14–15. St James' teaching is that the source of temptation is to be found in our own passions. Elsewhere he says that the world (cf. 1:27; 4:4) and the devil (4:7) are causes of temptation; but to actually commit sin the complicity of one's own evil inclinations is always necessary.

Concupiscence ("desire"), here as elsewhere in the New Testament (cf., e.g., Rom 1:24; 7:7ff; 1 Jn 2:16), means all the disordered passions and appetites which, as a result of original sin, have a place in men's hearts. Concupiscence as such is not a sin; but rather, according to the Council of Trent, "since it is left to provide a trial, it has no power to injure those who do not consent and who, by the grace of Jesus Christ, manfully resist"; and if it is sometimes called sin (cf. Rom 6:12ff) it is "only because it is from sin and inclines to sin" (*De peccato originali*, 5).

Using the simile of generation St James describes the course of sin from the stage of temptation to that of the death of the soul. When one gives in to the seduction of concupiscence sin is committed; this in turn leads to spiritual death, to the soul's losing the life of grace. This is the opposite process to the one described earlier (cf. vv. 2–12), which

begins with trials (temptations in the broad sense: cf. note on 1:2–4) and ends up in heaven; whereas in this passage, the process also begins with temptation but because of sin ends up with the death of the soul. John Paul II describes the process as follows: "Man also knows, through painful experience, that by a conscious and free act of his will he can change course and go in a direction opposed to God's will, separating himself from God (*aversio a Deo*), rejecting loving communion with him, detaching himself from the life-principle which God is, and consequently choosing *death*" (*Reconciliatio et paenitentia*, 17).

1:16–18. "The Father of lights": a reference to God as Creator of the heavenly bodies (cf. Gen 1:14ff; Ps 136:7–9) and, in the symbolism of light, as the source of all good things, material and, especially, spiritual. Unlike heavenly bodies, which change position and cast shadows, there is no variation or shadow in God: no evil can be attributed to him (cf. v. 13), but only good things.

"First fruits of his creatures": Christians, who have been recreated by God by "the word of truth" (the Gospel) already constitute the beginning of the new heaven and the new earth (cf. Rev 21:1) and are a sign of hope for all mankind and for the whole of Creation (cf. Rom 9:19–23).

---

a. Other ancient authorities read *variation due to a shadow of turning*

Doers of the word, not hearers only

Eccles 7:9
Sir 5:11

[19]Know this, my beloved brethren. Let every man be quick to hear, slow to speak, slow to anger, [20]for the anger of man does not work the righteousness of God. [21]Therefore put away all filthiness and rank growth of wickedness and receive with meekness the implanted word, which is able to save your souls.

Rom 2:13
1 Jn 3:18

[22]But be doers of the word, and not hearers only, deceiving yourselves.* [23]For if any one is a hearer of the word and not a

---

1:19–27. In the previous verse the sacred writer referred to the effectiveness of "the word of truth". Now he makes the point that although the Gospel has this effectiveness, it is not enough just to hear it: we need to listen to it with docility (vv. 19–21) and put it into practice (vv. 22–27). Further on he will emphasize this connexion between faith and works (cf. 2:14–26).

1:19–20. These counsels occur often in the wisdom books of the Old Testament (cf., e.g., Prov 1:5; 10:19; Sir 5:12–13; 20:5–8). To put doctrine into practice one needs to listen to it with a good disposition (v. 21). The letter will have more to say about prudence in speech (cf. 1:26; and especially 3:1ff).

"The anger of man does not work the righteousness of God": a Hebrew expression meaning that someone who gives way to anger is not acting justly in God's eyes.

Anger is one of the "capital" sins (one of the "seven deadly sins"), capital because they lead to many other sins; anger leads particularly to the evil desire for vengeance. Speaking of the effects of anger St Gregory the Great explains that it clouds one's judgment when making decisions, makes it difficult to get on with others, causes discord and makes it difficult to see where the truth lies. Moreover, "it deprives one of righteousness, as it is written, 'The anger of man does not work the righteousness of God'

(Jas 1:20) because when one's mind is not at peace, one's critical faculty is impaired and one judges to be right whatever one's anger suggests" (*Moralia*, 5, 45). This sin is avoided by the practice of the virtue of patience, of which St James spoke a few verses earlier (cf. 1:2–4, 12; also 5:7–11).

1:21. "First he calls", St Bede comments, "for the cleansing of mind and body from vice, so that those who receive the word of salvation can live in a worthy manner. A person who does not first turn his back on evil cannot do good" (*Super Iac. expositio,* ad loc.).

To listen docilely to the word of God one needs to try to keep evil inclinations at bay. Otherwise, pride—deceiving itself with all sorts of false reasons—rebels against the word of God (which it sees as a continuous reproach for a habit of sin it is unwilling to give up).

1:22–25. Holy Scripture frequently exhorts us to put the word of God into practice: "Everyone who hears these words of mine and does not do them will be like a man who built his house upon the sand" (Mt 7:26; cf., e.g., Ezek 33:10–11; Mt 12:50; Rom 2:13; Jas 2:14–26).

The comparison of the man looking in the mirror is a very good one: the word of God is frustrated unless it leads to examination of conscience and a firm resolution to mend one's ways. Those who are doers of the word will be "blessed";

doer, he is like a man who observes his natural face in a mirror; ²⁴for he observes himself and goes away and at once forgets what he was like. ²⁵But he who looks into the perfect law, the law of liberty, and perseveres, being no hearer that forgets but a doer that acts, he shall be blessed in his doing.

²⁶If any one thinks he is religious, and does not bridle his tongue but deceives his heart, this man's religion is vain.

Ps 19:8
Jn 13:17
Rom 8:2

Ps 34:14
Jas 3:2

---

our Lord says the same thing when he describes as blessed those who "hear the word of God and keep it" (Lk 11:28).

St James' counsels in this passage are a clear call for the consistency a Christian must seek at all times. Pope John Paul II comments: "These are very serious, very severe, statements; a Christian should always be genuine, should never be content with words alone. The mission he has received is a delicate one: he should be leaven in society, light of the world, salt of the earth. As time goes by, the Christian becomes more and more aware of his commitment, and the difficulties it entails: he discovers he has to swim against the tide, he has to bear witness to truths which are absolute, yet invisible; he has to lose his earthly life in order to gain eternity; he needs to feel responsible not just for himself but also for his neighbour—for whom he should light the way, and edify and save. However, he realizes that he is not alone in all this [...]. The Christian knows that not only did Jesus Christ, the Word of God, become man to reveal saving truth and redeem mankind; he has also chosen to stay with us on earth, mysteriously renewing the sacrifice of the Cross by means of the Eucharist and becoming spiritual food for the soul and accompanying it on its journey through life" (*Homily*, 1 September 1979).

1:25. "The perfect law, the law of liberty": that is, the good news brought by Christ, who has made us children of God (cf. Jn 1:12; 1 Jn 3:1ff) and set us free from every kind of servitude, both that of the Old Law (cf., e.g., Gal 2:4 and 4:21ff and notes on same) and subjection to the devil, to sin and to death.

It can also be regarded as a law of freedom because when man obeys it he is expressing his freedom to the fullest degree (cf. Jn 8:31ff), and he is happy in this life and will be blessed in the next (cf., e.g., Ps 1:1ff; 119:1ff). Thus, when a person sins and turns his back on this law, he becomes not a free man but a slave: "Such a person may show that he has acted according to his preferences," St Josemaría Escrivá explains, "but he does not speak with the voice of true freedom, because he has become the slave of his decision and he has decided for the worst, for the absence of God, where there is no freedom to be found.

"I tell you once again: I accept no slavery other than that of God's love. This is because, as I have told you on other occasions, religion is the greatest rebellion of men, who refuse to live like animals, who are dissatisfied and restless until they know their Creator and are on intimate terms with him. I want you to be rebels, free and unfettered, because I want you—it is Christ who wants us!—to be children of God. Slavery or divine sonship, this is the dilemma we face. Children of God or slaves to pride, to sensuality, to the fretful selfishness which seems to afflict so many souls" (*Friends of God*, 37–38).

1:26–27. St James now gives some examples of what doing "the word of truth"

²⁷Religion that is pure and undefiled before God and the Father is this: to visit orphans and widows in their affliction, and to keep oneself unstained from the world.

Impartiality

2 ¹My brethren, show no partiality as you hold the faith of our Lord Jesus Christ, the Lord of glory. ²For if a man with gold

1 Cor 2:8

(v. 18), that is, the Gospel, means—controlling one's tongue, being charitable and not letting oneself be stained by the world.

The Old Testament often refers to widows and orphans as deserving of special attention (cf. Ps 68:5; 146:9; Deut 27:19), and the first Christians made arrangements for the care of widows in the early communities (cf. Acts 6:1ff; 9:39; 1 Tim 5:3ff). Concern for widows and orphans is included in the works of mercy ("by which the temporal or spiritual wants of our neighbour are relieved": *St Pius X Catechism*, 943), which our Lord will take into account at the Last Judgment (cf. Mt 25:31–46).

"World" here has the pejorative meaning of "enemy of God and of Christians" (cf. also 4:4; and other passages of Scripture, e.g., Jn 1:10; 7:7; 16:8–11; Eph 2:2; 2 Pet 2:20); one needs to be constantly on the alert to avoid contamination. On other meanings of "world" in the Bible, see the note on John 17:14–16.

"God and the Father": this is the literal meaning of the Greek. In New Testament Greek the term "God" when preceded by the definite article normally means not the divine nature but the person of the Father. In this case by adding the words "and the Father" St James does not mean another, distinct, divine person; he is simply making explicit the meaning of the term "the God". It could also be translated by the paraphrase "before him who is God and Father".

2:1–13. Apparently some of the Christians to whom this letter was addressed were guilty of discriminating against people on the grounds of social standing—a clear instance of inconsistency between faith and actions, a key theme James has already touched on (cf. 1:19–27) and will develop later (cf. 2:14–26). He may well be taking an example from something that actually happened (vv. 1–4) to make the very vigorous point that discrimination is opposed to the Gospel (vv. 5–7) as indeed to the Law (vv. 8–11); and he makes it plain that this type of behaviour will be severely punished by God when he comes to judge (vv. 12–13).

2:1–4. God "is not partial and takes no bribe" (Deut 10:17). Discrimination among people is often condemned in the Old Testament—in the Law as well as in the Prophets and the Wisdom books (cf., e.g., Lev 19:15; Is 5:23; Mic 3:9–11; Ps 82:2–4). In the Gospel even our Lord's enemies admit that he is impartial and does not make unfair distinctions (cf. Mt 22:16).

In line with this teaching, the Church takes issue with every form of discrimination. "All men are endowed with a rational soul and are created in God's image; they have the same nature and origin and, being redeemed by Christ, they enjoy the same divine calling and destiny; there is here a basic equality between men and it must be given ever greater recognition. Undoubtedly not all men are alike as regards physical capacity

rings and in fine clothing comes into your assembly, and a poor man in shabby clothing also comes in, [3]and you pay attention to the one who wears the fine clothing and say, "Have a seat here, please," while you say to the poor man, "Stand there," or, "Sit at my feet," [4]have you not made distinctions among yourselves, and become judges with evil thoughts? [5]Listen, my beloved brethren. Has not God chosen those who are poor in the world to be rich in faith and heirs of the kingdom which he has promised to those who love him? [6]But you have dishonoured the poor man. Is it not the rich who

1 Cor 1:26
Rev 2:9

---

and intellectual and moral powers. But forms of social or cultural discrimination in basic personal rights on the grounds of sex, race, colour, social conditions, language or religion, must be curbed and eradicated as incompatible with God's design" (*Gaudium et spes*, 29).

2:1. "The faith of our Lord Jesus Christ, the Lord of glory": literally "the faith of our Lord Jesus Christ of glory." This phrase can be interpreted in slightly different ways depending on how one understands "of glory". The most likely interpretation is that this is an instance of a Semitic genitive used in place of the adjective "glorious" or "glorified"; in which case St James is referring to Jesus Christ who, after his ascension and resurrection, enjoys, also in his capacity as man, the highest honour and glory.

The RSV takes up the idea found in 1 Corinthians 2:8 where St Paul calls Christ "the Lord of glory": since in the Old Testament "glory" was the splendour of the majesty of Yahweh (cf. Ex 24:16), by applying this divine attribute to Christ his divinity is being explicitly asserted. If this is the correct translation, it may be a form of words taken from early Christian liturgy.

Some translate it in another way which puts even greater stress on Christ's divinity: "The faith of the glory [that is, the divinity] of our Lord Jesus Christ."

All these translations are compatible with one another and complementary to one another.

2:5–7. Many of the people to whom the letter was written must have been quite poor (cf. note on 1:2–4; 1 Cor 1:26–29). St James reminds them that God wants to make them rich in faith and heirs of the Kingdom of heaven. Jesus in fact had given as a sign of his messiahship the fact that the Gospel is proclaimed to the poor (cf. Mt 11:5; Lk 7:22) and he also taught that "Blessed are the poor in spirit, for theirs is the kingdom of heaven" (Mt 5:3). "Christ was sent by the Father 'to preach good news to the poor … to heal the contrite of heart' (Lk 4:18), 'to seek and to save the lost' (Lk 19:10). Similarly, the Church encompasses with her love all those who are afflicted by human misery and she recognizes in those who are poor and who suffer, the image of her poor and suffering founder. She does all in her power to relieve their need and in them she strives to serve Christ" (Vatican II, *Lumen gentium*, 8).

Of the rich, on the other hand, the apostle speaks with unusual harshness. As elsewhere in Scripture, those who deserve such severe condemnation are people who are bent on building up their possessions as if ownership were the only purpose in life, not minding what means they used, and oppressing and ill-treating the poor (cf. note on Lk 6:24).

oppress you, is it not they who drag you into court? [7]Is it not they who blaspheme that honourable name which was invoked over you?*

Lev 19:18
Mt 22:39
Mk 12:31

[8]If you really fulfil the royal law, according to the scripture, "You shall love your neighbour as yourself," you do well. [9]But if

Mt 5:19
Gal 3:10

you show partiality, you commit sin, and are convicted by the law as transgressors. [10]For whoever keeps the whole law but fails in one point has become guilty of all of it.* [11]For he who said, "Do

---

Behaviour of this type is so serious that it amounts to "blaspheming that honourable name by which you are called" (v. 7)—blasphemy by scandalous action rather than by words. This "name" can mean both the name "Jesus"—called down on them at Baptism—and that of "Christian", a name already being given to those first followers of the Master (cf. Acts 11:26).

What St James says here can in no sense be used to justify the "class struggle" which some materialistic doctrines propose. The Magisterium of the Church has often pointed out that the application of Christian principles should make for harmony and concord between the various groups in society (cf. Leo XIII, *Rerum novarum*, 14). James' words certainly do urge everyone to make a real effort to promote the human dignity of all: "The evil inequities and oppression of every kind which afflict millions of men and women today openly contradict Christ's Gospel and cannot leave the conscience of any Christian indifferent" (SCDF, *Libertatis conscientia*, 57).

2:8–11. The Apostle extends his argument against discrimination, recalling what is said in the Old Testament (with which his original readers would have been familiar, since many of them were Jewish converts to Christianity). As we have pointed out previously (cf. note on 2:1–4) all unjust discrimination is condemned in the Old Testament.

2:8. "The royal law" is spelled out in the book of Leviticus (19:18). St James calls it this perhaps because, in addition to commanding love of God above all things, it is the basis and root of all the other commandments (cf. Mt 22:34–40).

Jesus corrected narrow interpretations of that law of charity (cf. Mt 5:43–48; Lk 10:25–37) and formulated the "new commandment" at the Last Supper: "that you love one another, even as I have loved you, that you also love one another" (Jn 13:34). In proposing this new standard ("as I have loved you") our Lord gives new content and meaning to the precept of brotherly love. This commandment is the law of the new people of God, the Church (cf. *Lumen gentium*, 9).

2:10–11. Each and every commandment of the Law of God is an expression of his will. Therefore, any sin—even if it is against only one precept—is always an offence against God. And if the sin is a grave sin, it destroys the virtue of charity and the supernatural life of grace.

When explaining this point, St Augustine reminds us that charity is the fullness of the law (cf. Rom 13:9f); the Law and the Prophets are grounded on charity in its two dimensions of love of God and love of neighbour (cf. Mt 22:34–40).

"And no one loves his neighbour," he goes on, "unless he loves God and tries his best to get that neighbour (whom he loves as himself) to love God too. If he

not commit adultery," said also, "Do not kill." If you do not commit adultery but do kill, you have become a transgressor of the law. [12]So speak and so act as those who are to be judged under the law of liberty. [13]For judgment is without mercy to one who has shown no mercy; yet mercy triumphs over judgment.

Deut 5:17–18
Ex 20:13–14

Jas 1:25

Mt 5:7; 18:29, 34; 25:45f

2. FAITH AND GOOD WORKS

Faith without good works is dead

[14]What does it profit, my brethren, if a man says he has faith but has not works? Can his faith save him?* [15]If a brother or sister is

Mt 7:21; 21:29

---

does not love God, then he does not love himself, nor does he love his neighbour. That is why whoever would keep the whole law but fails in one point has become guilty of all of it, for he has acted against charity, on which the whole law depends. One becomes guilty of all the commandments when one sins against that (virtue) from which they all derive" (*Letter*, 167, 5, 16).

2:12. He again refers to the "law of liberty". Earlier (cf. 1:25 and note) he meant the new law brought by Jesus Christ; now the expression is used to mean the law of charity, on which we will be judged at the Last Day (cf. Mt 25:31–46 and notes).

2:13. Neglect and disdain for the poor implies acting without mercy, and anyone who acts like that will be judged without mercy. These words are a direct echo of what our Lord says: "Blessed are the merciful, for they shall obtain mercy" (Mt 5:7), and "With the judgment you pronounce you will be judged, and the measure you give will be the measure you get" (Mt 7:2).

Mercy "triumphs over [condemnatory] judgment": anyone who practises mercy will be confident and even happy

to face God's judgment because he knows that God will show him mercy.

Commenting on this verse, St Augustine says: "When the just King sits in judgment, who will claim to be pure in heart? Who will boast of being free from sin? What hope could there be if mercy did not prevail over judgment? But that mercy will be applied to those who are themselves merciful" (*Letter*, 167, 6, 20).

2:14–26. This passage forms the core of the letter. The sapiential method (often used in the Old Testament) and pedagogical style of the passage help to engrave the message on the readers' minds: unless faith is accompanied by works, it is barren, dead. This basic message, with different variances, is stated up to five times (vv. 14, 17, 18, 20, 26), in a cyclical, repetitive way.

The initial rhetorical question (v. 14) and the simple, vivid example of a person who is content with giving good advice to someone in urgent need of the bare essentials (vv. 15–16), catch the disciples' attention and predispose them to accept the core message, which is couched in the form of a sapiential maxim (v. 17).

The narrative retains its conversational tone, with a series of questions; we are given three examples of faith: firstly

1 Jn 3:17 ill-clad and in lack of daily food, ¹⁶and one of you says to them, "Go in peace, be warmed and filled," without giving them the things needed for the body, what does it profit? ¹⁷So faith by itself, if it has no works, is dead.

(a negative example), the faith of demons, which is of no avail (vv. 18–19); contrasting with this, the faith of Abraham, the model and father of believers (vv. 20–23); and finally, the faith of a sinner whose actions won her salvation, Rahab the prostitute (vv. 24–25). The last sentence once again repeats the essential idea: "faith apart from works is dead" (v. 26).

2:14. This teaching is perfectly in line with that of the Master: "Not every one who says to me, 'Lord, Lord', shall enter the kingdom of heaven, but he who does the will of my Father who is in heaven" (Mt 7:21).

A faith without deeds cannot obtain salvation: "Even though incorporated into the Church, one who does not however persevere in charity is not saved. He remains indeed in the bosom of the Church, but 'in body' not 'in heart'. All children of the Church should nevertheless remember that their exalted condition results not from their own merits but from the grace of Christ. If they fail to respond in thought, word, and deed to that grace, not only shall they not be saved, but they shall be the more severely judged" (Vatican II, *Lumen gentium*, 14).

In the Christian life, therefore, there needs to be complete consistency between the faith we profess and the deeds we do. "Unity of life", one of the key features of the spirituality of Opus Dei, tries to counter the danger of people leading a double life, "on the one hand, an inner life, a life related to God; and on the other, as something separate and distinct, their professional, social and family lives, made up of small earthly realities […].

There is only one life, made of flesh and spirit. And it is that life which has to become, in both body and soul, holy and filled with God: we discover the invisible God in the most visible and material things" (St Josemaría Escrivá, *In Love with the Church*, 52).

2:15–16. This very graphic example is similar to that in the First Letter of St John: "If any one has the world's goods and sees his brother in need, yet closes his heart against him, how does God's love abide in him?" (1 Jn 3:17); and the conclusion is also along the same lines: "Little children, let us not love in word or speech but in deed and in truth" (1 Jn 3:18). St Paul gives the same teaching: "the kingdom of God does not consist in talk but in power" (1 Cor 4:20). Actions, works, measure the genuineness of the Christian life; they show whether our faith and charity are real.

Almsgiving, for example, so often praised and recommended in Scripture (cf., e.g., Deut 15:11; Tob 4:7–11; Lk 12:33; Acts 9:36; 2 Cor 8:9), is very often a duty. Christ "will count a kindness done or refused to the poor as done or refused to himself […]. Whoever has received from the divine bounty a large share of temporal blessings whether they be external or material, or gifts of the mind, has received them for the purpose of using them for the perfecting of his own nature, and, at the same time, that he may employ them, as the steward of God's providence, for the benefit of others" (Leo XIII, *Rerum novarum*, 24).

2:17. As well as involving firm adherence to revealed truth, faith must influence a

[18]But some one will say, "You have faith and I have works." Gal 5:6 Show me your faith apart from your works, and I by my works will show you my faith. [19]You believe that God is one; you do well. Even the demons believe—and shudder.

Examples from the Bible

[20]Do you want to be shown, you shallow man, that faith apart from Gen 22:9 works is barren? [21]Was not Abraham our father justified by works, Heb 11:17

Christian's ordinary life and be a standard against which he measures his conduct When one's works are not in accordance with one's beliefs, then one's faith is dead.

Christian teaching also describes as "dead faith" the faith of a person in mortal sin: because he is not in the grace of God he does not have charity, which is as it were the soul of all the other virtues. "Faith without hope and charity neither perfectly unites a man with Christ nor makes him a living member of his body. Therefore it is said most truly that 'faith apart from works is dead' (Jas 2:17ff) and useless" (Council of Trent, *De iustificatione*, 7).

2:18. The apostle makes it crystal clear that faith without works makes no sense at all. "The truth of faith includes not only inner belief, but also outward profession, which is expressed not only by declaration of one's belief, but also by the actions by which a person shows that he has faith" (St Thomas, *Summa theologiae*, 2–2, 124, 5).

2:19. St James goes as far as to compare a faith without works with the kind of faith devils have, for they do believe: they are forced to believe by the evidence of the signs (miracles and prophecies, for example) which support Christian teaching (cf. *Summa theologiae*, 2–2, 5, 2). However, that faith is not saving faith; on the contrary, it causes them to cringe by

reminding them of divine justice and eternal punishment.

Commenting on this verse, St Bede says that it is one thing to believe God, another thing to believe in God, and another to believe "towards" God (*credere in illum*). "Believing him is believing that what he says is true. Believing in him is believing that he is God. Believing 'towards' him is loving him. Many people, even bad people, believe that God tells the truth; they believe it is the truth and they do not want to, are too lazy to, follow the way truth points. Believing that he is God is something the devils are able to do. But believing and tending towards him is true only of those who love God, who are Christians not in name only but whose actions and lives prove them to be so. For without love faith is of no avail. With love, it is the faith of a Christian; without love, it is the faith of the devil" (*Super Iac. expositio*, ad loc.).

2:20–26. The original addressees of the letter (Christians of Jewish background steeped in Scripture) would have been very familiar with the two examples from the Old Testament (Abraham and Rahab).

The patriarch Abraham is a model of faith (cf. especially Heb 11:8ff). St James highlights the fact that his faith was manifested in deeds (v. 22), so much so that he was ready to sacrifice his own son when God, to test him, asked him to do so (cf. Gen 22:1ff). The text of Genesis 15:6 quoted here (v. 23) is also used by

when he offered his son Isaac upon the altar? ²²You see that faith
was active along with his works, and faith was completed by
works, ²³and the scripture was fulfilled which says, "Abraham
believed God, and it was reckoned to him as righteousness"; and
he was called the friend of God. ²⁴You see that a man is justified by
works and not by faith alone. ²⁵And in the same way was not also

Gen 15:6
Rom 4:3
Is 41:8
2 Chron 20:7
Jn 8:39

St Paul in his polemic against the
Judaizers, to show that "first
justification" comes from faith and not
from works of the Mosaic Law (cf. Rom
4:1–25; Gal 3:6–9); that is, Abraham was
justified from the very moment he
believed in God; his works would not
have had any value without that direct
reference to God. In Abraham, as in
every Christian who acts consistently,
faith and works totally imbue each
another: works show forth faith, and faith
inspires and performs works (vv. 22, 24).

The story of Rahab (v. 25) is told in
the book of Joshua (2:1–21; 6:17–25):
this woman, who was living among the
Canaanites, saved the lives of two
Israelite spies whom Joshua had sent into
Jericho, and for this reason she and her
family were saved when the Israelites
took the city. Her actions showed her
faith (cf. Josh 2:9–14; Heb 11:31), and
led not only to her coming out unscathed
and becoming a member of the people of
Israel; it also won her the honour of
being one of the four foreign women
mentioned in the Gospel in our Lord's
ancestral tree (cf. Mt 1:5).

These two examples clearly show
that God calls all men to believe and that
all can and should manifest their faith by
exemplary living.

2:22–24. The Magisterium of the Church
quotes these verses when it teaches that
justification, righteousness, received as a
free gift in the sacrament of Baptism,
grows in strength as the Christian responds
to grace by keeping the commandments

of God and of the Church; the righteous,
the just, "increase in the very justice
which they have received through the
grace of Christ, their faith is completed
by works (cf. Jas 2:22), and they are
justified the more, as it is written: 'Let
the righteous still do right' (Rev 22:11),
[…] and again: 'You see that a man is
justified by works and not by faith alone
(Jas 2:24)" (Council of Trent, *De
iustificatione*, 10).

2:23. "It was reckoned to him as righteousness": St Paul (cf. Gal 3:6 and note)
uses these words of Genesis 15:6 to
explain that righteousness is attained not
just by Abraham's descendants but by all
who believe the word of God, whether
they be Jews or not; St James, from
another perspective, quotes this text to
show that Abraham's faith made him
righteous, that is, holy. Both teachings
are complementary. Abraham believed in
the divine promise that he would be the
father of a great people despite his age
and his wife's sterility; but that faith was
reinforced and manifested when it met
the test God set—that of sacrificing his
only son, while still believing in the
earlier promise. The same thing happens
in the case of the Christian: his initial
faith is strengthened by obedience to the
commandments, and he thereby attains
holiness.

"The friend of God": Scripture also
gives this touching title to Abraham (cf.
Is 41:8; Dan 3:35, New Vulgate) and our
Lord uses it to describe his apostles:
"I have called you friends" (Jn 15:15).

Rahab the harlot justified by works when she received the messengers and sent them out another way? [26]For as the body apart from the spirit is dead, so faith apart from works is dead.

Josh 2:4f; 6:17
Heb 11:31

Jas 2:17

3. PRACTICAL APPLICATIONS

Controlling one's tongue

3 [1]Let not many of you become teachers, my brethren, for you know that we who teach shall be judged with greater strictness. [2]For we all make many mistakes, and if any one makes no

Jas 1:26
Sir 14:1

These are not just isolated examples, for God calls all to be his friends; he wishes to be as intimate with everyone as he was with Abraham and the apostles: "We do not exist in order to pursue just any happiness. We have been called to penetrate the intimacy of God's own life, to know and love God the Father, God the Son, and God the Holy Spirit, and to love also—in that same love of the one God in three divine Persons—the angels and all men" (St Josemaría Escrivá, *Christ Is Passing By*, 133).

2:26. In speaking of "the spirit" St James is referring to the "breath of life", "breathing". The comparison (like all those in the letter) is very graphic: we recognise a body to be alive by its breathing; if it is not breathing it is a corpse; similarly, a faith that is alive expresses itself in actions, especially in acts of charity.

"Just as when a body moves we know it is alive," St Bernard explains, "so too good works show that faith is alive. The soul gives life to the body, causing it to move and feel; charity gives life to faith, causing it to act, as the Apostle says, 'faith working through love' (Gal 5:6). Just as the body dies when its soul leaves it, so faith dies when charity grows cold. Therefore, when you see someone who is

active in good works and happy and eager in his conduct, you can be sure that faith is alive in him: his life clearly proves it to be so" (*Second Sermon on the Holy Day of Easter*, 1).

3:1–18. There is now an apparently sudden change of subject; but in fact the themes dealt with in the letter from this point onwards are practical applications of the principle outlined in the second section (consistency between faith and works). Firstly, it deals with control of the tongue, prudent speech; after warning of occupational hazards of teachers (vv. 1–2), it denounces the sins the tongue can cause (vv. 2–12), and goes on to describe the characteristics of true and false wisdom (vv. 13–18).

3:1–2. St James draws attention to the responsibility that goes with holding a position of authority: all those who are teachers, in addition to answering to God for their own actions, are responsible to some degree for the actions of their disciples. That is why the Church has always encouraged prayer for those whose job it is to guide their brethren: "Nor should (lay people) fail to commend to God in their prayers those who have been placed over them, who indeed keep watch as having to render an account

37

mistakes in what he says he is a perfect man, able to bridle the whole body also. ³If we put bits into the mouths of horses that they may obey us, we guide their whole bodies. ⁴Look at the ships also; though they are so great and are driven by strong winds, they

---

of our souls, that they may do this with joy and not with grief (cf. Heb 13:17)" (Vatican II, *Lumen gentium*, 37).

"We all make many mistakes": Holy Scripture repeatedly draws attention to the sinful condition of man and the frequency with which he offends God (cf., e.g., Ps 19:13; 51:3ff; Prov 20:9; 1 Jn 1:8). The Council of Trent recalls these words of St James when it teaches that no one can go through life without committing some venial sin, "except by a special privilege granted by God, as the Church teaches happened in the case of the Blessed Virgin" (*De iustificatione*, can. 23; cf. chap. 16).

The great saints, from whom we can learn much, have attained holiness because they recognized that they were sinners: "I shall love you, Lord, and shall give thanks to you and confess your name," St Augustine exclaims, because "you have forgiven me such great sins and evil deeds [...]: for what might I have not done, seeing that I loved evil solely because it was evil? I confess that you have forgiven all alike—the sins I committed on my own motion, the sins I would have committed but for your grace [...]. If any man has heard your voice and followed it and done none of the things he finds me here recording and confessing, still he must not scorn me: for I am healed by the same doctor who preserved him from falling into sickness, or at least into such grievous sickness. But let him love you even more—seeing me rescued out of such sickness of sin, and himself saved from falling into such sickness of sin, by the one same Saviour" (*Confessions*, 2, 7).

3:2–12. The sacred writer focuses on sins of the tongue, possibly because of their frequency. In the wisdom books of the Old Testament these sins are referred to particularly often (cf., e.g., Prov 10:11–21; Sir 5:9–15; 28:13–26).

He basically makes three points—first, a positive point, by way of summing up what follows: "If any one makes no mistakes in what he says he is a perfect man" (v. 2). Then with three graphic comparisons (typical of this letter) he shows how difficult it is to control the tongue (vv. 3–6), but controlled it must be, otherwise great harm will be done (vv. 7–12).

"A perfect man" (v. 2): this does not mean that he cannot commit other sins; it implies that if one succeeds in restraining one's tongue one has self-control, which means that one is putting up good resistance to temptation.

3:3–6. Three simple, easy-to-understand examples (used also by other ancient writers in Greco-Latin and Jewish literature) show how something small—a horse's bit, a boat's rudder, a small fire—can have very big effects; the tongue has a similar influence in social life.

The *St Pius V Catechism*, recalling this teaching, says: "From these words we learn two truths. The fact is that sins of the tongue are very prevalent [...]. The other truth is that the tongue is the source of innumerable evils. Through the fault of the evil-speaker are often lost the property, the reputation, the life, and the salvation of the injured person, or of him who inflicts the injury. The injured person, unable to bear patiently the contumely, avenges it without restraint. The offender,

are guided by a very small rudder wherever the will of the pilot directs. ⁵So the tongue is a little member and boasts of great things. How great a forest is set ablaze by a small fire! ⁶And the tongue is a fire. The tongue is an unrighteous world among our members, staining the whole body, setting on fire the cycle of nature,ᵇ and set on fire by hell.ᶜ ⁷For every kind of beast and bird, of reptile and sea creature, can be tamed and has been tamed by humankind, ⁸but no human being can tame the tongue— a restless evil, full of deadly poison. ⁹With it we bless the Lord and Father, and with it we curse men, who are made in the likeness of God. ¹⁰From the same mouth come blessing and cursing. My brethren, this ought not to be so. ¹¹Does a spring pour forth from the same opening fresh water and brackish? ¹²Can a fig tree, my brethren, yield olives, or a grapevine figs? No more can salt water yield fresh.

Mt 15:11;
12:36f
Prov 16:27

Gen 9:2

Ps 140:4

Gen 1:27
Eph 4:29

Mt 7:16

---

on the other hand, deterred by a perverse shame and a false idea of what is called honour, cannot be induced to make reparation to him whom he has offended" (3, 9, 1). It should be remembered that if one unfairly damages another's reputation one has an obligation to make reparation by doing what one can to restore his or her good name.

"Do you know what damage you may cause by throwing stones with your eyes blindfolded? Neither do you know the harm you may cause—and at times it is very great—by letting drop uncharitable remarks that to you seem trifling, because your eyes are blinded by thoughtlessness or passion" (St Josemaría Escrivá, *The Way*, 455).

3:6. St James uses this graphic language to emphasize that if one does not control one's tongue it can cause much evil, affecting one's entire life. In itself very useful, the tongue can wreak havoc, so it is not surprising that the enemies of our sanctification seek to get control of it:

"though their voices sound like cracked bells, that have not been cast from good metal and have a very different tone from the shepherd's whistle call, they so distort speech, which is one of the most precious talents ever bestowed on men by God, a most beautiful gift for the expression of deep thoughts of love and friendship towards the Lord and his creatures, that one comes to understand why St James says that the tongue is 'an unrighteous world' (Jas 3:6). So great is the harm it can do—lies, slander, dishonour, trickery, insults, tortuous insinuations" (St J. Escrivá, *Friends of God*, 298).

3:9–12. The sacred writer uses further examples, equally simple and familiar to his readers, to stress the need for control of the tongue. Experience shows that it is as easy to put it to a good purpose as to an evil one. Besides, misuse of the tongue is a sign that one's heart is not in the right place: as our Lord already warned us, "out of the abundance of the heart the mouth speaks" (Mt 12:34).

b. Or *wheel of birth* **c.** Greek *Gehenna*

39

Gal 5:23
Jas 2:18
1 Pet 2:12
Rom 2:8
Eph 4:31
Col 3:3
Jas 1:5, 17

Is 32:17
Mt 5:9
Phil 1:11

True and false wisdom

¹³Who is wise and understanding among you? By his good life let him show his works in the meekness of wisdom. ¹⁴But if you have bitter jealousy and selfish ambition in your hearts, do not boast and be false to the truth. ¹⁵This wisdom is not such as comes down from above, but is earthly, unspiritual, devilish. ¹⁶For where jealousy and selfish ambition exist, there will be disorder and every vile practise. ¹⁷But the wisdom from above is first pure, then peaceable, gentle, open to reason, full of mercy and good fruits, without uncertainty or insincerity. ¹⁸And the harvest of righteousness is sown in peace by those who make peace.

3:13–18. These verses point out the qualities of Christian wisdom (cf. 1:5). After exhorting his readers to manifest their wisdom by their actions (v. 13), he attacks the signs of false wisdom (vv. 14–16) and explains the qualities of the true (vv. 17–18).

St Paul also makes a distinction between worldly wisdom—the wisdom of man when he veers away from his correct goal—and the wisdom of God, which reaches its highest expression on the cross (cf. 1 Cor 1:18 3:3). St James pays particular attention to the practical effects of godly wisdom—meekness, mercy and peace.

False wisdom, on the contrary, leads to bitter zeal, rivalry and resentment: it is "earthly" because it rejects things transcendental and supernatural; "unspiritual" (merely natural, "psychic" in the original Greek), as befits people who follow their nature as wounded by original sin, deprived of the help of the Spirit (cf. notes on 1 Cor 2:14–16; Jude 19–20); "devilish", in the sense that such people are inspired by the devil, who is envious (cf. Wis 2:24), "a liar and the father of lies" (Jn 8:44).

3:18. What this verse means is that the "peacemakers" of the Beatitudes (cf. Mt 5:6 and note) create around themselves an environment making for righteousness (holiness), and they themselves benefit from the peace they sow. "There can be no peace," John XXIII says, "between men unless there is peace within each of them: unless, that is, each one builds up within himself the order wished by God" (*Pacem in terris*, 165).

The "harvest of righteousness" is the equivalent of righteousness itself: it is keeping the law of the Gospel, doing good works, which show true wisdom. The passage is reminiscent of Isaiah 32:17–18: "and the effects of righteousness will be peace, and the result of righteousness, quietness and trust for ever. My people will abide in a peaceful habitation, in secure dwellings and in quiet resting places."

Every Christian who strives to live in accordance with his vocation is a sower of holiness and justice-with-peace: "Through your work, through the whole network of human relations," St J. Escrivá says, "you ought to show the charity of Christ and its concrete expression in friendship, understanding, human affection and peace. Just as Christ 'went about doing good' (Acts 10:38) throughout Palestine, so must you also spread peace in your family circle, in civil society, at work, and in your cultural and leisure activities" (*Christ Is Passing By*, 166).

The source of discord

4 ¹What causes wars, and what causes fightings among you? Is it not your passions that are at war in your members? ²You desire and do not have; so you kill. And you covet[d] and cannot obtain; so you fight and wage war. You do not have, because you do not ask. ³You ask and do not receive, because you ask wrongly, to spend it on your passions. ⁴Unfaithful creatures! Do you not

Rom 7:23
1 Pet 2:11

Rom 8:7
1 Jn 2:15

4:1—5:6. Contrasting with the peace possessed and spread by those who practise true wisdom (cf. 3:17–18), one often finds discord and contention among Christians which makes it difficult for them to live together in harmony. St James severely reproaches this sort of behaviour, pointing out that it originates in greed in all its various forms.

These verses are a further collection of teachings—warnings addressed to various groups in the Christian community, censuring the graver kinds of moral deviation, which all show that people are not practising the faith they profess. First comes discord (vv. 1–12); then, empty-headed boasting about one's own abilities (vv. 13–17); and, lastly, the injustice of the rich who oppress the weak (5:1–6).

In reproaching the faithful for dissension and division (vv. 1–12), the main causes are identified as greed and envy (vv. 1–3), disordered love of things of the world, and pride (vv. 4–10), and, stemming from that, complaints and evil speech (vv. 11–12).

4:1. "Wars" and "fighting" are an exaggerated reference to the contention and discord found among those Christians. "Passions", as elsewhere in the New Testament, means concupiscence, hedonism, pleasure-seeking (cf. v. 3; Lk 8:14; Tit 3:3; 2 Pet 2:13).

St James points out that if one fails to fight as one should against one's evil inclinations, one's inner disharmony overflows in the form of quarrelling and fighting. The New Testament often refers to the good kind of fight, which confers inner freedom and is a prerequisite for salvation (cf., e.g., Mt 11:12; Rom 7:14–25; 1 Pet 2:11).

"How can you be at peace if you allow passions you do not even attempt to control to drag you away from the 'pull' of grace? Heaven pulls you upwards; you drag yourself downwards. And don't seek excuses—that is what you are doing. If you go on like that, you will tear yourself apart" (St Josemaría Escrivá, *Furrow*, 851).

4:2–3. St James is describing the sad state to which free-wheeling hedonism (specifically, greed for earthly things) leads.

"You do not receive, because you ask wrongly": "He asks wrongly who shows no regard for the Lord's commandments and yet seeks heavenly gifts. He also asks wrongly who, having lost his taste for heavenly things, seeks only earthly things —not for sustaining his human weakness but to enable him to indulge himself" (St Bede, *Super Iac. expositio*, ad loc.).

4:4–6. The sacred writer warns that inordinate love of the world, which stems from ambition, is incompatible with the

---

d. Or *you kill and you covet*

Gen 2:7

Prov 3:34
Job 22:29

know that friendship with the world is enmity with God? Therefore whoever wishes to be a friend of the world makes himself an enemy of God. ⁵Or do you suppose it is in vain that the scripture says, "He yearns jealously over the spirit which he has made to dwell in us"? ⁶But he gives more grace; therefore it says,

---

love of God. "World" here has the meaning of "enemy of God", opposed to Christ and his followers (cf. note on 1:26–27). The teaching contained in these verses echoes that of our Lord: "No one can serve two masters; for either he will hate the one and love the other, or he will be devoted to the one and despise the other. You cannot serve God and mammon" (Mt 6:24).

The saints have frequently reminded us—by their lives as well as their teachings—that inordinate love of the world is incompatible with the love of God: "Worldly society has flowered from a selfish love which dared to despise even God, whereas the communion of saints is rooted in a love of God that is ready to trample on self" (St Augustine, *The City of God*, 14, 28).

"Unfaithful creatures!": the original Greek simply says "Adulterers" (fem.) and the New Vulgate, "Adulterers" (masc.). This echoes the symbol the prophets often use (cf., e.g., Hos 1:2ff; Jer 3:7–10; Ezek 16:1ff) of the marriage of God and his people sealed by the Covenant. St James, therefore, is not referring to the sin of adultery; he is berating those whose excessive love for the things of this world makes them unfaithful to God.

4:5. The original Greek is open to various interpretations and the quotation as given here is not to be found in the Bible. Translated word for word it means: "Jealously he loves the spirit which dwells in us." It is not clear who "loves"—God or the spirit; and "the spirit" may mean the soul or the Holy Spirit; moreover, the

jealousy can be either something good or something bad (like envy). It might perhaps be translated as "The Spirit who dwells in us jealously loves us" (which is how the New Vulgate translates it).

Although this sentence does not appear literally in the Bible, St James may be referring not so much to a specific passage as to an idea which often occurs in the Bible when it depicts God as a jealous lover (cf., e.g., Ex 20:5; 34:14; Zech 1:14; 8:2), who expects his love to be returned wholeheartedly; this very human kind of language is a most moving evocation of God's immense love for man. St Alphonsus teaches: "Since he loves us with infinite love, he desires all our love; that is why he is jealous when he sees others having a share in hearts which he wants entirely for his own. 'Jesus is jealous', St Jerome said (*Epistle*, 22), in the sense that he does not want us to love anything that is outside himself. And if he sees that some creature has a part of your heart, he is in a sense envious of it, as the apostle James writes, because he tolerates no rival for our love; he wants to have all our love" (*The Love of Jesus Christ*, chap. 11).

4:6. The sacred writer foresees the possibility that some may draw back from this "jealous" love God expects to be reciprocated: but God never expects the impossible; he gives us all the grace we need to do what he asks: "All my hope is naught," St Augustine exclaims, "save in your great mercy. Grant what you command, and command what you will" (*Confessions*, 10, 29).

"God opposes the proud, but gives grace to the humble." ⁷Submit yourselves therefore to God. Resist the devil and he will flee from you. ⁸Draw near to God and he will draw near to you. Cleanse your hands, you sinners, and purify your hearts, you men of double mind. ⁹Be wretched and mourn and weep. Let your

1 Pet 5:5

Eph 6:12
1 Pet 5:8f

Zech 1:3
Jas 1:8

However, only people who are humble are given this grace, and have it bear fruit. The proud, who are full of self-love, even fail to realize that they need grace, and so they do not ask for it, or do not ask for it properly. The second part of the verse is a literal quotation from Proverbs 3:34 (according to the Septuagint Greek): it is an example of the "poetic" form, with the characteristic antithetical parallelism of Hebrew verse. St Augustine, in his explanation of the fact that the Bible refers in places to the sins of prominent men, urges his readers to be humble, commenting that "there is scarcely a page in the sacred books which does not echo the fact that 'God resists the proud and gives grace to the humble'" (*De doctrina christiana*, 3, 23).

4:7–10. Some ways of countering pride are identified here: basically what is required is a sincere and deep conversion, which must begin with the humility of recognizing that we are sinners and in need of purification. The tone of these verses is reminiscent of the way the Old Testament prophets upbraid the people of Israel for their unfaithfulness to Yahweh.

To draw near to God the sinner needs purification. "Cleaning your hands" should not be understood as referring to the physical ablutions of the Jews (cf. Ex 30:19–21; Mk 7:1–5); but should be taken in a moral sense—purification from sins, and upright actions (e.g., Is 1:15–17; 1 Tim 2:8). Of all the possible ways of being purified and converted (for example, the penitential rite at Mass, a visit to a shrine, or fasting), "none is more signifi-

cant," John Paul II reminds us, "more divinely efficacious or more lofty and at the same time easily accessible as a rite than the sacrament of Penance. [...]. For a Christian, *the sacrament of Penance is the ordinary way* of obtaining forgiveness and the remission of serious sins committed after Baptism" (*Reconciliatio et paenitentia*, 28 and 31).

4:7. When someone resists the devil's temptations, the devil leaves him alone: he cannot force a man to commit sin. *The Shepherd of Hermas* (a work by an anonymous Christian writer, around the middle of the second century) elaborates on the same idea: "Be converted, you who walk in the commandments of the devil, commandments that are hard, bitter, cruel and foul. And do not fear the devil either, because he has no power against you [...]. The devil cannot lord it over those who are servants of God with their whole heart and who place their hope in him. The devil can wrestle with, but not overcome them. So, if you resist him, he will flee from you in defeat and confusion" (11th commandment, 4, 6 and 5, 2).

4:9. "Be wretched": "To acknowledge one's sin—penetrating still more deeply into the consideration of one's own personhood—*to recognize oneself as a sinner*, capable of sin and inclined to commit sin, is the essential first step in returning to God" (*Reconciliatio et paenitentia*, 13).

Mourning and weeping are the external expression of sincere repentance (cf. Mt 5:4 and note; Tob 2:6; Amos 8:10):

Mt 23:12
1 Pet 5:6

laughter be turned to mourning and your joy to dejection. [10]Humble yourselves before the Lord and he will exalt you.

[11]Do not speak evil against one another, brethren. He that speaks evil against a brother or judges his brother, speaks evil against the law and judges the law. But if you judge the law, you are not a doer of the law but a judge. [12]There is one lawgiver and judge, he who is able to save and to destroy. But who are you that you judge your neighbour?

Rom 14:4
Mt 10:28

Trust in divine providence

Prov 27:1
Lk 12:19f

Job 14:1f

Acts 18:21

[13]Come now, you who say, "Today or tomorrow we will go into such and such a town and spend a year there and trade and get gain"; [14]whereas you do not know about tomorrow. What is your life? For you are a mist that appears for a little time and then vanishes. [15]Instead you ought to say, "If the Lord wills, we shall live and we shall do this or that." [16]As it is, you boast in your

---

"You are crying? Don't be ashamed of it. Yes, cry: men also cry like you, when they are alone and before God. Each night, says King David, I soak my bed with tears. With those tears, those burning manly tears, you can purify your past and supernaturalize your present life" (St Josemaría Escrivá, *The Way*, 216).

4:11–12. Thinking evil of one's neighbour (judging him) and speaking evil of him (defaming him) goes against the commandment of charity, which sums up the Law and the Prophets (cf. Mt 22:3440). Therefore, anyone who acts like that breaks the whole Law: it means taking the law into one's own hands, usurping the place of God, the supreme Lawgiver and Judge. In other words it is for God to make laws and, in line with them, "to save and to destroy", that is, to reward and to punish.

4:13–17. Overweening self-confidence is a type of pride because it means one is forgetful of God who, in his providence, rules over the lives of men. St James reminds those who are totally caught up

in their business affairs that human life is something very impermanent (v. 14). He made the same point earlier with the simile of the flower of the grass (cf. 1:9–11); now he puts it in terms of the fleetingness of mist (a familiar Old Testament image: cf., e.g., Job 7:7–16; Ps 102:4; Wis 2:4). "Earthly life is a wearisome thing," St Gregory the Great reminds us, "more unreal than fables, faster than a runner, with many ups and downs caused by unreliability and weakness; we shelter in houses made of clay (in fact, life itself is mere clay); our fortitude, our resolution, has no substance; such rest and repose as we get in the midst of our activities and difficulties is of no help" (*Exposition on the seven penitential psalms*, Ps 109, prologue).

A Christian should trustingly abandon himself into the hands of God, but that does not in any sense mean that he may irresponsibly opt out of his duties or avoid exercising his rights.

4:15. "If the Lord wills": this expression is to be found elsewhere in the New Testament; St Paul uses the same words

arrogance. All such boasting is evil. [17]Whoever knows what is right to do and fails to do it, for him it is sin.

Lk 12:47
Rom 14:23

A warning to the rich

5 [1]Come now, you rich, weep and howl for the miseries that are coming upon you. [2]Your riches have rotted and your garments are moth-eaten. [3]Your gold and silver have rusted, and their rust will be evidence against you and will eat your flesh like fire. You

Lk 6:24
Mt 6:19
Sir 29:10
Prov 16:27

(cf. 1 Cor 4:19) or ones like them, when speaking about his personal plans (cf. Acts 18:21; Rom 1:10; 1 Cor 16:7). It is a saying which has passed into popular Christian speech and it shows a readiness to leave one's future in God's hands, trusting in divine providence.

4:17. As elsewhere in the letter, St James ends this passage with a general maxim (cf. 1:12; 2:13; 3:18). In this instance, to emphasize the need to prove one's faith and one's grasp of the faith by action (cf. 2:14–16), he gives a warning about sins of omission. Once again, the Master's teachings are reflected in what the sacred writer says: "the servant who knew his master's will, and did not make ready or act according to his will, shall receive a severe beating" (Lk 12:47).

5:1–6. With exceptional severity and energy the sacred writer again (cf. 2:5–7) criticizes the sins of the well-to-do. In tones reminiscent of the Prophets (cf., e.g., Is 3:13–26; Amos 6:1ff; Mic 2:1ff), he reproves their pride, vanity and greed (vv. 2–3) and their pleasure-seeking (v. 5), warning them that the judgment of God is near at hand (vv. 3, 5). The opening exhortation—"weep and howl" —is a very forceful call to repentance.

The Church has constantly taught that we have a duty to do away with unjust inequalities among men, which are frequently denounced in Scripture. The Second Vatican Council made an urgent

call for a more just, fraternal society, a call for solidarity: "To fulfil the requirements of justice and equity, every effort must be made to put an end as soon as possible to the immense economic inequalities which exist in the world and increase from day to day, linked with individual and social discrimination, provided, of course, that the rights of individuals and the character of each people are not disturbed" (*Gaudium et spes*, 66).

People who are well-to-do should use their resources in the service of others. In this connexion, the Church teaches that "they have a moral obligation not to keep capital unproductive and in making investments to think first of the common good. [...] The right to private property is inconceivable without responsibilities to the common good. It is subordinated to the higher principle which states that goods are meant for all" (SCDF, *Libertatis conscientia*, 87).

5:2–3. Greed, an inordinate desire for material things, is one of the seven deadly sins. An avaricious person offends against justice and charity and becomes insensitive to his neighbour's needs, so keen is he on his self-aggrandisement. "If you are inclined to avarice," says St Francis de Sales, "think of its folly: it makes us slaves to that which was intended to serve us. Remember how we must leave everything when we die; perhaps those who get our wealth then will only

Lev 19:23
Deut 24:14, 15
Is 5:9

Jer 12:3
Lk 16:19–25

have laid up treasure[e]* for the last days. [4]Behold, the wages of the labourers who mowed your fields, which you kept back by fraud, cry out; and the cries of the harvesters have reached the ears of the Lord of hosts. [5]You have lived on the earth in luxury and in

---

squander it, and even to their ruin" (*Introduction to the Devout Life*, 4, 10).

Our Lord also speaks about the moth and the rust which consume earthly treasures, and tells us that the true treasure is good works and upright actions, which will earn us an everlasting reward from God in heaven (cf. Mt 6:19–21).

"You have laid up treasure for the last days": a reference to the Day of Judgment, as in v. 5: "you have fattened your hearts in a day of slaughter" (cf. e.g., Is 34:6; Jer 12:3; 25:34). It can also be translated as "you have laid up treasure in the last days", which would be a reference to the present time, which (ever since the coming of the Messiah) is seen as in fact the last days, the beginning of the eschatological era. The two renderings are compatible because they both have reference to the Judgment.

5:4. Cheating workers of their earnings was already condemned in the Old Testament (cf., e.g., Lev 19:13; Deut 24:14–15; Mal 3:5). It is one of the sins which "cries out to heaven" for immediate, exemplary punishment; the same applies to murder (cf. Gen 4:10), sodomy (Gen 18:20–21) and oppression of widows and orphans (Ex 22:22–24).

The Church has often reminded the faithful about the duty to pay fair wages: "remuneration for work should guarantee man the opportunity to provide a dignified livelihood for himself and his family on the material, social, cultural and spiritual level to correspond to the role and the productivity of each, the relevant

economic factors in his employment, and the common good" (Vatican II, *Gaudium et spes*, 67).

"The Lord of hosts": a common Old Testament description of God, manifesting his omnipotence, as Creator and Lord of the whole universe; it is used to acclaim God in the *Sanctus* of the Mass: "Lord God of power and might" ("Dominus Deus Sabaoth").

5:5. This description of the lifestyle of these rich people (vv. 2, 3, 5) recalls the parable of the rich man and Lazarus (cf. Lk 16:19ff). Those who live in this way do well to listen to the Master's warning: "Take heed to yourselves lest your hearts be weighed down with dissipation and drunkenness and cares of this life, and that day come upon you suddenly like a snare" (Lk 21:34).

Against the hedonism condemned by the sacred writer, Christians should be conscious of the duty to promote a just society: "Christians engaged actively in modern economic and social progress and in the struggle for justice and charity must be convinced that they have much to contribute to the prosperity of mankind and to world peace. Let them, as individuals and as group members, give a shining example to others. Endowed with the skill and experience so absolutely necessary for them, let them preserve a proper sense of values in their earthly activity in loyalty to Christ and his Gospel, in order that their lives, individual as well as social, may be inspired by the spirit of the Beatitudes, and in particular by the spirit of poverty.

---

e. Or *will eat your flesh, since you have stored up fire*

46

pleasure; you have fattened your hearts in a day of slaughter. ⁶You
have condemned, you have killed the righteous man; he does not
resist you.

Hos 1:6

4. FINAL COUNSELS

A call for constancy

⁷Be patient, therefore, brethren, until the coming of the Lord.
Behold, the farmer waits for the precious fruit of the earth, being

Deut 11:14
Jer 5:24

"Anyone who in obedience to Christ seeks first the kingdom of God will derive from it a stronger and purer love for helping all his brethren and for accomplishing the task of justice under the inspiration of charity" (*Gaudium et spes*, 72).

5:6. "The righteous man": according to St Bede (cf. *Super Iac. expositio,* ad loc.), this refers to our Lord, who is just *par excellence* and is described as such in other passages of Scripture (cf., e.g., Acts 3:14; 7:52). This interpretation is quite appropriate, given the fact that in the needy we should see Jesus Christ himself (cf. Mt 25:31–45); they often suffer at the hands of those who refuse to recognize even their most elementary rights: "The bread of the needy is the life of the poor; whoever deprives them of it is a man of blood. To take away a neighbour's living is to murder him; to deprive an employee of his wages is to shed blood" (Sir 34:21–22).

"Every man has the right to possess a sufficient amount of the earth's goods for himself and his family. This has been the opinion of the Fathers and Doctors of the Church, who taught that men are bound to come to the aid of the poor and to do so not merely out of their superfluous goods.[...] Faced with a world today where so many people are suffering from

want, the Council asks individuals and governments to remember the saying of the Fathers: 'Feed the man dying of hunger, because if you do not feed him you are killing him!' and it urges them according to their ability to share and dispose of their goods to help others, above all by giving them aid which will enable them to help and develop themselves" (*Gaudium et spes*, 69).

5:7–11. Just before he ends his letter, St James again (cf. 1:2–4, 12) exhorts his readers to be patient, perhaps in case some are tempted to avenge themselves on the rich. He uses the simile of the farmer, who patiently waits for the earth to yield the fruits of his work: in the same kind of way the oppressed will be rewarded for all their afflictions when the Lord comes. St James encourages them also by reminding them of the patience and long-suffering of the prophets and of Job.

Christian hope, and the patience it induces, enables people to put up with injustice in this present life; but it is not an easy way out of one's responsibilities nor an invitation to be passive. A Christian should strive to make this world a place of justice and peace, but should realize it is a transient place, and not make these temporal ideals an absolute goal. "God did not create us to build a lasting city here on earth. [...] Nevertheless, we

1 Thess 3:13

Mt 24:33

Mt 5:12

patient over it until it receives the early and the late rain. [8]You also be patient. Establish your hearts, for the coming of the Lord is at hand. [9]Do not grumble, brethren, against one another, that you may not be judged; behold, the Judge is standing at the doors. [10]As an example of suffering and patience, brethren, take the prophets who spoke in the name of the Lord. [11]Behold, we call those happy

children of God ought not to remain aloof from earthly endeavours, for God has placed us here to sanctify them and make them fruitful with our blessed faith, which alone is capable of bringing true peace and joy to all men wherever they may be [...]. We urgently need to christianize society. We must imbue all levels of mankind with a supernatural outlook, and each of us must strive to raise his daily duties, his job or profession, to the order of supernatural grace. In this way all human occupations will be lit up by a new hope that transcends time and the inherent transience of earthly realities" (St Josemaría Escrivá, *Friends of God*, 210).

5:7–9. St James' words show how vividly the early Christians realized that the Christian life should be a time for watchfulness and for looking forward to the Parousia of the Lord, when our redemption will be finally sealed (cf. Lk 21:28). Jesus did not choose to reveal the precise moment of his coming (cf. Mt 24:36); he stressed, rather, the need to be watchful, to make sure it found us ready (cf. Mt 24:42, 44; 25:13). Therefore, every Christian should live in the expectation of that event which surely will come, though he knows not when. This is also what the Apostle means when he says "the coming of the Lord is at hand" and "the Judge is standing at the doors", for he may come at any moment.

5:10–11. The lives of the prophets are a very good model of patience and

endurance in adversity. Some of them in particular (Elijah, Isaiah, Jeremiah) underwent great suffering on account of their obedience to God.

"You have seen the purpose of the Lord": this is the interpretation of St Bede and St Augustine, referring to the example of patience set by Jesus in his passion and death on the cross. Most commentators prefer the other possible translation, "You have seen the outcome the Lord gave him", referring to Job, who bore patiently the trials God sent to him (cf. Job 42:10ff), because, for one thing, it avoids having to give the term "Lord", which appears twice in the same verse (v. 11), two different meanings—Jesus Christ and God one and three.

5:11. "The Lord is compassionate and merciful": Holy Scripture often describes the Lord as a God of mercy, attributing to him human sentiments like "abounding in steadfast love", "bowels of mercy", meaning that he has tender, even maternal, feelings towards us (cf., e.g., Ex 34:6; Joel 2:13; Lk 1:78).

St Thomas Aquinas, who often says that divine omnipotence is displayed particularly in the form of mercy (cf. *Summa theologiae*, 1, 21, 4; 2–2, 30, 4) explains very simply and graphically that God's mercy is abundant and infinite: "To say that a person is merciful is like saying that he is sorrowful at heart (*miserum cor*), that is, he is afflicted with sorrow by the misery of another as though it were his own. Hence it follows that he endeavours to dispel the misery of

who were steadfast. You have heard of the steadfastness of Job, Ps 103:8; 111:4
Job 1:21f;
Jas 1:12 and you have seen the purpose of the Lord, how the Lord is compassionate and merciful.

On oath-taking

¹²But above all, my brethren, do not swear, either by heaven or by earth or with any other oath, but let your yes be yes and your no be no, that you may not fall under condemnation. Mt 5:34–37

The value of prayer. The sacrament of the Anointing of the Sick

¹³Is any one among you suffering? Let him pray. Is any cheerful? Let him sing praise. ¹⁴Is any among you sick? Let him call for the Mk 6:13

---

the other person as if it were his own; and this is the effect of mercy. God cannot feel sorrow over the misery of others, but it does most properly belong to him to dispel that misery, whatever form that shortcoming or deprivation takes" (*Summa theologiae*, 1, 21, 3).

In Christ, Pope John Paul II taught, the mercy of God is very clear to see: "*he himself makes it incarnate* and personifies it. *He himself, in a certain sense, is mercy.* To the person who sees it in him—and finds it in him—God becomes 'visible' in a particular way as the Father 'who is rich in mercy' (Eph 2:4)" (*Dives in misericordia*, 2).

5:12. This exhortation is almost an exact echo of the words of the Lord: "Let what you say be simply 'Yes' or 'No'; anything more than this comes from evil" (Mt 5:37). The Jews of the time tended to take oaths far too readily and had developed an elaborate casuistry about them (cf. note on Mt 5:33–37); our Lord criticized these abuses, and St James repeats his teaching. However, that does not mean that oath-taking is always wrong: in fact Holy Scripture itself praises it when it is done in the right way for good reasons (cf. Jer 4:2), and St Paul some-

times resorts to it (cf., e.g., Rom 1:9; 2 Cor 1:23). Hence the Church teaches that it is lawful and even does honour to God to take an oath when it is strictly necessary and provided one acts in accordance with truth and justice.

St James' "let your yes be yes and your no be no" is in fact a summing up of the virtue of sincerity, a virtue which is very pleasing to God (cf. Jn 1:47) and essential in human relationships.

5:13–18. In these final counsels, St James has most to say on the subject of prayer. He teaches that it is a necessary and effective counter to sadness ("suffering": v. 13); the prayer of priests, while anointing the sick with oil, is the sacrament of Anointing (vv. 14–15); prayer for others helps bring forgiveness of sins (v. 16). All this is supported by the example of Elijah (vv. 17–18).

5:13. "Suffering": the Greek word, which can be translated as "experiencing sadness", includes the idea of suffering under some evil, so the "sadness" can be taken as some type of affliction, or sickness of the soul.

St Bede describes the attitude a Christian should adopt when he or she feels overwhelmed by the "pest" of sadness, regardless of its cause: "Have recourse to the Church; kneel in prayer before the Lord, asking him to send the grace of his consolation, and do not imbibe the world's sadness, which only leads to death" (*Super Iac. expositio*, ad loc.). Sadness, gloominess, is a powerful ally of the devil and one of the subtlest weapons he uses to lead a person to commit sin; one needs to react against it immediately.

"Being children of God, how can we be sad? Sadness is the end product of selfishness. If we truly want to live for God, we will never lack joy, even when we discover our errors and wretchedness. Cheerfulness finds its way out into our life of prayer, so much so that we cannot help singing for joy. For we are in love, and singing is a thing that lovers do" (St Josemaría Escrivá, *Friends of God*, 92).

14–15. The Church's Magisterium teaches that this text promulgates the sacrament of the Anointing of the Sick: cf. the Council of Trent: "This holy anointing of the sick was initiated as a true and proper sacrament of the New Testament by Christ our Lord; it is implied in St Mark (cf. Mk 6:13) and it is commended to the faithful and promulgated by the Apostle, St James, the brother of the Lord [...] (Jas 5:14f). In these words, as the Church has learned from the apostolic Tradition transmitted to her, he teaches the matter, the form, the proper minister and the effects of this life-giving sacrament" (*De Sacramento extremae unctionis*, chap. 1; cf. can. 1).

The matter of the sacrament is "oil blessed by a bishop, because anointing very fittingly symbolizes the grace of the Holy Spirit, who anoints the soul of the sick person in an invisible manner" (ibid.). It is true that among ancient peoples (including the Jews: cf. Is 1:6; Jer 8:21–22; Lk 10:34) oil was much appreciated for its curative powers; hence the symbolism of this sacramental sign. But St James is looking at medicinal effects on the soul rather than on the body, for he says that the sick man will be saved and his sins will be forgiven. The Church expressly teaches that the anointing stands for the grace of the Holy Spirit. The oil of the sick is solemnly blessed by the bishop in the Chrism Mass; in case of necessity it can also be blessed by the priest at the time he administers the Anointing (cf. *The Rite of Anointing of the Sick*, 21).

The form of the sacrament is the prayer which the priest recites as he anoints the sick person on the forehead and hands. The Greek words of St James —"let them pray over him, anointing him"—are so couched that they lead one to conclude that from the very beginning the praying and the anointing took place simultaneously and therefore the formula "pray over" refers to a liturgical gesture.

As far as the minister of the sacrament is concerned, the Council of Trent, referring to these verses, says: "They indicate that the proper ministers of this sacrament are the presbyters of the Church. This does not refer to the older men nor to the more influential men in the community but to the bishops or the priests duly ordained by the bishops through the laying on of hands of the presbyterate (cf. 1 Tim 4:14)" (*De Sacramento extremae unctionis*, chap. 3; cf. can. 4). The term "elder" which St James uses also means someone older in age; but here as in other New Testament passages (cf., e.g., Acts 11:10; 14:23; 15:2; 20:17; 1 Tim 5:17–19) it clearly refers to the bishops and priests of the Church.

elders of the church, and let them pray over him, anointing him
with oil in the name of the Lord; ¹⁵and the prayer of faith will save   Mk 16:18

As regards the effects of the sacrament, "Furthermore the complete effect of this sacrament is explained in the words: 'and the prayer of faith will save the sick man, and the Lord will raise him up, and if he be in sins, they shall be forgiven him' (Jas 5:15). For this effect is the grace of the Holy Spirit, whose anointing takes away sins, if there are any still to be expiated, and removes the traces of sin: and it comforts and strengthens the soul of the sick person. It gives him great confidence in the divine mercy. Encouraged by this, the sick man more easily bears the inconvenience and trials of the illness and more easily resists the temptations of the devil who lies in wait for his heel. This anointing occasionally restores health to the body if health would be of advantage to the salvation of the soul" (ibid., chap. 2).

Finally, as regards the recipient of the sacrament and when it should be administered, the words of the letter point to an illness of some seriousness, because the priests are asked to go to the sick person's house. The Second Vatican Council says that this sacrament is not only for those who are at the point of death and that "as soon as anyone of the faithful begins to be in danger of death from sickness or old age, the fitting time for him to receive this sacrament has certainly already arrived" (*Sacrosanctum Concilium*, 73). The Code of Canon Law lays down that "pastors of souls and those who are close to the sick are to ensure that the sick are helped by this sacrament in good time" (can. 1001).

It is important, therefore, to avoid delaying it unduly through fear of causing anxiety or upset. "In public and private catechesis, the faithful should be encouraged to ask for the anointing and, as soon as the time for the anointing comes, to receive it with complete faith and devotion" (*The Rite of Anointing the Sick*, 13).

This sacrament is a wonderful expression of divine mercy and of God's tender loving care for every single soul: "our merciful Redeemer willed that his servants should always be provided with salutary safeguards against all weapons of all enemies. Accordingly he prepared great helps in the other sacraments to enable Christians to keep themselves throughout their lives untouched by any serious spiritual harm, and likewise he protected them at the end of life with the invincible strength of the sacrament of extreme unction. For even if our adversary seeks occasions throughout the whole of life and goes about that he may devour our souls in any way he can (cf. 1 Pet 5:8), there is no time at which he is more vehemently intent on using all the forces of his cunning to destroy us completely and, if possible, to disturb our trust in the divine mercy, than when he sees the end of life approaching us" (Council of Trent, *De Sacramento extremae unctionis*, prologue).

5:15. "Will save the sick man": from the way St James uses the same verb elsewhere (cf. 2:21; 2:14; 4:12; 5:20) we can see that he is referring to the salvation of the soul. Secondarily, and to the degree that it makes for spiritual health, this sacrament can also heal the body; it seems clear that the sacred writer does not mean to say that physical health will always be restored, as if the Anointing of the Sick were a guarantee that one would not die. And it is quite clear that, by

the sick man, and the Lord will raise him up; and if he has committed sins, he will be forgiven.* [16]Therefore confess your sins to one another, and pray for one another, that you may be healed. The prayer of a righteous man has great power in its

virtue of the grace of the sacrament, the sick person is strengthened to face the trauma of illness and death with supernatural outlook and joy. "Nothing conduces more to a tranquil death than to banish sadness, await with a joyous mind the coming of our Lord, and be ready willingly to surrender the deposit entrusted whenever it shall be his will to demand it back. To free the minds of the faithful from this solicitude, and fill the soul with pious and holy joy is, then, an effect of the sacrament of Extreme Unction" (*St Pius V Catechism*, 2, 6, 14).

"If he has committed sins, he will be forgiven": although the sacrament of Anointing of the Sick is a sacrament "of the living", that is, it should be received in the state of grace, Catholic teaching, based on these words, says that Anointing can forgive the mortal sins of a sick person who is repentant but has not been able to go to Confession (cf., e.g., *Summa theologiae*, Supplement, 30, 1). Hence the importance of conferring this sacrament "upon sick people who have lost consciousness or lost the use of reason, if as Christian believers they would have asked for it were they in control of their faculties" (*Rite of Anointing of the Sick*, 14).

5:16. "Therefore confess your sins to one another": it is impossible to say exactly what type of confession is being referred to. Some—St Augustine, for example (cf. *In Ioann. Evang.*, 58, 5)—interpret these words as referring to a pious custom of confessing sins to others in a public act of contrition at which people prayed for one another; in which case it could be the

origin of the penitential rite at the beginning of Mass. Others, including St Thomas (cf. *Summa theologiae*, Supplement, 6, 6), apply these words to sacramental confession; in which case one would have to understand it as meaning confession to priests. St Bede in his commentary links these two possible interpretations while distinguishing between venial and mortal sin: "In this sentence a distinction should be made: we should confess to each other our lesser, daily sins, and believe that we are saved by the daily prayer of others. But, as the law lays down, we should show to the priest the uncleanness of graver leprosy and be sure to purify ourselves in the manner and for the period that his decision specifies" (*Super Iac. expositio*, ad loc.).

Without intending to define the meaning of this text, the Council of Trent refers to it when it teaches that it is a matter of divine law that all mortal sins be confessed in the sacrament of Penance. "From the time of the institution of the sacrament of Penance, already explained, the universal Church has always understood that integral confession of sins (cf. Jas 5:16; 1 Jn 1:9; Lk 17:14) was also instituted by the Lord, and that it is by divine law necessary (for the forgiveness) of all falls committed after Baptism, for our Lord Jesus Christ, when he was about to ascend from earth to heaven, left priests to take his place (Mt 16:19; 18:18; Jn 20:23), as presidents and judges, before whom Christ's faithful should confess all the mortal sins they might commit, so that by the power of the keys they (priests) might pass sentence of absolution or retention of sins" (*De Sacramento paenitentiae*, chap. 5).

effects. [17]Elijah was a man of like nature with ourselves and he prayed fervently that it might not rain, and for three years and six months it did not rain on the earth. [18]Then he prayed again and the heaven gave rain, and the earth brought forth its fruit.

1 Kings 17:1

1 Kings 18:42

Concern for one another

[19]My brethren, if any one among you wanders from the truth and some one brings him back, [20]let him know that whoever brings back a sinner from the error of his way will save his soul from death and will cover a multitude of sins.

Gal 6:1

Prov 10:12
1 Pet 4:8

5:17–18. As a palpable example of the power of prayer, St James mentions Elijah, whose prayer obtained that no rain should fall in Israel for a period, and then that it should come in abundance (cf. 1 Kings 17–18; Sir 48:3).

He thereby demonstrates the immense power of prayer, even for obtaining God's help in our material needs. We must remember that good prayer identifies our will with that of God, who is almighty. This has always been the way the saints have understood it: "God has never and will never refuse anything to those who ask him for his graces in the right way," the Curé of Ars says. "Prayer is the great recourse we have for escaping from sin, for persevering in grace, for moving God's heart and drawing down upon ourselves all manner of heavenly blessings, whether for our soul or to meet our temporal needs" (*Selected Sermons*, Fourth Sunday after Easter).

5:19–20. St James' letter ends with an encouraging exhortation to apostolic concern for those who stray from the right path. This is something extremely important, causing St Teresa of Avila to exclaim: "Whenever I read in the lives of saints of how they converted souls, I seem to feel much more devout, tender and envious of them than when I read of all the martyrdoms that they suffered. This is an inclination given me by our Lord; and I think he prizes one soul which by his mercy, and through our diligence and prayer, we may have gained for him, more than all the other services we can render him" (*Book of Foundations*, 1, 7). The Second Vatican Council teaches that apostolic concern stems from the Christian vocation itself and therefore is something all Christians should have; referring to the apostolate of lay people, it says specifically that it is "a sharing in the salvific mission of the Church. Through Baptism and Confirmation all are appointed to this apostolate by the Lord himself" (*Lumen gentium*, 33).

Introduction to the First Letter of St Peter

ST PETER THE APOSTLE

The Gospels and the Acts of the Apostles give us the main features of St Peter's character, but do not provide enough information for a biography of the Apostle.

He was originally called Simeon, in Hebrew (cf. Acts 15:14; 2 Pet 1:1), or Simon, the Greek form of the same name;[1] but Jesus surnamed him Cephas (cf. Jn 1:42). From this word, which in Aramaic (the language mostly spoken by the Jews of the time) means stone or rock, comes the name Peter, the Greek for rock.

Like most of our Lord's first disciples, Simon Peter was a native of Bethsaida (cf. Jn 1:44), a city of Galilee on the north-east shore of Lake Tiberius or Gennesaret. Like his father John[2] and his brother Andrew, he was a fisherman (cf. Mt 4:18). We also know that he was married, because Jesus cured his mother-in-law, who was living in Capernaum (cf. Mt 8:14).

Before meeting Jesus, he had very probably been a disciple of the Baptist, along with his brother Andrew (cf. Jn 1:35, 40). It was Andrew who brought him to Jesus (cf. Jn 1:40–42), thereby beginning a relationship which was to give a new direction to his life.

We can take it that he was present at the first miracle Jesus worked, at the wedding in Cana (cf. Jn 2:1–11), after which he went down with him to Capernaum (cf. Jn 2:12). He continued to work as a fisherman, listening to our Lord's teaching and witnessing his miracles (cf. Lk 4:31–5:7) up to the time when he was called to be one of the Twelve. Peter answered the call immediately, along with Andrew and the two sons of Zebedee, James and John: they left everything to follow Christ (cf. Lk 5:11; Mt 4:22; Mk 1:18).

He now was part of the Lord's circle of disciples. Prior to the Sermon on the Mount, after spending the night in prayer (cf. Lk 6:12), Jesus "called his disciples, and chose from them twelve, whom he named apostles" (Lk 6:13), which means "sent out". The apostles are listed four times in the New Testament and Simon Peter heads each list.[3] Within the apostolic college he, with James and John, constituted an inner group, the only ones to witness the resurrection of the daughter of Jairus (cf. Mk 5:37), the transfiguration of our Lord (cf. Mk 9:2), and his agony in the garden of Olives (cf. Mk 14:33).

---

1. Cf. Mt 16:17; Lk 22:31; Jn 1:42; 21:15–17.   **2.** Cf. Jn 1:42; 21:15–17. In Mt 16:17 he is called Jona, which was a shortened form of the Hebrew *Johanan* (John).   **3.** Cf. Mt 10:2–4; Mk 3:16–19; Lk 6:14–16; Acts 1:13.

Peter often acts as the spokesman for the apostles: he asks Jesus to explain the parable about purity of heart (cf. Mt 15:15); he asks about what reward they will get for having left everything (cf. Mt 19:27); after the eucharistic discourse in the synagogue of Capernaum, which led many disciples to abandon the Master, it is Peter again who speaks on behalf of the apostles: "Lord, to whom shall we go? You have the words of eternal life; and we have believed, and have come to know, that you are the Holy One of God" (Jn 6:68–69).

One episode at Caesarea Philippi is particularly important—when our Lord asked the Twelve, "But who do you say that I am?" and Simon Peter replied, "You are the Christ, the Son of the living God" (Mt 16:15–16). Christ went on to make a solemn promise to Peter that he would have charge of his Church: "And I tell you, you are Peter, and on this rock I will build my church, and the powers of death shall not prevail against it. I will give you the keys of the kingdom of heaven, and whatever you bind on earth shall be bound in heaven, and whatever you loose on earth shall be loosed in heaven."[4]

Although Jesus had foreknowledge of Peter's weakness and denials, he made this revelation to him in the Upper Room: "Simon, Simon, behold Satan demanded to have you, that he might sift you like wheat, but I have prayed for you that your faith may not fail; and when you have turned again, strengthen your brethren."[5] Finally, after his resurrection, Christ confers on Peter those powers of nourishing and governing the whole Church in his name.[6]

After our Lord's ascension, Peter, without any debate, is the leading apostle; it is he who proposes and presides over the election of Matthias to take the place of the traitorous Judas, specifying the requirements for candidacy (cf. Acts 1:15–22); he delivers the first address to evangelize the people on the day of Pentecost (cf. Acts 2:14–40); he speaks out before the Sanhedrin to justify the apostles' preaching (cf. Acts 3:6–7; 5:15; 9:36–41); he condemns Ananias and Sapphira (cf. Acts 5:1–11) as he does Simon the magician (cf. Acts 8:18–24); instructed by the Lord in a vision, he receives the first pagan family into the Church, that of Cornelius (cf. Acts 10:9–48; 11:1–18). And St Paul, after his conversion and despite receiving the Gospel in a revelation from Jesus Christ (cf. Gal 1:11–12), went up to Jerusalem around the year 39, to see Cephas (as he usually called him), and stayed with him for two weeks (cf. Gal 1:18–19)—a clear sign of the veneration St Paul had for the man chosen by the Lord to be the visible head of the Church.

The Jewish authorities, too, were aware of the leading place St Peter had in the early Church, as can be seen from the fact that, around the year 43, Herod Agrippa I had him imprisoned with the intention of putting him to death (cf. Acts 12:3–4). On that occasion the Church "made earnest prayer" to God for him (Acts 12:5); after he was miraculously released from prison "he departed

---

4. Mt 16:18–19; cf. note on Mt 16:13–20. **5.** Lk 22:31–32; cf. note on Lk 22:31–34. **6.** Cf. Jn 21:15–17 and note on same.

and went to another place" (Acts 12:17)—probably Antioch or Rome. We do know that he spent some time in Antioch (cf. Gal 2:11–14), but it is not clear whether it was at this juncture (tradition tells us that he occupied the see of Antioch for a while). We do know for certain that he was present at the apostolic Council of Jerusalem in the year 49 (cf. Acts 15:7–11), at which, once again, he played a key role in promoting the unity of the Church.

There is evidence to support an ancient tradition of St Peter spending a period in Rome, as its bishop, and suffering a martyr's death there under the emperor Nero. What is not clear is when exactly he arrived in Rome or how long he stayed there; nor is the precise date of his martyrdom known. Some commentators think that he went to Rome twice—once, when he left Jerusalem, around the year 49, the date of the Council. Prior to the year 60 he would have returned to Rome, although he was probably away from the city for periods, on missionary journeys. This theory would explain why he is not mentioned in the greetings in St Paul's Letter to the Romans (in 57–58), nor in connexion with Paul's first imprisonment in Rome (in 61–63). Other scholars, however, think that St Peter went to Rome only once, during the reign of Nero (54–68).

As far as his death is concerned, it is certain that he suffered martyrdom in Rome under Nero (the tradition is that he was crucified, head down). On the basis of information supplied by Eusebius,[7] and by St Jerome, some put the likely date at the year 67, which was when St Paul also died; however, others suggest the year 64, when, after the burning of Rome, Nero was responsible for the persecution and death of very many Christians.

A very ancient tradition, supported by archaeological excavations, says that the tomb of the prince of the Apostles lies under the altar of St Peter's basilica.

THE AUTHOR

The greeting at the start of the letter gives the author as the apostle St Peter (cf. 1 Pet 1:1), a witness of the sufferings of Christ (cf. 1 Pet 5:1). This is consistent both with the external testimony of Tradition and with examination of the text itself.

Throughout Christian antiquity, no doubts were raised about the Petrine authorship of the letter or about its being a canonical, inspired, text. As far back as the end of the second century, St Irenaeus of Lyons quotes from it several times, attributing it expressly to St Peter.[9] The same is true of Clement of Alexandria (d. 214),[10] the author of the first commentary on the letter.[11]

In addition to the explicit testimonies, there are implicit ones of an even earlier time—the first half of the second century. Although they do not

---

7. Cf. *Chronicon*, book 2. 8. *On Famous Men*, 1, 5. 9. Cf. *Against Heresies*, 4, 9, 2; 16, 5; 5, 7, 2.
10. Cf. *Stromata*, 4, 7, 47. 11. Cf. *Hypothyposeis*.

mention the author, they do show that this letter was regarded even then as having the authority of an inspired document. Thus, St Polycarp cites it a number of times in his *Letter to the Philippians*, as does Papias of Hierapolis, according to fragments of his writing contained in the work of Eusebius of Caesarea.[12] Eusebius (d. 339 or 340) summarizes Christian tradition prior to his time when he says that this epistle belongs to those New Testament writings accepted by all and rejected by none.[13]

All the ancient canons (lists of inspired books) which have come down to us mention this letter (all, that is, except the Muratorian Canon; but this exception may be due to the fact that part of that document is missing). Thus, the epistle appears in the canons of the provincial councils of Laodicea (*c.*360), Hippo (393), and the third and fourth councils of Carthage (397 and 419), as also in Pope St Innocent I's letter to Exuperius, bishop of Toulouse (405).

Examination of the content of the letter supports its Petrine origin: there are very obvious similarities between the teaching contained in it and the discourses of St Peter recorded in the Acts of the Apostles; for example: the portrayal of Jesus as the Servant of Yahweh (cf., e.g., 1 Pet 2:22–25; Acts 3:13) and the cornerstone rejected by the builders (cf. 1 Pet 2:4–8; Acts 4:11); and the resurrection of our Lord as the kernel of the Christian faith and of the proclamation of the Gospel.

Silvanus' part in the letter. "By Silvanus," St Peter says at the end of his letter, "a faithful brother as I regard him, I have written briefly to you" (1 Pet 5:20). This seems to be the Silvanus who worked with St Paul in the evangelization of Asia Minor (cf. 2 Cor 1:9; 1 Thess 1:1; 2 Thess 1:1), who is called Silas in the Acts of the Apostles (cf., e.g., Acts 15:22ff; 16:19, 25). He would therefore have known very well the people the letter was addressed to.

St Peter's very brief mention of Silvanus does not make it quite clear what role he played in connexion with the letter; he may simply have been the bearer and commentator of the letter; he may have been an amanuensis who took down the apostle's dictation (which was Tertius' role in the Letter to the Romans: cf. Rom 16:22); or he may have acted as editor or redactor, who faithfully put into writing ideas given him by St Peter.

St Jerome uses the last-mentioned possibility to explain the differences in style between the First and Second Letters of St Peter: "As the need arose, he [Peter] used different interpreters."[14] Some modern scholars also favour this theory because it may best explain the letter's flowing Greek, the ease with which the author quotes and draws inspiration from the Greek version of the Old Testament (the Septuagint), and the coincidences noticeable between this letter and certain letters of St Paul (particularly Romans and Ephesians). This theory does seem to be the best one.

---

12. Cf. *Ecclesiastical History*, 3, 39, 17.   **13.** Cf. ibid., 3, 1; 3, 25, 2.   **14.** *Epist. ad Hedibiam*, 120, 11.

Introduction to the First Letter of St Peter

In any event, if Silvanus was in fact the redactor of the epistle, that does not take anything away from its authenticity as a Petrine text, for St Peter clearly makes it his own (cf. 1 Pet 1:1; 5:12).

IMMEDIATE READERSHIP AND DATE OF COMPOSITION

The letter is addressed to a number of Christian communities in different parts of Asia Minor (cf. 1:1). No indications are given as to whether St Peter knew these Christians personally (the region in question had been evangelized by St Paul, accompanied in fact by Silvanus: cf. Acts 15:40ff). These young communities were located in a hostile environment, which could have made it difficult for them to persevere in the faith. It is possible that when the Apostle learned of the trials they were experiencing he decided it would be good to write them some words of encouragement.

From the letter itself it is clear that quite a number of these Christians were converts from paganism. For example, there are references to their "former ignorance" (1:14) about God, who "called (them) out of darkness into his marvellous light" (2:9), so that those who were formerly no people are now become "God's people" (cf. 2:10). These and other features of the letter (cf. 1:18; 2:25; 4:2–4) suggest that these were first-generation Christians, who had only recently embraced the faith—which also explains why St Peter frequently reminds them of their Baptism (cf. 1:3, 23; 2:2; 3:21).

As regards the date, certain things point to the letter's having been written around the year 64. For example, the opening greeting (cf. 1:1) implies that Christianity has already spread through Asia Minor, and therefore the letter should be dated after St Paul's last journey in the region (50–57). Also, there is no mention of St Paul, which seems to indicate that he had already left Rome, after being set free from captivity in the spring of 63. On the other hand, the letter was probably written prior to the persecution under Nero (July 64), because that is not mentioned. As indicated at the end of the letter, it was written in "Babylon" (5:13), undoubtedly a reference to Rome, the capital of the Empire, often given the symbolic name of "Babylon" (cf. Rev 14:8; 16:19; 17:5; 18:2, 10, 21).

CONTENT

The main purpose of the letter seemingly was to console and exhort Christians to stand firm in the midst of difficulties. It does not have any very clear structure. Very often doctrinal points are developed in the course of the exhortation. However, the fact that it follows no particular plan does not mean that it is not a single, coherent whole.

The *prologue* (1:1–12) consists of the usual greeting (1:1–2) and an introductory hymn of thanksgiving (1:3–12), which mentions the difficulties of those Christians who are being exhorted to perseverance.

The body of the letter (1:13–5:11) can be divided into three sections, followed by final exhortations.

1. *The first part* (1:13—2:10) is a stirring invitation to seek holiness. This is based on two main points—the holiness of God who called them (1:13–16) and the blood of Christ which rescued them from sin (1:17–21). Holiness should express itself in charity (1:22–25) and in their effort to grow in the Christian life (2:1–3), conscious of the fact that, like living stones, they form the edifice of the Church (2:4–10).

2. *The second part* (2:11—3:12) identifies the kinds of obligations Christians have in society—exemplary lives to be led by all in a pagan environment (2:11–12); citizens' duties to legitimate authority (2:13–17); servants' duties to their masters (2:18–25); the duties of husband and wife in family life (3:1–7); and the duty of all to practise the greatest fraternity (3:8–12).

3. *The third part* (3:13—4:19) expands on the way Christians should cope with persecution and trials: the baptized have a part to play in the redemptive mystery of Christ. When they suffer unjustly they can count themselves blessed (3:13–17), for Christ suffered unto death before he was glorified (3:18–22). The Christian, who is a member of Christ's body, has broken with sin (4:1–6) and has to practise charity (4:7–11). This section ends by speaking about the spiritual value of suffering unjust persecution (4:12–19).

4. At the end of the letter St Peter addresses a series of *exhortations* to priests (5:1–4) and to all the faithful (5:5–11), encouraging all to put their trust in the Lord.

As in other New Testament letters, the *epilogue* (5:12–14), sends greetings from the church of the sender and concludes with some words of blessing.

TRIALS

St Peter may have been spurred to write this letter by the various trials (cf. 1:6–7) these Christians were experiencing, including unjust accusation (cf. 2:12–15), revilement (cf. 3:9–17) and abuse (cf. 4:4); he goes so far as to describe these trials as a "fiery ordeal" (cf. 4:12–16) which he fears may cause them to waver.

It is unlikely that he is referring to official persecution: the persecution instigated by Nero did not extend to the provinces of Asia Minor; empire-wide persecution did not occur until much later in the time of Domitian (d. 96) and Trajan (d.117). These latter persecutions were so severe that he would have written in more dramatic terms if he had been referring to them. He must therefore mean opposition in different forms from the pagan world around them, a world which felt affronted by the lifestyle of these recent converts (cf. 4:4) and which therefore discriminated against them in various ways.

These Christian communities felt alienated by their fellow-citizens (cf. 2:11–12); but the clash of lifestyles also occurred within the family circle, where slaves had to bear injustice from their masters (cf. 2:18–25) and wives intolerance from their husbands (cf. 3:1–3).

The letter is clearly written in a tone of consolation and exhortation. The trials they have to bear have a positive side: they should avail of them to draw closer to God; he, not men, is their true Judge (cf. 4:19). They should realize that their imitation of Jesus will bring good results and will even attract their persecutors to the faith (cf. 2:12). The sacred writer does not confine himself to giving occasional advice on humility (cf. 5:5–7) but tells them, in line with our Lord's teaching (cf. Mt 5:10–12), that they are blessed, and encourages them to bear their sufferings joyfully (cf. 4:13). He develops a particularly profound and consoling idea: the Christian is built into Christ and shares in his paschal mystery; just as Jesus, in order to redeem man, underwent his passion and death and afterwards was raised to everlasting life, so too Christians will attain their own salvation, and that of many others, by bearing trials well. Jesus Christ is their model and it is also he who gives full meaning to trials as Christian experiences (cf. 4:12–19).

BAPTISM

Although he explicitly mentions Baptism only once (cf. 3:21), St Peter frequently alludes to this sacrament which makes us members of Jesus Christ and marks the start of a new life: by God's "great mercy we have been born anew to a living hope" (1:3). These references help to identify elements of baptismal liturgy and pre-baptismal catechetical instruction. From his teaching we can notice three things: Baptism means a rebirth; it sets one free from sin (it is prefigured in the liberation of the Israelites from Egypt); the salvation of Noah is a "type" of the salvation effected by this sacrament.

In the New Testament Baptism is often depicted as a *new birth* (cf., e.g., Jn 3:3ff; Tit 3:5; 1 Jn 2:29). St Peter sees Christians as "born anew" of imperishable seed (cf. 1:23; 1:3) and he encourages them, as "newborn babes" (2:2), to live in goodness and simplicity, desirous of the spiritual nourishment that they receive from the Word of God and from the sacraments.

Baptism is also *liberation from the slavery of sin*. Christians have broken with sin (cf. 4:1–6) and have passed from slavery to the freedom of the children of God, because they have been ransomed "with the precious blood of Christ, like that of a lamb without blemish or spot" (1:19; cf. note on 1:1–2).

Without formally citing them, the letter contains many references which recall the exodus of the Israelites from the land of Egypt, as if that ancient liberation worked by God prefigured what happens in Baptism. Thus, St Peter teaches the Christians that previously they were not a people but now they are "God's own people" (2:10); previously they lived in ignorance, but now they are called to holiness (cf. 1:14–15). The mention of the "lamb without blemish or spot" (1:19) recalls the paschal lamb (cf. Ex 12:5) whose blood the Israelites smeared on the lintels of their doors; and the advice to "gird up" their minds (cf. 1:13) seems to be an allusion to the passages in which the Israelites are told to eat the paschal lamb girded as for a journey (cf. Ex 12:11).

Moreover, Christians are "a chosen race, a royal priesthood, a holy nation, God's own people" (2:9): the text is interwoven with a quotation from the book of Exodus (cf. Ex 19:5–6), which explains the consequences of God's Covenant with his people, and another from Isaiah (cf. Is 43:20–21) which recalls the epic journey of the Israelites in the wilderness. The new people of God (cf. 2:10), born through Baptism, have a duty—a stricter one than that imposed on the Israelites—to imitate God's holiness (cf. 1:15–16; Lev 19:2; 20:7–8) and to give up their former concupiscence (cf. 1:14).

Reference to the events of the exodus to show what happens at Baptism is something very common in the Tradition of the Church: "Reflect with me", St Cyril of Jerusalem taught neophytes in the fourth century, "on the passage from the old things to the new, the passage from figure to reality. There Moses was sent by God to Egypt; here Christ is sent to the world from the bosom of his Father. There it was a question of bringing the chosen people out of Egypt; here Christ must set free those who in the world were enslaved by sin; there the blood of the lamb deflected the exterminator; here the blood of the immaculate Lamb, Jesus Christ, acts as a refuge against the demons."[15] And the liturgy includes the reading of the account of the passage of the Red Sea (cf. Ex 14:15—15:1) in the Easter Vigil, in which Baptism is solemnly administered.

Finally, the letter mentions *the salvation of Noah as a type of Baptism*. The only time the letter explicitly uses the word "Baptism" (cf. 3:21) is when it compares the salvation of Noah and his family from the flood with that of the Christian faithful, who are saved by the water of Baptism (cf. 3:18–22). St Peter is not saying that there is an exact parallel between both events, but he is clearly teaching about the efficacy of the sacrament of Baptism.

Water on its own only serves to remove dirt (cf. 3:21); the sacrament of Baptism cleanses the soul of original sin and of every other sin, purifying the heart from all stain by bathing the body with pure water (cf. Heb 10:22). By receiving Baptism one is asking God "for a clear conscience, through the

---

15. *Mystagogical Catechesis*, 1, 3.

resurrection of Jesus Christ" (3:21): these words imply, above all, a moral cleansing in the Christian; but they may also contain a reference to the commitment to keep the faith which the neophyte professed; they may even refer to what later came to be known as the baptismal "character".[16]

OTHER DOCTRINAL ASPECTS

Possibly following the style of a baptismal catechism, the letter includes doctrinal points important for helping Christians to stay true to their faith (cf. 5:9).

For example, it recalls (though not systematically) the dogma of the Blessed Trinity (cf. 1:2–12; 4:14); the divinity of Jesus Christ with his title of *Kyrios*, Lord (cf. 1:3; 2:3; 3:15), and his redemptive work: by his passion, death and resurrection he has obtained salvation for all mankind (cf. 1:17–21; 3:18–22); in Baptism the faithful become members of him in such a way as to have a share in his sufferings and glory (cf. 2:18–25; 3:13ff).

Although the Church is not named as such, it is present throughout the letter: Christians, who are brothers to one another, are living stones in the spiritual building which has Christ as its cornerstone (cf. 2:4–10); they are the new priestly people established by God (cf. 2:9); Christ is their Shepherd (cf. 2:25) and in his name pastors must tend souls disinterestedly and lovingly (cf. 5:1–4).

Hope of eternal life should encourage Christians on their earthly pilgrimage (cf. 1:1, 17; 2:11); they have been reborn so as to obtain an imperishable inheritance (cf. 1:4); the difficulties and trials they experience will not last for long, for the hour will come when the faithful will receive their definitive, glorious reward, and when the guilty will be punished (cf. 4:17–19). This hope of theirs is a distinctive mark of believers and they should always be ready to explain it to others (cf. 3:15).

These truths of our faith form the basis of the apostle's exhortations, which are sometimes addressed to Christians in general and sometimes to particular groups—servants (cf. 2:18–25), women (cf. 3:1–6), husbands (cf. 3:7), priests (cf. 5:1–4), young people (cf. 5:5). Particular stress is laid on humility (cf. 2:18–25; 3:8–9; 5:5ff) and on the joy which should govern the Christian life, no matter how difficult times are (cf. 1:2–12; 4:12–19).

---

16. Cf. note on 1 Pet 3:21.

THE FIRST LETTER OF PETER

The Revised Standard Version, with notes

Greeting

1 ¹Peter, an apostle of Jesus Christ, To the exiles of the Dispersion in Pontus, Galatia, Cappadocia, Asia, and Bithynia,* ²chosen and destined by God the Father and sanctified by the Spirit for obedience to Jesus Christ and for sprinkling with his blood:
May grace and peace be multiplied to you.

Jas 1:1
Rom 8:29
Heb 12:24
2 Thess 2:13

Praise and thanksgiving to God

³Blessed be the God and Father of our Lord Jesus Christ! By his great mercy we have been born anew to a living hope through the

Eph 2:4

1:1–2. In his greeting the sacred writer uses the name conferred on him by Jesus: Peter is the Greek translation of the Aramaic word *cephas*, which means rock (cf. 1 Jn 1:42 and note). He introduces himself as "an apostle of Jesus Christ", a trustworthy witness to our Lord's life.

The "Dispersion" (Diaspora) originally referred to Jews who were resident outside Palestine, but here the term is given a deeper meaning: St Peter addresses those who are "exiles of the Dispersion", that is, Christians, who are living on this earth like wayfarers journeying towards their lasting homeland, heaven. On this idea, often found in Scripture (cf., e.g., Gen 47:9; the entire book of Exodus; Ps 39:13; 119:19; Heb 11:13), he will insist further (cf. 1:17; 2:11).

The regions mentioned in v. 1 were in Asia Minor (present-day Turkey). Perhaps the first news they received of Christianity came from Jews who had been converted on the day of Pentecost and were domiciled in these places (cf. Acts 2:9). Later, St Paul evangelized part of this region.

Verse 2 explains the sublime choice that has been made of Christians: by an eternal design of God they have been chosen from all eternity (cf. Rom 8:28–30; Eph 1:4–6) and sanctified by the Holy Spirit. Their election has a double purpose—to obey Jesus Christ by faith and good works, and to enable them to be "sprinkled with his blood", that is, take a

full share of the fruits of Redemption. The words are evocative of the events on Sinai: when Moses read the book of the Covenant to the people, they pledged obedience to Yahweh and then Moses sprinkled them with the blood of the sacrifices to seal the Covenant (cf. Ex 24:7–8). By referring to obedience and to sprinkling with blood, the apostle is reminding them that Christ brought about the new and enduring Covenant, sealed by the blood he shed on the cross. This whole verse, therefore, is really a short, profound profession of faith in the Blessed Trinity: to the Father is attributed the choice made from all eternity; to the Son, redemption; to the Holy Spirit, sanctification.

The grace and peace he wishes his readers is a type of Christian greeting, often used by St Paul (cf. note on Rom 1:7; also 2 Pet 1:2): it expresses a wish for God's blessing (which comes in the form of sanctifying grace and the gifts of the Holy Spirit) and inner peace, the effect of the reconciliation with God which Jesus has brought about.

1:3–12. This passage, a hymn of praise and gratitude to God, developing what is proclaimed in v. 2, is more explicit about the action of each person of the Blessed Trinity: by making his choice of Christians, God the Father has destined us to a marvellous heritage in heaven (vv.

Col 1:5, 12

Rom 5:2
2 Cor 4:17
Heb 12:11

resurrection of Jesus Christ from the dead, ⁴and to an inheritance which is imperishable, undefiled, and unfading, kept in heaven for you, ⁵who by God's power are guarded through faith for a salvation ready to be revealed in the last time. ⁶In this you rejoice,ᵃ though now for a little while you may have to suffer various trials,

---

3–5); to attain this we need to love and believe in Jesus Christ our Lord (vv. 6–9); the Holy Spirit, who earlier proclaimed salvation by the mouth of the Old Testament prophets, is now, through those who preach the Gospel, announcing that salvation has arrived (vv. 10–12).

1:3–5. When the fruits of the Redemption are applied to us, a kind of rebirth takes place. St Peter is the only New Testament writer to use the Greek term translated here "we have been born anew" (cf. also 1:23); but the same idea occurs elsewhere: St John speaks of the action of the Holy Spirit at Baptism as causing one to be born again (cf. Jn 3:1ff; also, e.g., 1:12–13; 1 Jn 2:29; 3:9); St Paul refers to "a new creation" to describe the effects of Redemption (cf., e.g., Gal 6:15; 2 Cor 5:17); and St James calls Christians the "first fruits of his creatures" (Jas 1:16–18).

Through this being born again, God destines us "to a living hope", which centres on the inheritance of heaven, here described as "imperishable" (it is eternal), "undefiled" (it contains no evil) and "unfading" (it will never grow old). The sacred writer uses these adjectives of negation to show that heavenly things are not subject to any of the imperfections and defects of earthly things.

For those Christians who stay true to their calling, this inheritance is "kept in heaven". This key theme will be addressed in various parts of the letter (cf. 2:18–25; 3:13–17; 4:12–19; 5:5–11); the letter is very much aimed at encouraging the faithful to bear sufferings with joy, knowing

that they are a means to and a guarantee of heaven.

1:3. God brought about the work of Redemption "by his great mercy". For "God, who is rich in mercy, out of the great love with which he loved us, even when we were dead through our trespasses, made us alive together with Christ" (Eph 2:4–5). And just as the work of Creation is a manifestation of God's omnipotence, so his new Creation is an expression of his mercy (cf. *Summa theologiae*, 2–2, 30, 4; cf. the note on 2 Cor 5:17).

"Through the resurrection of Jesus Christ from the dead": the resurrection of our Lord marks the climax of his salvific work, for it assures men of their redemption and their own resurrection. In its Easter liturgy the Church joyfully reminds us of this: "He is the true Lamb who took away the sins of the world. By dying he destroyed our death; by rising he restored our life" (*Easter Preface*, I).

1:6–9. Hope of obtaining the inheritance of heaven gives Christians joy in the midst of trials which test their faith. At the centre of that faith is Jesus, whom they strive to love above all, thereby attaining "unutterable and exalted joy", a foretaste of the joy of heaven itself.

Exhortations to be joyful in the midst of affliction occur often in the New Testament (cf., e.g., Mt 5:11–12; 2 Cor 1:3–7; Jas 1:2) and reflect a deep Christian conviction, which St Bede refers to in his commentary: "St Peter says that it is

a. Or *Rejoice in this*

[7]so that the genuineness of your faith, more precious than gold which though perishable is tested by fire, may redound to praise and glory and honour at the revelation of Jesus Christ. [8]Without having seen[b] him you[c] love him; though you do not now see him you[c] believe in him and rejoice with unutterable and exalted joy. [9]As the outcome of your faith you obtain the salvation of your souls.

Prov 17:3
Rom 2:7, 10
Jas 1:3; Mal 3:3

Jn 17:20; 20:29
2 Cor 5:7
Rom 6:22

[10]The prophets who prophesied of the grace that was to be yours searched and inquired about this salvation; [11]they inquired

good to suffer trials because eternal joys cannot be obtained except through the afflictions and sorrows of this passing world. 'For a little while', he says, however, because when one receives an eternal reward, the afflictions of this world—which appeared so heavy and bitter—seem then to have been very short-lived and slight" (*Super 1 Pet. expositio*, ad loc.).

Christian joy is the fruit of faith, hope and love. "You should realize that God wants us to be happy and that, if you do all you can, you will be happy, very, very happy, although you will never be a moment without the Cross. But that Cross is no longer a gallows. It is the throne from which Christ reigns" (St Josemaría Escrivá, *Friends of God*, 141).

1:7. The refining of gold by fire is often referred to in Scripture (cf., e.g., Ps 66:10; Prov 17:3; 1 Cor 3:12–13; Rev 3:18) to explain that the sufferings of this life help to improve the quality of one's faith. "If I experience pain," St Augustine teaches, "relief will come in due course. If I am offered tribulation, it will serve for my purification. Does gold shine in the craftsman's furnace? It will shine later, when it forms part of the collar, when it is part of the jewellery. But, for the time being, it puts up with being in the fire because when it sheds its impurities it will acquire its brilliant shine" (*Enarrationes in Psalmos*, 61, 11).

The thought of Christ coming in glory (cf. 1:5–13; 4:13) should greatly encourage the Christian to bear trials cheerfully.

1:10–12. These verses of thanksgiving (vv. 3–12) end with a reference to the role of the Holy Spirit in salvation: he acted in the Old Testament through the prophets by announcing salvation, and now, through preachers of the Gospel, he reveals that it has come about.

The passage is a clear acknowledgment of the unity and continuity of the Old and New Testaments: in the Old the sufferings and subsequent glorification of Christ are proclaimed, in such a way that "what the prophets predicted as future events," says St Thomas, "the apostles preached as something which had come true" (*Commentary on Eph* 2:4). "The economy of the Old Testament was deliberately orientated to prepare for and declare in prophecy the coming of Christ, Redeemer of all men, and of the messianic Kingdom (cf. Lk 24:44; Jn 5:39; 1 Pet 1:10) [...]. God, the inspirer and author of the books of both Testaments, in his wisdom has so brought it about that the New should be hidden in the Old and that the Old should be made manifest in the New. For although Christ founded the New Covenant in his blood (cf. Lk 22:20; 1 Cor 11:25), still the books of the Old Testament, all of them caught up into the

b. Other ancient authorities read *known*   **c.** Or omit *you*

Is 53; Mt 13:17
Lk 24:27

Eph 3:10
what person or time was indicated by the Spirit of Christ* within them when predicting the sufferings of Christ and the subsequent glory. ¹²It was revealed to them that they were serving not themselves but you, in the things which have now been announced to you by those who preached the good news to you through the Holy Spirit sent from heaven, things into which angels long to look.

1. A CALL TO HOLINESS

Christians are called to be saints

Lk 12:35
¹³Therefore gird up your minds, be sober, set your hope fully upon the grace that is coming to you at the revelation of Jesus Christ.

Gospel message, attain and show forth their full meaning in the New Testament (cf. Mt 5:17; Lk 24:27; Rom 16:25–26; 2 Cor 3:14–16) and in their turn, shed light on it and explain it" (Vatican II, *Dei Verbum*, 15–16).

These verses show the Holy Spirit's role as cause and guide of the evangelizing activity of the Church. In the early days of the spread of Christianity, as described in Acts, the action of the third Person of the Blessed Trinity was palpable.

1:12. The Greek word translated at the end of this verse as "look" contains the idea of bending over carefully in order to get a better look. This metaphor, then, depicts the angels in heaven contemplating with joy the mystery of salvation. St Francis de Sales, referring to this passage, exclaims: "Now in this complacency we satiate our soul with delights in such a manner that we do not yet cease to desire to be satiated [...]. The fruition of a thing which always contents never lessens, but is renewed and flourishes incessantly; it is ever agreeable, ever desirable. The perpetual contentment of heavenly lovers produces a desire perpetually content" (*Treatise on the Love of God*, 5, 3).

1:13—2:10. Having focused their attention on the sublimity of the Christian calling, St Peter exhorts the faithful to a holiness in keeping with it. He provides some reasons why they should strive for holiness—the holiness of God (vv. 13–16) and the price paid for their salvation, the blood of Christ (vv. 17–21). He then goes on directly to refer to the importance of love (vv. 22–25); and he encourages them to grow up in their new life (2:1–3) so that as "living stones" they can form part of the spiritual building of the Church, which has Christ as its cornerstone (vv. 4–10).

1:13–16. Israel was chosen by God from all the peoples of the earth to implement his plan of salvation: he set the people of Israel free from the slavery of Egypt, established a covenant with them and gave them commandments about how to live. These commandments in their highest form tell them to be holy as God is holy (cf. Lev 19:2). However, those events in the life of Israel were only an imperfect foreshadowing of what would happen when Jesus Christ came: Christians constitute the new chosen people; by Baptism they have been set free from sin and have been called to live in a fully holy way, with God himself as their model.

¹⁴As obedient children, do not be conformed to the passions of your former ignorance, ¹⁵but as he who called you is holy, be holy yourselves in all your conduct; ¹⁶since it is written, "You shall be holy, for I am holy."

Rom 12:2
Eph 4:17; 2:3

Lev 11:44;
19:2; 20:7

The blood of Christ has ransomed us

¹⁷And if you invoke as Father him who judges each one impartially according to his deeds, conduct yourselves with fear

Jer 3:19; Mt 6:9
Rom 2:11
2 Cor 5:11

The Second Vatican Council solemnly declared that all are called to holiness (cf., e.g., *Lumen gentium*, 11, 40, 42). St Josemaría Escrivá, who anticipated the Council's teaching on this and other points, had constantly preached about this universal call to holiness: "Christ bids all without exception to be perfect as his heavenly Father is perfect. For the vast majority of people, holiness means sanctifying their work, sanctifying themselves in it, and sanctifying others through it—thereby finding God as they go about their daily lives [...]. Since the foundation of the Work in 1928, my teaching has been that sanctity is not the reserve of a privileged few; all the ways of the earth, every state in life, every job, every honest occupation, can be divine" (quoted in Bernal, 3, 3).

1:13. "Gird up your minds": a metaphor based on the custom of the Jews, and Middle Easterners in general, of gathering up their rather full garments prior to setting out on a journey, to let them walk with greater ease. In the account of the Exodus we are told that God laid it down that when the Israelites celebrated the Passover they should do so with their loins girt, their sandals on and a staff in their hand (cf. Ex 12:11), because they were about to start on the journey to the promised land. St Peter evokes this image (which our Lord also used: cf. Lk 12:35ff), because Baptism, the new Exodus, marks the start of the Christian pilgrimage to

heaven, our lasting home (cf. 1:17; 2:11); and he applies it to sobriety: we need to control our feelings and inclinations if we are to walk with joy along the route which will take us to the glorious coming of the Lord.

"The revelation of Jesus Christ": this is a reference, above all, to his eschatological coming at the end of time. The revelation of Jesus began with his incarnation and will reach its climax at the end of this world. Therefore, the "grace" mentioned should be understood not only as sanctifying grace but also the whole ensemble of benefits the Christian receives at Baptism, which will find their full expression in heaven.

1:14. "Your former ignorance": the writer contrasts his hearers' present position with their former one. He does not mean that prior to Baptism they were perverse and ignorant, but that the Christian vocation brings such clear knowledge of God and so many aids to practise virtue that their previous position can be viewed as one of concupiscence and ignorance. "The followers of Christ, called by God, not in virtue of their works but by his design and grace, and justified in the Lord Jesus, have been made sons of God in the baptism of faith and partakers of the divine nature, and so are truly sanctified" (Vatican II, *Lumen gentium*, 40).

1:17–21. The Christian has attained the honour of being a son or daughter of

Is 52:3
1 Cor 6:20; 7:23

Heb 9:14
Jn 1:29
Rom 16:25f
Rom 4:24
Col 1:27

throughout the time of your exile. [18]You know that you were ransomed from the futile ways inherited from your fathers, not with perishable things such as silver or gold, [19]but with the precious blood of Christ, like that of a lamb without blemish or spot. [20]He was destined before the foundation of the world but was made manifest at the end of the times for your sake. [21]Through him you have

God. The sacred writer summarizes God's plan for man's salvation, which comes about in Christ: from all eternity, it was God's design to save men through Christ; this design was made manifest "at the end of the times", when our Lord offered himself as an expiation for the sins of men, and then rose from the dead and was glorified. This is a further reason why Christians should grow in their desire for holiness.

"You were ransomed" (v. 18): the image of ransoming used here to explain Redemption is probably taken from sacred manumission (common at the time in Asia Minor and Greece) whereby slaves were set free through a sum of money being deposited in the temple. When exhorting Christians not to return to their former sins, St Paul also stresses the great size of the ransom (cf. 1 Cor 6:20 and note). The amount of the ransom, St Ambrose points out, "was not reckoned in terms of money but in terms of blood, for Christ died for us; he has set us free with his precious blood, as St Peter also reminds us in his letter [...]; precious because it is the blood of a spotless Lamb, the blood of the Son of God, who has ransomed us not only from the curse of the Law, but also from that never-ending death which impiety implies" (*Expositio Evangelii sec. Lucam*, 7, 117).

"The blood of Christ, like that of a lamb without blemish or spot" (v. 19): in the sacrifice of Jesus was fulfilled the prophecy of Isaiah about the Messiah's expiatory suffering; and it also finally completed the liberation of the Israelite first-born in Egypt through the blood of the paschal lamb (Ex 12; cf. Introduction to this letter). So, when in the New Testament the figure of the Lamb is applied to Christ, this is a way of referring to the atoning sacrifice of the cross and, also, the spotless innocence of the Redeemer (cf. note on Jn 1:29).

1:17. "If you invoke as Father": this may be a reference to the saying of the Our Father, which Christians may have recited at the Baptism ceremony from the very beginning. We do know (cf. the *Didaché*, or *Teaching of the Twelve Apostles*, an anonymous text of the apostolic era) that Christians used to pray the Our Father three times a day (cf. 8, 3). Frequent reflection on the fact that God is our Father fills us with peace and joy and stirs us to act as befits children of such a Father, knowing that God sees us and judges our actions. Therefore, divine filiation can never be taken as a kind of safe-conduct which allows us to be casual about our duties: "Worldly souls are very fond of thinking of God's mercy. And so they are encouraged to persist in their follies.

"It is true that God our Lord is infinitely merciful, but he is also infinitely just: and there is a judgment, and he is the Judge" (St Josemaría Escrivá, *The Way*, 747).

1:21. The resurrection of Jesus is the basis of Christian faith and hope and is the main proof of Jesus' divinity and his divine mission (cf., e.g., 1 Cor 15 and

confidence in God, who raised him from the dead and gave him glory, so that your faith and hope are in God.[d]

Brotherly love

[22]Having purified your souls by your obedience to the truth for a sincere love of the brethren, love one another earnestly from the heart. [23]You have been born anew, not of perishable seed but of imperishable, through the living and abiding word of God; [24]for

1 Jn 3:9
Jas 1:18

> "All flesh is like grass
> and all its glory like the flower of grass.
> The grass withers, and the flower falls,
> [25] but the word of the Lord abides for ever."

Is 40:6, 7
Jas 1:10f

Is 40:8

That word is the good news which was preached to you.

Like newborn babies

2 [1]So put away all malice and all guile and insincerity and envy and all slander. [2]Like newborn babes, long for the pure spiritual milk, that by it you may grow up to salvation; [3]for you have tasted the kindness of the Lord.

Eph 4:22
Jas 1:21

Mt 18:3
1 Cor 3:2
Heb 5:12f

Ps 34:9

---

notes on same). The apostles were, first and foremost, witnesses of our Lord's resurrection (cf. Acts 1:22; 2:32; etc.), and the proclamation of the Resurrection was the core of apostolic catechesis (cf. the discourses of St Peter and St Paul in the Acts of the Apostles).

Jesus Christ rose from the dead by his own power, the power of his divine person (cf. *Creed of the People of God*, 12); the *St Pius V Catechism* points out that "we sometimes, it is true, read in Scripture that he was raised by the Father; but this refers to him as man, just as those passages, on the other hand, which say that he rose by his own power relate to him as God" (1, 6, 8).

1:22–25. Fraternal love is one of the main signs of holiness. Jesus said that this love would be the distinguishing mark of Christians, and the apostles often repeat this teaching in the instruction they impart (cf., e.g., 1 Cor 13; Jas 2:8; 1 Jn).

The new people of God, Vatican II says, "are reborn, not from a corruptible seed, but from an incorruptible one through the word of the living God (cf. 1 Pet 1:23); the law of this people is the new commandment to love as Christ loved us (cf. Jn 13:34)" (*Lumen gentium*, 9).

2:1–3. The liturgy applies this text to the newly baptized (cf. Second Sunday of Easter, entrance antiphon): they are like babies recently born to the new life of grace (cf. 1:23). These verses are an exhortation to have the sincerity and simplicity of children.

Just as little children clamour for their food, Christians should long for the spiritual nourishment that lies in the Word of God and the sacraments. St Bede comments: "Just as children have a natural desire for their mother's milk [...], so should you desire to know the rudiments of the faith [...], so that by learning well you may come to receive the living Bread

d. Or *so that your faith is hope in God*

The priesthood that all believers share

Acts 4:11
Eph 2:21f
Rom 12:1

⁴Come to him, to that living stone, rejected by men but in God's sight chosen and precious; ⁵and like living stones be yourselves

---

that has come down from heaven, through the sacraments of the Lord's incarnation; these sacraments cause you to be born again and give you nourishment that enables you to contemplate the majesty of God" (*Super 1 Pet. expositio*, ad loc.).

Psalm 34, to which St Peter refers in v. 3 says, "Taste and see that the Lord is good" (v. 8); by applying these words to Christ, his divinity is being asserted (cf. note on 1:10–12). Among the early Christians it was quite usual for Holy Communion to be given during the baptismal ceremony (in which this psalm was sung in honour of the Eucharist). "This hymn", St Cyril of Jerusalem teaches, "is a divine melody inviting us to partake of the divine mysteries: 'O taste and see the Lord is good.' It is not your tongue but your sound faith that forms your judgment. For it is not bread and wine that you are tasting, but the body and blood which they contain" (*Mystagogical Catechesis*, 5, 20).

2:2. "Like new-born babies": although this simile applies here to people who have only recently received Baptism, all Christians should throughout their lives have the simplicity and trust of children. "Unless you turn and become like children, you will never enter the kingdom of heaven" (Mt 18:3). Spiritual childhood, whereby we always see ourselves as small children in God's eyes, is one way of growing in intimacy with him. "In our interior life", St Josemaría Escrivá recommends, "it does all of us good to be *quasi infantes*, like those tiny tots who seem to be made of rubber and who even enjoy falling over because they get up right away and are running around again, and

also because they know their parents will always be there to console them whenever they are needed.

"If we try to act like them, our stumbling and failures in the interior life (which, moreover, are inevitable) will never result in bitterness. Our reaction will be one of sorrow but not discouragement, and we'll smile with a smile that gushes up like fresh water out of the joyous awareness that we are children of that Love, that grandeur, that infinite wisdom, that mercy, that is our Father. During the years I have been serving our Lord, I have learned to become a little child of God. I would ask you to do likewise, to be *quasi modo geniti infantes*, children who long for God's word, his bread, his food, his strength, to enable us to behave henceforth as Christian men and women" (*Friends of God*, 146)

"Spiritual milk": this may be an allusion to the promises God made to the chosen people to bring them into "a land flowing with milk and honey" (Ex 3:8), and it could be that from those words the custom grew in the early baptismal liturgy of giving the recently baptized milk mixed with honey (a custom suppressed towards the end of the fourth century). The expression refers to all the graces our Lord gives in Baptism to enable a person attain salvation.

2:4–10. Baptism makes us members of the Church. The sacred writer uses the idea of constructing a building (vv. 4–8) to explain that Christians together go to make up the one, true people of God (vv. 9–19). The whole passage is built on quotations from the Old Testament, possibly ones used in early apostolic catechesis.

built into a spiritual house, to be a holy priesthood, to offer
spiritual sacrifices acceptable to God through Jesus Christ. [6]For it
stands in scripture:

Is 28:16

> "Behold, I am laying in Zion a stone, a cornerstone chosen

Rom 9:33

> and precious,
> and he who believes in him will not be put to shame."

[7]To you therefore who believe, he is precious, but for those who do
not believe,

Ps 118:22
Mt 21:42

> "The very stone which the builders rejected
> has become the head of the corner,"

[8]and

Is 8:14f

> "A stone that will make men stumble,
> a rock that will make them fall";

for they stumble because they disobey the word, as they were
destined to do.

Ex 19:6
Deut 7:6
Eph 5:8

[9]But you are a chosen race, a royal priesthood, a holy nation,

Phil 2:15

God's own people,[e] that you may declare the wonderful deeds of him

Acts 26:18

The Church is like a spiritual building of which Christ is the cornerstone, that is, the stone which supports the entire structure (cf. *Lumen gentium*, 6). Christians have to be living stones united to Christ by faith and grace, thereby forming a solid temple in which "spiritual sacrifices" are offered which are "acceptable to God" (v. 5). The closer their union with Christ, the stronger the building: "All of us who believe in Christ Jesus", Origen explains, "are called 'living stones' [...]. For if you, who are listening to me, want to prepare yourself better for the construction of this building, and be one of the stones closest to the foundation, you need to realize that Christ himself is the foundation of the building we are describing. As the Apostle Paul tells us, 'no other foundation can any one lay than that which is laid, which is Jesus Christ' (1 Cor 3:11)" (*In Iesu nave*, 9, 1).

2:8. Applying to Christ what the prophet Isaiah says of Yahweh (cf. Is 8:14; note on 1 Pet 2:13), St Peter shows how, for

those who do not believe in Christ, the cornerstone becomes a "stone that will make men stumble, a rock that will make them fall"; Simeon prophesied as much to the Blessed Virgin in the temple (cf. Lk 2:34).

"As they were destined to do": this does not mean that God predestined some to damnation. God wants all men to be saved (cf. 1 Tim 2:4), and that was why Jesus Christ became man; but for someone to be saved, his free response is necessary, and man can oppose God's salvific plan and reject grace. It should be remembered that in the language of the Bible, particularly the Old Testament, sometimes no distinction is made between what God orders or wills and what he simply allows to happen (cf. Rom 9:14–33 and notes on same).

2:9–10. In contrast with those who reject faith (vv. 7–8), believers form the true Israel, the true people of God; in it the titles applied to Israel in the Old Testament find their full meaning: they

e. Greek *a people for his possession*

75

Hos 1:6; 9; 2:3,
25
Rom 9:25
who called you out of darkness into his marvellous light. [10]Once you were no people but now you are God's people; once you had not received mercy but now you have received mercy.

---

are "a chosen race" (cf. Ex 19:5–6), a people convoked by God to sing his praises (cf. Is 43:20–21). Their election is not only something Christians should glory in; it makes demands on them: Christians are set apart for God, they belong to him (cf. 1 Cor 6:19), for the blood of Christ has been paid as their ransom (cf. 1 Pet 1:18–21). So, they must not remain passive; they have to preach the greatness of God and draw many other souls to him: "the Good News of the Kingdom which is coming and which has begun is meant", says Pope Paul VI, "for all people of all times. Those who have received the Good News and who have been gathered by it into the community of salvation can and must communicate and spread it" (*Evangelii nuntiandi*, 13).

In this people there is only one priest, Jesus Christ, and one sacrifice, that which he offered on the cross and which is renewed in the Mass. But all Christians, through the sacraments of Baptism and Confirmation, obtain a share in the priesthood of Christ and are thereby equipped to mediate in a priestly way between God and man and to take an active part in divine worship; by so doing they can turn all their actions into "spiritual sacrifices acceptable to God" (1 Pet 2:5). Theirs is a true priesthood, although it is essentially different from the ministerial priesthood of those who receive the sacrament of Order: "Though they differ essentially and not only in degree, the common priesthood of the faithful and the ministerial or hierarchical priesthood are none the less ordered one to another; each in its own proper way shares in the one priesthood of Christ. The ministerial priest, by the sacred power that he has,

forms and rules the priestly people; in the person of Christ he effects the eucharistic sacrifice and offers it to God in the name of all the people. The faithful indeed, by virtue of their royal priesthood, participate in the offering of the Eucharist. They exercise that priesthood, too, by the reception of the sacraments, prayer and thanksgiving, the witness of a holy life, abnegation and active charity" (Vatican II, *Lumen gentium*, 10; cf. *Presbyterorum ordinis*, 2).

And the same Council says, apropos of those "spiritual sacrifices" (v. 5) by which Christians sanctify the world from within, that "all their works, prayers and apostolic undertakings, family and married life, daily work, relaxation of mind and body, if they are accomplished in the Spirit—indeed even the hardships of life if patiently borne—all these become spiritual sacrifices acceptable to God through Jesus Christ (cf. 1 Pet 2:5). In the celebration of the Eucharist these may most fittingly be offered to the Father along with the body of the Lord. And so, worshipping everywhere by their holy actions, the laity consecrate the world itself to God" (*Lumen gentium*, 34).

2:10. A passage from the book of Hosea is applied to the faithful: Yahweh tells the prophet to name two of his children "Not pitied" and "Not my people" (Hos 1:6, 8), to symbolize the unfaithfulness of the people of Israel, for which they deserved to be rejected by God. However, a little further on (Hos 2:22f), when he speaks of the new covenant he is thinking of making, Yahweh says, "I will have pity on Not pitied, and I will say to Not my people, 'You are my people'; and he shall say,

2. THE OBLIGATIONS OF CHRISTIANS

Setting an example for pagans

¹¹Beloved, I beseech you as aliens and exiles to abstain from the passions of the flesh that wage war against your soul. ¹²Maintain

Ps 39:13
Gal 5:17, 24

'Thou art my God'". St Peter indicates that this prophecy has found its fulfilment in the Church, the new people of God.

"Christ instituted this new covenant, namely the new covenant in his blood (cf. 1 Cor 11:25); he called a race made up of Jews and Gentiles which would be one, not according to the flesh, but in the Spirit, and this race would be the new people of God. For those who believe in Christ, who are reborn, not from a corruptible seed, but from an incorruptible one through the word of the living God (cf. 1 Pet 1:23), not from flesh, but from water and the Holy Spirit (cf. Jn 3:5–6), are finally established as a 'chosen race, a royal priesthood, a holy nation ... who in times past were not a people, but now are the people of God' (1 Pet 2:9–10)" (*Lumen gentium*, 9).

2:11—3:12. After outlining the fact that their vocation requires Christians to be holy, the apostle goes on to describe how their conduct will attract Gentiles to the faith (2:11–12)—exemplary behaviour in social and civic life, obeying lawful authority (vv. 13–17); obedience of servants to masters (vv. 18–25); and mutual respect between husband and wife (3:1–7). Finally, he encourages all to practise fraternal charity (3:8–12).

2:11–12. The letter contains many appeals to Christians to stay true to the faith even when pagans criticize them (2:12), cause them to suffer (3:13–15), or insult them for following Christ (4:14). Some authors, reading these remarks as referring to state persecution unleashed by Roman emper-

ors—especially Domitian (d. 96) and Trajan (d. 117)—give the letter a much later date, even a second-century date; but all the information available to us favours a much earlier date, around the year 64 (cf. Introduction). St Peter seems to be referring rather to the trials the faithful met at the hands of their fellow-citizens. At that time Christians often encountered misunderstanding, rejection and discrimination, and even the loss of property (cf., e.g., Acts 19:23–31; 2 Thess 2:14).

This context explains why the apostle encourages these recent converts (he once again reminds them they are wayfarers: cf. 1:1, 17) to lead exemplary lives, so that those among whom they live, although they may initially misinterpret their conduct, will end up glorifying God: "Let your light so shine before men, that they see your good works and give glory to your Father who is in heaven" (Mt 5:16). Good example is enormously effective in drawing souls closer to God. St John Chrysostom exhorted his flock in this way: "There would be no need for preaching if our life were a beacon of virtues—no call for words if we had deeds to show. There would be no pagans if we were truly Christians—if we kept Jesus Christ's commandments, if we put up with unjust treatment and deception, if we blessed those who cursed us, if we returned good for evil. No one would be such a monster not to embrace the true religion immediately if we really lived like that" (*Hom. on 1 Tim*, 10).

In addition to being mindful of exterior difficulties, St Peter does not

Jas 3:13
Mt 5:16
Is 10:3
good conduct among the Gentiles, so that in case they speak against you as wrongdoers, they may see your good deeds and glorify God on the day of visitation.

Obedience to civil authority

Rom 13:1, 7
Tit 3:1
¹³Be subject for the Lord's sake to every human institution,[f] whether it be to the emperor as supreme, ¹⁴or to governors as sent by him to punish those who do wrong and to praise those who do right. ¹⁵For it is God's will that by doing right you should put to

---

forget that the greatest danger lies in personal evil inclinations which "wage war against your soul" (v. 11). Constant effort is called for if one is to control one's passions and overcome temptation (cf., e.g., Mt 10:38–39; 1 Cor 9:24–27; 1 Tim 6:12): "There are people who want to be humble," St Gregory the Great teaches, "but without being despised; who want to be content with their lot, provided they have all they need; to be chaste, but without mortifying their body; to be patient, provided no one offends them. When they try to acquire virtues but avoid the effort which virtues involve, it is as if, with no experience of combat on the battlefield, they want to win the war without moving from the city" (*Moralia*, 7, 28).

"The day of visitation": this may refer to the time when the Lord will come in glory at the end of the world; but from the context it seems, rather, to refer to his coming to the hearts of the Gentiles through the grace of conversion (cf. Lk 19:44).

2:13–17. Christians should be exemplary in all their dealings with others, obeying the emperor and other people in authority "for the Lord's sake". Jesus taught the obligation of conscientious fulfilment of civic duties (cf. Mt 22:21–22; 17:24–27);

and St Paul, echoing the Master's teaching, reminds us that all authority comes from God (Rom 13:1–7; cf. Jn 19:11). The first Christians, in the midst of trials and persecutions, were heroically faithful to their civic duties; not only did they not react violently against unjust persecution, but they prayed for their persecutors (cf. note on Rom 13:1–7).

As regards relations between citizen and State, the Magisterium of the Church teaches that, on the side of the State, authority "must be exercised within the limits of the moral order and directed toward the common good (understood in the dynamic sense of the term) according to the juridical order legitimately established or due to be established. Citizens, then, are bound in conscience to obey (cf. Rom 13:5). Accordingly, the responsibility, the dignity, and the importance of civic rulers is clear.

"When citizens are under the oppression of a public authority which oversteps its competence, they should still not refuse to give or to do whatever is objectively demanded of them by the common good; but it is legitimate for them to defend their own rights and those of their fellow citizens against abuses of this authority within the limits of the natural law and the law of the Gospel" (Vatican II, *Gaudium et spes*, 74).

---

f. Or *every institution ordained for men*

silence the ignorance of foolish men. ¹⁶Live as free men, yet without using your freedom as a pretext for evil; but live as servants of God. ¹⁷Honour all men. Love the brotherhood. Fear God. Honour the emperor.

Duties towards masters. Christ's example

¹⁸Servants, be submissive to your masters with all respect, not only to the kind and gentle but also to the overbearing. ¹⁹For one is approved if, mindful of God, he endures pain while suffering unjustly. ²⁰For what credit is it, if when you do wrong and are beaten for it you take it patiently? But if when you do right and suffer for it you take it patiently, you have God's approval. ²¹For

---

2:16. By obeying political authority, the faithful are not surrendering their freedom; on the contrary, they are correctly using, in generous service of God and of others, the freedom which Christ has won for them. St Peter encourages them to "live as free men", conscious that they are "servants of God".

The Second Vatican Council teaches that Christians "should be a shining example by their sense of responsibility and their dedication to the common good; they should show in practice how authority can be reconciled with freedom, personal initiative with the solidarity and the needs of the whole social framework, and the advantages of unity with profitable diversity" (*Gaudium et spes*, 75).

2:17. The Christian's social and political duties are summed up here in four points. "Honour all men": that is, treat them as befits their human dignity (cf. *Gaudium et spes*, 12–22). "Love the brotherhood," that is, everyone in the Church, thereby keeping our Lord's new commandment (cf. 1 Pet 1:22; Jn 13:34). "Fear God," the source of all wisdom, avoiding all selfishness (cf. Prov 1:7; 1 Jn 4:17–18 and note). "Honour the emperor": give to Caesar the things that are Caesar's (cf. Mt 22:21 and note).

2:18–25. The writer now addresses all domestic servants (the Greek word means all who work in household tasks). He exhorts them to obey their masters, even if they are harsh (v. 18), because God is pleased if they put up with unfairness for his sake (vv. 19–20); in doing so they are imitating the example of Jesus (vv. 21–25). St Paul, when addressing slaves in his letters (cf. Eph 5:5–9; Col 3:22–24), never encourages them to rebel. Christian teaching on social issues is not based on class struggle but on fraternal love: love eventually does away with all discrimination, for all men have been created in the image of God and are equal in his sight. This peaceable policy gradually made for the suppression of slavery, and it will also lead to the solution of all social problems (cf. *Gaudium et spes*, 29).

The fact that St Peter addresses only servants and does not go on to say anything to masters (as St Paul usually does: cf. Eph 6:5–9; Col 3:23ff) has led some commentators to suggest that most of the Christians addressed in this letter must have been people of humble condition.

2:21–25. This passage is a beautiful hymn to Christ on the cross. Christ's sufferings, which fulfil the prophecies about the Servant of Yahweh contained in the book

<table>
<tr><td>Is 53:9
Jn 8:46</td><td>to this you have been called, because Christ also suffered for you, leaving you an example, that you should follow in his steps. ²²He</td></tr>
</table>

Is 53:9
Jn 8:46

Is 53:12
Mt 5:39

Is 53:4, 5, 12
2 Cor 5:21
Heb 9:28
Rom 3:24f; 6:11

Is 53:6
Ezek 34:5
Jn 10:12
1 Pet 5:4

to this you have been called, because Christ also suffered for you, leaving you an example, that you should follow in his steps. ²²He committed no sin; no guile was found on his lips. ²³When he was reviled, he did not revile in return; when he suffered, he did not threaten; but he trusted to him who judges justly. ²⁴He himself bore our sins in his body on the tree,ᵍ that we might die to sin and live to righteousness. By his wounds you have been healed. ²⁵For you were straying like sheep, but have now returned to the Shepherd and Guardian of your souls.

---

of Isaiah (52:13 53:12), have not been in vain, for they have a redemptive value. He has taken our sins upon himself and brought them with him onto the cross, offering himself as an atoning sacrifice. This means that we are free of our sins ("dead to sin") and can live "to right-eousness", that is, can live for holiness with the help of grace.

The example of the suffering Christ is always a necessary reference point for Christians: however great the trials they experience, they will never be as great or as unjust as those of our Lord. Reflecting on Christ's suffering led St Bernard to comment: "I have come to see that true wisdom lies in meditating on these things [...]. Some have provided me with whole-some, if bitter, drink, and I have used others as gentle and soothing unction. This gives me strength in adversity and helps me to be humble in prosperity; it allows me to walk with a sure step on the royal road of salvation, through the good things and the evil things of this present life, free from the dangers which threaten to right and left" (*Sermons on the Song of Songs*, 43, 4).

2:25. The messianic prophecy about the Servant of Yahweh includes the image of the scattered flock (cf. Is 53:6), to which Jesus alludes in his allegory of the Good Shepherd (cf. Jn 10:11–16). St Peter, to

whom our Lord had given charge of his flock (cf. Jn 21:15–19), would have had a special liking for imagery connected with shepherding.

Jesus Christ is "the Shepherd and Guardian of your souls" and "the chief Shepherd" (1 Pet 5:4). The etymology of the Greek word—*epíscopos* (guardian)—means "overseer"; the word was used in civic life to designate those who were responsible for seeing that the law was kept. In the Dead Sea manuscripts the Hebrew equivalent (*mebaqqer*) is used to designate the religious leaders of the schismatic community of Qumran. Whatever might be the origin of the term, in the New Testament the word *epíscopos* is often used to mean the pastor of the Church (cf., e.g., Acts 20:28; see the note on 1 Pet 5:1–4). Here St Peter applies to Christ the words the prophet Ezekiel places on the lips of God: "I will seek out my sheep, and I will rescue them from all places where they have been scattered" (Ezek 34:12). Our Lord found-ed the Church as a sheepfold "whose sheep, although watched over by human shepherds, are nevertheless at all times led and brought to pasture by Christ himself, the Good Shepherd and prince of shepherds (cf. Jn 10:11; 1 Pet 5:4), who gave his life for his sheep (cf. Jn 10:11–16)" (Vatican II, *Lumen gentium*, 6).

g. Or *carried up ... to the tree*

Exemplary family life

3 ¹Likewise you wives,* be submissive to your husbands, so that some, though they do not obey the word, may be won without a word by the behaviour of their wives, ²when they see your reverent and chaste behaviour. ³Let not yours be the outward adorning with braiding of hair, decoration of gold, and wearing of fine clothing, ⁴but let it be the hidden person of the heart with the imperishable jewel of a gentle and quiet spirit, which in God's sight is very precious. ⁵So once the holy women who hoped in God used to adorn themselves and were submissive to their husbands, ⁶as Sarah obeyed Abraham, calling him lord. And you are now her children if you do right and let nothing terrify you.

⁷Likewise you husbands, live considerately with your wives, bestowing honour on the woman as the weaker sex, since you are joint heirs of the grace of life, in order that your prayers may not be hindered.

Eph 5:22
1 Cor 7:16

1 Pet 2:12

Is 3:18, 24
1 Tim 2:9
Rev 17:4

Gen 18:12
Prov 3:25

Love of the brethren

⁸Finally, all of you, have unity of spirit, sympathy, love of the brethren, a tender heart and a humble mind. ⁹Do not return evil for

Rom 12:16

3:1–7. The counsels and appeals in this passage are not meant to cover all aspects of the sacrament of Marriage; in contrast with the morality of the time, St Peter simply exhorts married people, both men and women, to live in a Christian way, and offers them practical advice.

"Joint heirs of the grace of life" (v. 7): St Peter identifies the source of the dignity of women, who up to then (especially in the East) were regarded as inferior to men: according to Christian teaching man and woman are equal in dignity, because both are children of God and have the same supernatural destiny. The essential equality of men and women does not gainsay their different roles in marriage.

3:1–2. Again he reminds them of the importance of good example (cf. 2:11–12). Throughout the history of the Church, many women have converted husbands who were pagans or separated from God.

St Augustine movingly describes the example of his mother, St Monica: "she served (her husband) as her lord. She made every effort to win him to you, speaking of you to him by her behaviour, by which you made her beautiful to her husband, respected and loved by him and admirable in his sight. For she bore his acts of unfaithfulness quietly, and never had any jealous scene with her husband about them. She hoped that your mercy would come upon him and that he believing in you might become chaste [...]. The upshot was that towards the very end of his life she won her husband to you; and once he was a Christian she no longer had to complain of the things she had had to bear with before he was a Christian" (*Confessions*, 9, 9).

3:8–12. St Peter now addresses the faithful in general, emphasizing their membership of the Church. The exhortation ends with a quotation from Psalm 34

Mt 5:39, 44
1 Thess 5:15

Ps 34:13–17
Jas 1:26

evil or reviling for reviling; but on the contrary bless, for to this you have been called, that you may obtain a blessing. ¹⁰For

>"He that would love life
>and see good days,
>let him keep his tongue from evil
>and his lips from speaking guile;
>¹¹ let him turn away from evil and do right;
>let him seek peace and pursue it.
>¹² For the eyes of the Lord are upon the righteous,
>and his ears are open to their prayer.
>But the face of the Lord is against those that do evil."

3. THE CHRISTIAN'S ATTITUDE TO SUFFERING

Rom 8:34

Mt 5:10

Undeserved suffering is a blessing

¹³Now who is there to harm you if you are zealous for what is right? ¹⁴But even if you do suffer for righteousness' sake, you will

---

(vv. 12–16), a psalm he quoted earlier (cf. 2:3).

Love is the virtue that must govern the Christian life (vv. 8–9; cf. 1:22–25). This theological virtue influences all the moral virtues (St Peter here makes mention of unity, fraternity, compassion and humility, all of which replace the law of vengeance). He also stresses that their Christian calling dictates the way they should act: they have been chosen to inherit the blessings of God and therefore they in their turn should bless, not curse, others.

3:13—4:19. The sacred writer now makes a series of appeals designed to give hope to Christians suffering unjustly on account of Jesus' name: he reminds them that every baptized person is called to share in the paschal mystery of Christ, that is, in his sufferings and in his glorification; just as he, after suffering

unjustly, was glorified (3:18–22), so too those who now suffer for Christ will have a part in his glorious triumph (4:13–14).

The section begins and ends speaking about the Christian meaning of tribulation (3:13–17 and 4:12–19): trials should not make them feel cowed or ashamed, nor should they come as a surprise; on the contrary, they should fill them with joy and lead them to glorify God for letting them partake in our Lord's suffering.

The apostle also points to one of the reasons for the misunderstandings they experience: after Baptism they have broken with their previous sinful life and that is something pagans cannot understand (4:1–6). Also, Christians should remember that life is something very transient, and therefore they should practise prayer and charity (4:7–11).

3:13–17. These verses act as an introduction to the central theme of this section

be blessed. Have no fear of them, nor be troubled, [15]but in your hearts reverence Christ as Lord. Always be prepared to make a defence to any one who calls you to account for the hope that is in you, yet do it with gentleness and reverence; [16]and keep your conscience clear, so that, when you are abused, those who revile your good behaviour in Christ may be put to shame. [17]For it is better to suffer for doing right, if that should be God's will, than for doing wrong.

Is 8:13
1 Pet 1:3

1 Pet 2:12

(3:13—4:19). They seem to be directed to people who are surprised to encounter persecution despite doing good (v. 13). Opposition should not dismay them; their calumniators will come to realize their mistake (v. 16).

St Peter's words of advice have a very positive ring about them; they are really an application of the beatitude in which our Lord says, "Blessed are you when men revile you and persecute you and utter all kinds of evil against you falsely on my account. Rejoice and be glad, for your reward is great in heaven" (Mt 5:11–12).

St Peter's teachings have a perennial value for disciples of Christ, for (as history clearly shows) fidelity to the Master brings with it persecution (cf. Jn 15:18–22; 2 Tim 3:12), sometimes open and violent persecution, sometimes persecution of a more subtle type, in the form of calumny, humiliation and other hazards.

3:15. "Reverence Christ as Lord": literally, "Hallow", as in the Our Father. The words imply recognition of the divinity of Jesus Christ: he is called Lord (*Kyrios*), a name proper to God; and they are told to "glorify" or "reverence" him, that is, render him the worship that is due to God alone. Even in the midst of difficulties the entire Christian life should be a hymn of praise to God; by acting in this way, Christians are living out their

holy, royal priesthood (1 Pet 2:4–10; cf. Vatican II, *Presbyterorum ordinis*, 1).

"To account for the hope that is in you": he is not referring to defending oneself before the courts, for official persecution had not yet become widespread in Asia Minor (cf. note on 2:11–12). He seems, rather, to be referring to the obligation to bear witness to their faith and hope, for all baptized persons should always, by word and example, make their faith known to others.

3:18–22. This passage may include parts of a Creed used in early Christian baptismal instruction. It very clearly expresses the essence of faith in Jesus Christ, as preached from the beginning by the apostles (cf. Acts 2:14–36; 1 Cor 15:1ff) and as articulated in the Apostles' Creed: "He was crucified, died and was buried. He descended into hell; the third day he rose again from the dead. He ascended into heaven and sits at the right hand of God the Father Almighty."

Jesus Christ, who suffers for the sins of mankind—"the righteous for the unrighteous"—and then is glorified, gives meaning to the sufferings of Christians. "Oh, how great thanks am I bound to return to you for having shown me and all the faithful the right and good way to your everlasting kingdom! For your life is our life; and by holy patience we walk on to you, who are our crown. If you had not gone before and taught us, who

1 Pet 2:21, 24
Rom 6:10
Heb 9:28

1 Pet 4:6
2 Pet 3:9
Gen 7:7, 17

Christ's suffering and glorification

[18]For Christ also died[h] for sins once for all, the righteous for the unrighteous, that he might bring us to God, being put to death in the flesh but made alive in the spirit; [19]in which he went and preached to the spirits in prison, [20]who formerly did not obey, when God's patience waited in the days of Noah, during the

---

would care to follow? Alas, how many would have stayed afar off and a great way behind if they had not had before their eyes your wonderful example!" (*The Imitation of Christ*, 3, 18).

3:18. "Christ has died for sins once for all": our Lord's sacrifice is unrepeatable (cf. Heb 9:12–28; 10:10) and superabundantly sufficient to obtain the remission of all sins. The fruits of the cross are applied to man, in a special way, by means of the sacraments, particularly by taking part in the Mass, the unbloody renewal of the sacrifice of Calvary.

"Being put to death in the flesh but made alive in the spirit": there is disagreement among commentators as to what "flesh" and "spirit" mean here. Some identify them with our concepts of body and soul—"dead as regards the body, alive as regards the soul". Others see them as equivalent to the humanity-divinity of our Lord: "dead as far as his human nature is concerned, alive (continues to live) as far as his divinity is concerned". Finally, having regard to the meaning these terms have in the Old Testament, the phrase may refer to the earthly condition of our Lord compared with the glorious condition he had after his resurrection; in which case it would be an early form of words used to convey the idea that Jesus Christ, on dying, left his mortal condition behind for ever in order to move into his glorious, immortal state through his resurrection (cf. 1 Cor 15:35–49).

3:19–20. "In which", that is, in the spirit. The ambiguity of the original text (referred to in the previous note) continues, so it is possible to understand the "in which" in the three ways outlined. Some take it as meaning that Christ went to preach to the spirits in prison "with his soul", separated from his body; for some he went "in his glorious condition", which is not incompatible with the resurrection in the strict sense happening afterwards.

In any event, these verses are one of the clear references in the New Testament to our Lord descending into hell (cf. also Mt 12:38–41; Acts 2:24–36; Rom 10:6–7; Eph 4:8–9; Rev 1:18). After dying on the cross, Jesus Christ went to bring his message of salvation "to the spirits in prison": many Fathers and commentators are inclined to the view that this is a reference to the just of the Old Testament who, not being able to enter heaven until the Redemption took place, were kept in the bosom of Abraham, which is also called the "limbo" of the just (cf. *St Pius V Catechism*, 1, 6, 1–6).

The reference to the contemporaries of Noah is probably explained by the fact that, for the Jews of the time, those people (along with the people of Sodom and Gomorrah: cf. Mt 24:36–39; Lk 17:26–30) were the classic inveterate sinners. By bringing in this reference St Peter is teaching that the Redemption embraces all men: even the contemporaries of Noah, if they repented, could have attained salvation through the merits of Christ.

h. Other ancient authorities read *suffered*

building of the ark, in which a few, that is, eight persons, were saved through water. ²¹Baptism, which corresponds to this, now saves you, not as a removal of dirt from the body but as an appeal to God for a clear conscience, through the resurrection of Jesus Christ, ²²who has gone into heaven and is at the right hand of God, with angels, authorities, and powers subject to him.

Heb 10:22

Eph 1:21
Ps 110:1

The Christian has broken with sin

4 ¹Since therefore Christ suffered in the flesh,ⁱ arm yourselves with the same thought, for whoever has suffered in the fleshⁱ

Rom 6:2, 7

3:21–22. The waters of the Flood are a figure of Baptism: in the same way as Noah and his family were saved by being in the Ark, now men are saved through Baptism, which makes them members of Christ's Church.

"As an appeal to God for a clear conscience, through the resurrection of Jesus Christ": the obvious meaning of this is that the Christian asks for perseverance in the good way of life he entered into at Baptism. However, the Greek word translated as "appeal", a rarely used one, contains the idea of "commitment". It is possible that this may be a reference to a part of the baptismal rite—for example, the profession of faith the neophyte made, and his promise to stay true to it. Or it may refer to a permanent effect of Baptism whereby the Christian is given a share in "the resurrection of Christ": it would not be surprising if St Peter were referring to what later came to be known as the baptismal "character". In fact, the context suggests something permanent and indelible: just as Noah's salvation was a lasting one and there was never again a flood, so too the condition of the Christian is something permanent; now that he has risen Jesus can never die again (cf. Rom 6:3) and neither can the baptized return to their former sinful condition.

Verse 22, possibly taken from a baptismal hymn, is a very concise account of

the glorification of Christ. After descending into hell, he arose and ascended into heaven, where he is seated "at the right hand of God": this phrase, already common in early Christian catechesis (cf., e.g., Mt 22:41–46; Mk 16:19; Acts 2:33) means that our Lord, who is equal to the Father in his divinity, also, as man, occupies at his side the place of honour over all other created beings. This universal lordship of Christ is further emphasized by the statement that all heavenly beings are subject to him (cf. Phil 2:10; Eph 1:21); three degrees of angels are mentioned, that is, all the angels, because the number three symbolizes totality.

4:1–6. The apostle continues his exposition, possibly following the pattern of baptismal instruction. Christians have to identify with Christ, dead and risen: they have died with him, to rise with him (cf. Rom 6:3); their lives can no longer be the way they were before Baptism, even if the change of lifestyle results in their being misunderstood and reviled. They should remember that they will in due course appear before the Judge of the living and the dead, Jesus Christ.

"Whoever has suffered in the flesh has ceased from sin" (v. 1): this looks like a legal adage, meaning that one who has suffered the pain of death has paid for all his crimes (cf. Rom 6:7). St Peter

i. Other ancient authorities add *for us*; some *for you*

85

1 Jn 2:16f
Tit 3:3
Rom 1:28

Acts 10:42

1 Pet 3:19
Rom 8:10
1 Cor 5:5

1 Cor 10:11
Prov 10:12
1 Cor 13:7

has ceased from sin,* ²so as to live for the rest of the time in the flesh no longer by human passions but by the will of God. ³Let the time that is past suffice for doing what the Gentiles like to do, living in licentiousness, passions, drunkenness, revels, carousing, and lawless idolatry. ⁴They are surprised that you do not now join them in the same wild profligacy, and they abuse you; ⁵but they will give account to him who is ready to judge the living and the dead. ⁶For this is why the gospel was preached even to the dead, that though judged in the flesh like men, they might live in the spirit like God.

A call for charity

⁷The end of all things is at hand; therefore keep sane and sober for your prayers. ⁸Above all hold unfailing your love for one another,

---

would have adapted it to give it a theological meaning: Christians, by dying mystically with Christ in Baptism, have had all their sins forgiven and therefore it does not make sense to continue to live in them (cf. Rom 6:1ff; 1 Jn 3:9; 5:18).

This new mode of behaviour has led to opposition from pagans, who cannot understand why they have given up the vices they previously indulged in. Some of the sins mentioned (sins not common among Jews), and the reference to abuse by Gentiles, suggest that the letter was originally written to Christian converts from paganism. The reaction of the pagans to their behaviour, constituting as it does a moral reproach for their sinful lives, is nothing new: Why did Cain kill Abel, St John asks himself, and he replies, "Because his deeds were evil and his brother's righteous" (1 Jn 3:12). This type of reaction is always liable to occur.

In this connexion the apostle reminds them that Judgment is nigh (cf. note on 4:7), and that judgment will show everything up in its true light. He who "is ready to judge the living and the dead" (v. 5) is Jesus Christ; in many other passages of the New Testament it reads "who will come to judge (cf. 5:4; Acts 10:42; 2 Tim 4:1): this must have been a standard formula in early

Christian catechesis, which passed into the Apostles' Creed.

4:6. "The gospel was preached even to the dead": it is not easy to work out what this means; it may be an allusion to our Lord descending into the bosom of Abraham (cf. 3:19–20). However, St Peter is possibly referring to Christians who have already died without seeing, in this life, the final victory of Christ: the preaching they heard, and their lives according to the Gospel (which brought them insults from their contemporaries), have not been in vain.

In either case, St Peter would be referring to those who remained faithful to God, whose life seemed folly to people without supernatural outlook. This passage is evocative of the following text from the book of Wisdom: "The souls of the righteous are in the hand of God, and no torment will ever touch them. In the eyes of the foolish they seemed to have died, and their departure was thought to be an affliction, and their going from us to be their destruction; but they are at peace. For though in the sight of men they were punished, their hope is full of immortality" (Wis 3:1–4).

4:7–11. "The end of all things is at hand": the incarnation of Jesus Christ marked

since love covers a multitude of sins. ⁹Practise hospitality ungrudgingly to one another. ¹⁰As each has received a gift, employ

Jas 5:20
1 Pet 1:22
Lk 12:42

the beginning of the last days, a period which extends to the end of the world and the Last Judgment (cf. note on 1 Jn 2:18). That is why the last stage of the world "is at hand", or, as some translate it, "has arrived".

Because the End is imminent (cf. 4:5), St Peter urges them to practise prayer and charity, Christ's "new commandment" (cf. Jn 13:34–35), and also hospitality, which was highly valued among the Semites and encouraged among Christians (cf., e.g., Rom 12:13; 1 Tim 3:2; 5:10).

This readiness to make available to others the gifts one has received from God, will cause God to be glorified in everything through Jesus Christ (v. 11). The passage ends with a doxology or hymn in praise of Christ (possibly as a formula used in early liturgy and familiar to the first Christians). As elsewhere in the New Testament, the doxology does not appear at the end of the letter (cf. Rom 1:25; 9:5; Gal 1:5; Eph 3:21); in fact only three epistles end with a doxology (Romans, Jude and 2 Peter). Therefore, the fact that the doxology comes at this point does not mean that it originally marked the end of the letter; it may indicate that St Peter has been following up to this point the structure of an early form of baptismal catechesis. The themes dealt with in the rest of the letter, the style, and even the vocabulary, all support the view that the same author is writing throughout.

4:8. "Love covers a multitude of sins": this quotation from the Old Testament (Prov 10:12; cf. Jas 5:20) can be taken to refer both to other people's sins (which charity understands and forgives) and to one's own. After teaching us to pray in

the Our Father, "Forgive us our trespasses as we forgive those who trespass against us", our Lord added: "if you forgive men their trespasses, your heavenly Father also will forgive you" (Mt 6:12, 14). And, when he pardoned the sinful woman, he said, "her sins, which are many, are forgiven, for she loved much" (Lk 7:47).

The Church teaches that perfect love for God wins pardon for sins, but it stresses that that love includes a desire to receive the sacrament of Penance, for one cannot love God without wanting to do what he has laid down: "The Sacred Council also teaches that even if it sometimes happens that a person has this contrition made perfect by charity and becomes reconciled to God prior to receiving this sacrament, his reconciliation should not be attributed to his contrition but rather to his desire for the sacrament which is included in his contrition" (Council of Trent, *De sacramento paenitentiae*, chap. 4).

4:10–11. The Christian receives various gifts from God, that is, charisms or graces given mainly for the benefit of others: they should not be kept for oneself but used for the purpose for which they were intended.

Speaking of the apostolic action of the faithful, the Second Vatican Council recalls that "the Holy Spirit sanctifies the people of God through the ministry and the sacraments. However, for the exercise of the apostolate he gives the faithful special gifts besides (cf. 1 Cor 12:7), 'apportioning them to each one as he wills' (1 Cor 12:11), so that each and all, putting at the service of others the grace received, may be 'as good stewards of God's varied grace' (1 Pet 4:10), for the

it for one another, as good stewards of God's varied grace: ¹¹whoever speaks, as one who utters oracles of God; whoever renders service, as one who renders it by the strength which God supplies; in order that in everything God may be glorified through Jesus Christ. To him belong glory and dominion for ever and ever. Amen.

1 Pet 1:6f
Acts 5:41
Rom 8:17

2 Tim 2:12
Jas 1:2

Is 11:2
Ps 89:51f

The Christian meaning of suffering

¹²Beloved, do not be surprised at the fiery ordeal which comes upon you to prove you, as though something strange were happening to you. ¹³But rejoice in so far as you share Christ's sufferings, that you may also rejoice and be glad when his glory is revealed. ¹⁴If you are reproached for the name of Christ, you are blessed,

building up of the whole body in charity (cf. Eph 4:16). From the reception of these charisms, even the most ordinary ones, there arises for each of the faithful the right and duty of exercising them in the Church and in the world for the good of men and the development of the Church" (*Apostolicam actuositatem*, 3).

4:12–19. St Peter now returns to the main theme of this part of the letter (3:13 4:19)—the trials Christians unjustly suffer on account of being followers of Christ (cf. 1:6–7; 2:18–25; 3:13–17). They should not be surprised or ashamed by this; rather, it should make them happy and lead them to glorify God, for if they share in Christ's suffering it means they will also share in his exaltation. St John of Avila wrote: "God wants to open our eyes and have us realize what favours are being done us in things the world regards as disadvantages, and how honoured we are to be scoffed at for seeking the honour of God, and what great reward awaits us for our present depression, and how God's gentle, sweet and loving arms are opened wide to receive those wounded in doing battle on his behalf" (*Letter*, 58).

Moreover, the "spirit of God" will rest on them (v. 14): our Lord promised

the special assistance of the Holy Spirit to persecuted Christians hauled before courts on account of their faith (cf. Mt 10:19–20); St Peter here calls him "the spirit of glory", because his indwelling in the Christian is a guarantee and an anticipation of eternal glory (cf. 2 Cor 1:22).

Before the divine judgment which lies ahead (it is one of the frequent themes of the letter) no one can be complacent (vv. 17–18). The Apostle's severe warnings are reminiscent of those Jesus gave the women of Jerusalem on his way to Calvary: "if they do this when the wood is green, what will happen when it is dry?" (Lk 23:31). However, if one has suffered on Christ's account in this life it is clear that one can approach the judgment with greater confidence (cf. Mt 5:11–12; 10:32).

4:13. "To the prospect of the Kingdom of God," Pope John Paul II teaches, "is linked hope in that glory which has its beginning in the Cross of Christ. The Resurrection revealed this glory—eschatological glory—which in the Cross of Christ was completely obscured by the immensity of suffering. Those who share in the suffering of Christ are also called, through their own sufferings, to share *in glory*" (*Salvifici doloris*, 22).

because the spirit of glory[j] and of God rests upon you. [15]But let none of you suffer as a murderer, or a thief, or a wrongdoer, or a mischief-maker; [16]yet if one suffers as a Christian, let him not be ashamed, but under that name let him glorify God. [17]For the time has come for judgment to begin with the household of God; and if it begins with us, what will be the end of those who do not obey the gospel of God? [18]And

> "If the righteous man is scarcely saved,
>
> where will the impious and sinner appear?"

[19]Therefore let those who suffer according to God's will do right and entrust their souls to a faithful Creator.

Lk 10:6; Acts 5:41; 1 Pet 2:20
Acts 11:26;
26:28; Phil 1:20
Ezek 9:6; Jer 25:29; Lk 23:31
1 Cor 11:32
2 Thess 1:8
Prov 11:31
Lk 23:46

4. FINAL EXHORTATIONS

To priests

5 [1]So I exhort the elders among you, as a fellow elder and a witness of the sufferings of Christ as well as a partaker in the glory that is to be revealed. [2]Tend the flock of God that is your

Mt 17:5
Rom 8:17
2 Jn 1
Jn 21:16
Acts 20:28
Philem 14
Tit 1:7

4:16. This is one of the three places in the New Testament in which Christ's disciples are described as "Christians" (cf. Acts 11:26; 26:28). As St Luke explains in Acts, they were first given this name in Antioch, the capital of the Roman province of Syria (cf. Acts 11:26).

Being a Christian should never cause one to be cowed or ashamed; it should be a motive for gratitude to God and for holy pride: "Christians who become cowed or inhibited or envious in the face of the licentious behaviour of those who have not accepted the Word of God, show that they have a very poor idea of the faith. If we truly keep the law of Christ—that is, if we make the effort to do so, because we will not always fully succeed—we will find ourselves endowed with a wonderful gallantry of spirit that does not need to look elsewhere to discover the full meaning of human dignity" (St Josemaría Escrivá, *Friends of God*, 38).

5:1–4. In many New Testament texts, the Greek terms *presbyteros* and *epískopos* mean the same, being used indiscriminately to designate pastors of local communities (cf., e.g., Acts 11:30; 20:28; and notes on same). From the second century on, the terminology became fixed: *epískopoi* (bishops) have the fullness of the sacrament of Order and are responsible for local churches; *presbyteroi* (elders, later designated priests) carry out the priestly ministry as co-workers of the bishops. The Acts of the Apostles tell us that Paul and Barnabas ordained priests in the various churches of Asia Minor (cf. Acts 14:23), to which St Peter is now writing (1 Pet 1:1).

The leader of the apostles here addresses them formally. Although he refers to himself as one of them—a "fellow elder [priest]"—he is distinguishing himself as a witness of the sufferings of Christ and "a partaker in the glory that

j. Other ancient authorities insert *and of power*

2 Cor 1:24
Tit 2:7
Phil 3:17
1 Cor 9:25
Heb 13:20
1 Pet 2:25

charge,[k] not by constraint but willingly,[l] not for shameful gain but eagerly, [3]not as domineering over those in your charge but being examples to the flock. [4]And when the chief Shepherd is manifested you will obtain the unfading crown of glory.

Prov 3:34; Jn
13:4, 14; Eph
5:21; Jas 4:6

To all the faithful

[5]Likewise you that are younger be subject to the elders. Clothe

---

is to be revealed" (this is possibly an allusion to the Transfiguration, at which he was given a foretaste of that glory: cf. Mt 17:1ff; 2 Pet 1:16–18).

St Peter's exhortations (vv. 2–3) recall those of our Lord when he spoke about the Good Shepherd (Jn 10:1ff) and when he told Peter after the Resurrection, "Feed my lambs.... Feed my sheep" (Jn 21:15–17). The Magisterium of the Church has often drawn inspiration from these words when reminding pastors of their duties: "As to the faithful, they (the priests) should bestow their paternal attention and solicitude on them, whom they have begotten spiritually through baptism and instruction (cf. 1 Cor 4:15; 1 Pet 1:23). Gladly constituting themselves models of the flock (cf. 1 Pet 5:3), they should preside over and serve their local community in such a way that it may deserve to be called by the name which is given to the unique People of God in its entirety, that is to say, the Church of God (cf. Cor 1:2; 2 Cor 1:21; and passim). They should be mindful that by their daily conduct and solicitude they display the reality of a truly priestly and pastoral ministry both to believers and unbelievers alike, to Catholics and non-Catholics; that they are bound to bear witness before all men of the truth and of the life, and as good shepherds seek after those too (cf. Lk 15:4–7) who, whilst having been baptized in the catholic Church, have given up the practice of the sacraments,

or even fallen away from the faith" (*Lumen gentium*, 28; cf. No. 41).

If they approach their responsibilities in this way, they will have no reason to fear the Judgment (v. 4); the Lord will make himself present to them as "the chief Shepherd", whom they have tried to imitate in their care of the flock, and they will receive "the unfading crown of glory" (cf. note on Jas 1:12). "When the moment comes for them to enter God's presence, Jesus will go out to meet him. He will glorify forever those who have acted on earth in his Person and in his name. He will shower them with that grace of which they have been ministers" (St Josemaría Escrivá, *In Love with the Church*, 50).

5:3. St Gregory the Great teaches that the pastor of souls "should always give the lead, to show by his example the way to life, so that his flock (who follow the voice and the actions of the pastor) are guided more by example than by words; his position obliges him to speak of elevated things, and also to manifest them personally; the word more easily gains access to the hearts of hearers when it carries with it the endorsement of the life of him who when giving instructions assists in their fulfilment by his own example" (*Regulae pastoralis*, 2, 3).

5:5–11. The apostle concludes his exhortation with a call to humility, which should express itself in complete docility

---

k. Other ancient authorities add *exercising the oversight* l. Other ancient authorities add *as God would have you*

yourselves, all of you, with humility toward one another, for "God
opposes the proud, but gives grace to the humble."

⁶Humble yourselves therefore under the mighty hand of God,   Job 22:29
that in due time he may exalt you. ⁷Cast all your anxieties on him,   Ps 55:23
for he cares about you. ⁸Be sober, be watchful. Your adversary the   Mt 6:25

---

in the face of the trials God permits (vv.
6–7). This last piece of advice is often
found in Scripture: "Cast your burden
on the Lord, and he will sustain you"
(Ps 55:22); Jesus also teaches that we
should trust in God's fatherly providence
(cf. Mt 6:19–34). "You have such care for
each one of us", St Augustine exclaims,
"as if you had no others to care for"
(*Confessions*, 3, 11).

However, abandonment in God does
not mean irresponsibility, so St Peter
reminds them there is always need to be
watchful against the assaults of the devil,
who will pounce on us if we lower our
guard (v. 8).

The description of the devil (etymo-
logically the word means liar, detractor:
cf. Rev 12:9–10) as a roaring lion seeking
someone to devour has often been taken
up by the saints. "He moves round each
one of us", St Cyprian says, "like an
enemy who has us surrounded and is
checking the walls to see if there is some
weak, unsecured part, where he can get
in" (*De zelo et livore*).

Christians "firm in the faith" will
resist the attacks of the devil. The trials
they suffer (cf. 1:6–7; 4:13; 5:1–4) serve
to purify them and are a pledge of the
glory God will give them: "For this
momentary affliction is preparing for us
an eternal weight of glory beyond all
comparisons" (2 Cor 4:17). "So great is
the good that I hope for, that any pain is
for me a pleasure" (St Francis of Assisi,
Reflections on Christ's Wounds, 1).

5:5. "You who are younger": it is not clear
whether he is addressing people who are

young in age, or Christians who are not
"elders" (priests), that is, lay people.

"God opposes the proud, but gives
grace to the humble": a quotation from
Proverbs (cf. Jas 4:6 and note on same),
containing an idea which runs right
through the Old Testament (cf., e.g., Job
12:19; Ps 18:88; 31:34) and the teachings
of Christ (cf., e.g., Lk 14:11). The Blessed
Virgin proclaims this truth in the
Magnificat: "he has put down the mighty
from their thrones, and exalted those of
low degree" (Lk 1:52).

"Humility is the source and foundation of every kind of virtue," the Curé
of Ars teaches; "it is the door by which
all God-given graces enter; it is what
seasons all our actions, making them so
valuable and so pleasing to God. Finally,
it makes us masters of God's heart, to the
point, so to speak, of making him our
servant; for God has never been able to
resist a humble heart" (*Selected Sermons*,
10th Sunday after Pentecost).

5:8. For the third time, St Peter exhorts
the faithful to be sober; earlier he referred
to the importance of sobriety so as to put
one's hope in heavenly things (1:13) and
to help one to pray (4:7). Now he stresses
that it puts us on guard against the devil.

Man should use the goods of this
world in a balanced, temperate way, so as
to avoid being ensnared by them, thereby
forgetting his eternal destiny: "Detach
yourself from the goods of the world.
Love and practise poverty of spirit: be
content with what enables you to live a
simple and sober life. Otherwise, you
will never be an apostle" (St Josemaría
Escrivá, *The Way*, 631).

1 Thess 5:6
Jas 4:7
Rev 5:5

Eph 6:11, 13

1 Thess 2:12

devil prowls around like a roaring lion, seeking some one to devour. ⁹Resist him, firm in your faith, knowing that the same experience of suffering is required of your brotherhood throughout the world. ¹⁰And after you have suffered a little while, the God of all grace, who has called you to his eternal glory in Christ, will himself restore, establish, and strengthen^m you. ¹¹To him be the dominion for ever and ever. Amen.

Words of farewell

Acts 15:22–27
Heb 13:22

Acts 12:12
2 Jn 13

¹²By Silvanus, a faithful brother as I regard him, I have written briefly to you, exhorting and declaring that this is the true grace of God; stand fast in it. ¹³She who is at Babylon,* who is likewise chosen, sends you greetings; and so does my son Mark. ¹⁴Greet one another with the kiss of love.

Peace to all of you that are in Christ.

5:12. Silvanus, called Silas in the Acts of the Apostles (Acts 15:22) accompanied St Paul on his second apostolic journey through Asia Minor and Greece (cf. Acts 15:36—18:22); he was therefore well known to the Christians addressed in this letter.

From the reference St Peter makes to him here, it is not possible to say for sure whether Silvanus was simply the bearer of the letter, or acted as an amanuensis who took down the apostle's dictation, or was an editor or redactor of ideas the apostle gave him (on this subject, see the Introduction to this letter).

5:13. "Babylon": this is a symbolic way of referring to Rome, the prototype of the idolatrous and worldly city of the era. Some centuries earlier Babylon had been the subject of severe reproaches and threats by the prophets (cf., e.g., Is 13:47; Jer 50–51). In the book of Revelation Rome is also referred to by this name (cf. e.g., Rev 17–18).

The Mark referred to is the author of the Second Gospel. Tradition says that he

acted as St Peter's interpreter in Rome. The apostle calls him "son", meaning that he was spiritually his son, and implying that they had been close to each other for a long time.

5:14. "The kiss of love": St Paul also, at the end of some of his letters, refers to the "holy kiss" (cf. Rom 16:16; 1 Cor 16:20; 2 Cor 13:12; 1 Thess 5:26), a mark of supernatural charity and shared faith. With this meaning the gesture passed into primitive eucharistic liturgy (cf. note on 1 Cor 16:20).

The final words, "Peace to all of you that are in Christ", are similar to the way St Paul ends many of his letters; since the first age of the Church it has been used in liturgical celebrations. St Cyril of Jerusalem, for example, ends his baptismal catechism with these words: "May the God of peace hallow you entirely, and your body and your soul remain unsullied until the coming of our Lord Jesus Christ, to whom be glory for ever and ever. Amen" (*Mystagogical Catechesis*, 5, 23).

---

m. Other ancient authorities read *restore, establish, strengthen and settle*

Introduction to the Second Letter of St Peter

THE AUTHOR

At the start of the letter the writer introduces himself by his two names—Simon (in the original, Simeon, the Semitic form: cf. Acts 15:14) and Peter—adding reference to his vocation, "apostle of Jesus Christ". In the course of the letter he makes some allusions to himself: he was an eyewitness of the transfiguration of Jesus (cf. 1:16–18); this is the second time he is writing to his readers (cf. 3:1), a reference no doubt to 1 Peter; he calls St Paul "our beloved brother" (3:15); and he speaks about his death, possibly referring to Jesus' prophecy of his martyrdom (cf. Jn 21:18–19).

Despite this information, this is the New Testament text whose authenticity has been most debated. In the first two centuries Tradition provides no clear reference to St Peter being its author; from the third and fourth century onwards there are numerous testimonies to Petrine authorship, among them those of Clement of Alexandria (d. 214), according to Eusebius.[1] Towards the middle of the third century, Origen, who was aware of the doubts about the letter's authenticity, quotes 2 Peter 1:4 as words of St Peter;[2] and elsewhere he remarks that "Peter proclaims with the trumpets of his two epistles."[3] Dating from the same period is the testimony of Firmilian, bishop of Caesarea in Cappadocia, in his *Letter to Cyprian*.[4]

In his *Ecclesiastical History* Eusebius of Caesarea includes this letter among the "disputed" New Testament writings, that is, those not accepted by all, although accepted by most;[5] he himself did not regard it as canonical.[6] On the other hand, several fourth-century writers—including St Athanasius, St Basil, St Gregory Nazianzen, and Didymus of Alexandria—made use of it in their works.

What St Jerome has to say is particularly interesting. On the one hand, he mentions doubts about its Petrine authorship and the reasons for those doubts: Peter "wrote two epistles which are called 'catholic', the second of which many say is not his, because of the difference in style from the first."[7] At another point he offers a solution to this difficulty: "The two epistles which bear Peter's name differ from one another in both style and character. From which we conclude that, in accordance with his needs, he used different secretaries."[8]

---

1. Cf. *Ecclesiastical History*, 6, 14, 1.   **2.** Cf. *In Lev. hom.*, 6, 4.   **3.** *In Iesu nave*, 7, 1.   **4.** Cf. 75, 6.
5. Cf. *Ecclesiastical History*, 3, 25, 3.   **6.** Cf. ibid., 3, 3, 1.   **7.** *On Famous Men*, 1.   **8.** *Epist. ad Hedibiam*, 120, 11.

Introduction to the Second Letter of St Peter

The main difficulties about attributing the letter to St Peter come from study of the text itself. The vocabulary and style are noticeably different from those in the First Letter of St Peter, with expressions that seem better suited to a later period; there is the mention of the apostles and "fathers";[9] the letter's view of the second coming of Christ seems to be different;[10] St Paul's letters are, in 2 Peter, already regarded as Scripture (cf. 3:15–16); finally, the letter seems to have been written after the Letter of St Jude, from which it seems to quote.

These difficulties do not rule out St Peter as the author. In fact, there are also notable similarities between the letter and 1 Peter[11] and also between it and the discourses of Peter recorded in Acts.[12] For this reason some Catholic authors suggest that 2 Peter was written in Rome, around the year 64 or 67, shortly before the apostle was martyred.

It is also possible that an anonymous disciple of St Peter, under the inspiration of the Holy Spirit, chose to pass on certain teachings which were in line with those of the apostle. By using Peter's name and authority, he would be resorting to a device common at the time (pseudonymous writing), well aware that the ideas he was giving were not his own but those of the apostle Peter. In this case, the redactor would not be trying to usurp St Peter's name but rather to acknowledge the paternity of ideas contained in the letter.

If the letter was in fact written pseudonymously, it could date from around the years 80–90. However, there are insufficient grounds for dating the letter well into the second century, as some have tried to do.

As far as its being an inspired and therefore canonical letter is concerned, it is of secondary importance whether it was written by St Peter or by an anonymous disciple of his. The letter appears in the earliest lists of canonical books, such as those of the Council of Laodicea (360), Hippo (393), the third and fourth Councils of Carthage (397 and 419) and the letter of Pope Innocent I (405). The Council of Trent issued a declaration to the effect that this letter and the other texts of the Bible are inspired.[13]

IMMEDIATE READERSHIP

As it says in its opening words, this letter is addressed "to those who have obtained a faith of equal standing with ours" (2 Pet 1:1), that is, Christians in general. Some expressions suggest that the immediate addressees may have been the Christian community of Greece or Asia Minor. For example, we know for a fact that St Paul also wrote to those Christians (cf. 3:15–16);

9. Cf. 2 Pet 3:2–4 and notes on same.   10. Cf. 2 Pet 3:1–10 and notes on same.   11. Cf., e.g., 1 Pet 1:7–9 and 2 Pet 3:1–10; 1 Pet 1:10–12 and 2 Pet 1:19–21; 1 Pet 22 and 2 Pet 1:12; 1 Pet 3:20 and 2 Pet 2:5.   12. Cf. Acts 2:14ff; 3:11ff; 5:29ff; 10:34ff.   13. Cf. *De libris sacris*.

besides, one gets the impression that the writer knows them personally (cf. 1:12–16) and that they were the same persons as those to whom he wrote the First Letter (cf. 3:1). Although originally addressed to particular groups of the faithful, the general tone of the letter shows that the sacred writer had in mind Christians in general.

It is not easy to say where the letter was written. If it was written by St Peter, he must have written it from Rome, where he was living. If it was by a disciple, it could have been written from Rome or else from somewhere in Asia Minor or Egypt. We do not have enough information to be sure.

LINKS BETWEEN 2 PETER AND THE LETTER OF ST JUDE

When 2 Peter and Jude are compared, one immediately notices similarities in the way the ideas are developed: even the wording is the same at times. Specifically, between 2 Peter 2:1–3:3 and Jude 4–18 the parallels are such that the only explanation seems to be that the two texts are linked in some way.

The most likely answer is that 2 Peter is dependent on Jude. Thus, it tends to explain and paraphrase ideas which appear in a much more concise form in Jude; it omits allusions or quotations from Jewish apocryphal writings (especially the *Book of Enoch*) which appear in Jude, and logically the letter which omits these would be the later one; the text of 2 Peter is more elaborate: for example, when it refers to the punishment inflicted by God (cf. 2:4–8) it keeps to a chronological order (angels, the Flood, Sodom), whereas in the parallel passage in Jude (cf. Jud 5–7) that is not the case (his order is: Israelites in the wilderness, angels, Sodom).

These and other little things suggest that the author of this letter was familiar with that of Jude.

CONTENT

The epistle has a fairly clear structure. It begins with a greeting similar to that in other New Testament writings (1:1–2) and ends with an exhortation to perseverance (3:17–18). The body of the letter has three distinct parts: the *first part* (1:3–21) is an appeal for fidelity to teaching received; the *second part* (2:1–22) is a long denunciation of false teachers, immoral people who try to corrupt others; the *third part* (3:1–16) deals with the second coming of Christ; it refutes false views and expounds the true teaching.

From the doctrinal point of view, we might point particularly to what it has to say about the Parousia, its refutation of erroneous theories on that subject, and consequent exhortation.

Introduction to the Second Letter of St Peter

THE FINAL COMING OF THE LORD

The main doctrinal point controverted by the false teachers was the Parousia of the Lord (cf. 3:3–4). This is a subject which comes up often in the New Testament, particularly in the First Letter of St Peter, where the apostle bases his appeal for fidelity in the midst of trials on hope of the next life. The author of 2 Peter faces right into this subject, first, making it quite clear that the Lord will come; and he takes issue with the arguments put forward by the false teachers.

His unequivocal teaching about the coming of Christ at the end of time is based firstly on the episode of the Transfiguration, which was an anticipation of Christ's glorious manifestation (cf. 1:16–18); also, the word of the prophets and of the Old Testament in general confirms this truth (cf. 1:19), because their constant teaching is that God will reward the good and punish the wicked.

One of the false teachers' arguments was that the Parousia was too long in coming. Without going into the ins and outs of this subject, the sacred writer clearly teaches that time is something very relative from the point of view of the eternity of God, for whom "one day is as a thousand years" (3:8), and if God puts off the final moment he does so in his mercy, "not wishing that any should perish" (3:9). One thing is clear: they must remain watchful, for the Day of the Lord will come without warning (cf. 3:10).

Another of their objections was that so much time had gone by and there was as yet no sign of the natural phenomena which were meant to herald the total change the end would bring (cf. 3:3–4). The sacred writer reproaches them for their lack of faith: God created the world by his word alone and in the same way brought about the punishment of the Flood, which involved vast ecological changes (cf. 3:5–6). Therefore, we must believe that it will be his word too that will cause all creation to undergo the profound change which will bring about "new heavens and a new earth" (cf. 3:7, 10, 12, 13).

As regards the specific form the glorious coming of Christ will take and the details of same, the letter contains expressions which are difficult to interpret. It is possible that the sacred writer is using obscure language (as our Lord himself did: cf. Mt 24:36ff and par.) to encourage the faithful to be vigilant, and also to underline the sublimity of this mysterious design of God's.

That Jesus Christ will come in glory to judge the living and the dead has formed part of the Church's creed from the very beginning and was solemnly defined as a dogma of faith by Benedict XII in the constitution *Benedictus Deus* (AD 1336).

THE FALSE TEACHERS

In chapter 2 the sacred writer describes false teachers as men who are greedy (cf. 2:3, 14), dissipated (cf. 2:13), blinded by passion (cf. 2:10, 14, 18), and seducers (cf. 2:14, 18, 19). In chapter 3 he emphasizes, rather, their doctrinal errors: they are scoffers who do not believe in the second coming of Jesus Christ (cf. 3:3–4). By their evil conduct and their false theories they deny the Lord (cf. 2:1) and lead many to perdition (cf. 2:14, 18, 19).

There is no reason to think that the author is taking issue with organized heresy (as some have suggested, to support the theory that this is a text written much later on). Scarcely any details are given about these heresies, whereas St John, for example, does give details in his letters.[14]

The author is mainly concerned to forewarn Christians and thereby draw them away from the moral depravity of the false teachers.

MORAL CONDUCT

In view of the loose morality being promoted by the false teachers, the sacred writer stresses fidelity to the teaching they have received (cf. 1:2, 3, 8; 2:20, 21; 3:18) and perseverance in virtue (cf. 1:5–7; 2:21; 3:11, 14).

At the beginning of the letter (cf. 1:5–7) he gives a list of virtues.[15] This is not meant to cover all Christian morality; it is simply a short, practical survey. Faith, the beginning of the Christian life, is listed first; charity, its climax, comes at the end; and six other inter-connected virtues are listed, like links in the one chain.

Throughout the letter there is much emphasis on motives: on the one hand, the Christian calling (cf. 1:3, 10) and the initiative of God, who gives us promises and a share in his divine nature (cf. 1:4), require us to respond by growing in virtue and avoiding the sins of the past (1:9); on the other hand, the goal that lies ahead (access to the eternal Kingdom of the Lord: cf. 1:11) should encourage us to persevere in good living. If we remember the prophecy of the coming of Christ we will remain vigilant at all times (cf. 1:12–21) and persevere in godliness (cf. 3:11), for we do not know when that time will come (cf. 3:10).

---

14. Cf. "Introduction to the First Letter of St John", below.　**15.** Similar lists appear elsewhere in the New Testament (cf., e.g., Rom 5:3; Gal 5:22–23; Rev 2:19).

THE SECOND LETTER OF PETER

The Revised Standard Version, with notes

Greeting

1 ¹Simon Peter, a servant and apostle of Jesus Christ,
To those who have obtained a faith of equal standing with ours
in the righteousness of our God and Saviour Jesus Christ:ᵃ
Acts 15:14

²May grace and peace be multiplied to you in the knowledge of
God and of Jesus our Lord.
Jude 2

1. A CALL TO FIDELITY

Divine largesse

³His divine power has granted to us all things that pertain to life
and godliness, through the knowledge of him who called us toᵇ his
1 Pet 2:9
2 Cor 4:4, 6

1:1–2. As in other New Testament writings and in ordinary letters of the time, the opening greeting gives the name of the sender, that of the addressees and the greeting as such.

"Simon": the original Greek text says "Simeon", using the Hebrew form of the same name (cf. Acts 15:14). To this he adds that of "Peter", the name the Lord gave him when he promised to make him the head of the apostles (cf. Jn 1:42).

The original addressees of the letter may have been the faithful of the communities of Greece or Asia Minor (cf. the Introduction).

The greeting contains two words frequently used in this setting—"grace and peace" (cf. 1 Pet 1:2 and note)—which sum up the benefits the Christian has received. The true "knowledge of God and of Jesus" is a frequent point of reference in the letter (cf. 1:1, 8; 2:20; 3:18). It is not just intellectual knowledge, but rather the knowledge that comes from familiarity with the Lord and conduct consistent with the faith (cf. 1:5–7). The author emphasizes this point from the very start, because he wants to forestall the influence of false teachings which undermine the faith.

"The righteousness of our God and Saviour Jesus Christ": this may be a reference to God the Father *and* Jesus; but, given that the Greek text uses only one definite article, it is probably a title of Jesus Christ, whom he calls "God and Saviour", in the same way as elsewhere he describes him as "Lord and Saviour" (1:11; 2:20; 3:2, 18). Thus, the divinity of Jesus Christ, which is often proclaimed in the New Testament, is openly acknowledged at the very start of the letter.

1:3–21. The first part of the letter is an appeal for steadfastness and for growth in Christian life. Firstly, Peter encourages his readers to pursue virtue; the reasoning he uses is both simple and profound (vv. 3–11): by his power, God has chosen the apostles and conferred on them wonderful graces in which all the faithful share (vv. 3–4); they must respond to this divine initiative by practising virtue so as to reach the goal and fullness to which the Christian is called (vv. 5–11).

He goes on (vv. 12–21) to remind them that hope in our Lord's second coming is something well founded, something that belongs to the deposit of faith: the transfiguration of our Lord was a foretaste of

---

a. Or *of our God and the Saviour Jesus Christ*   **b.** Or *by*

own glory and excellence, [4]by which he has granted to us his precious and very great promises, that through these you may escape from the corruption that is in the world because of passion, and become partakers of the divine nature.*

Christian virtues

Gal 5:6
1 Thess 4:9

[5]For this very reason make every effort to supplement your faith with virtue, and virtue with knowledge, [6]and knowledge with self-

---

his final coming (vv. 16–18); it was something foretold in many prophecies and no one has the right to argue against it (vv. 19–21). Therefore, the final coming of the Lord is something quite certain and helps to keep our hope alive.

1:3–4. In these verses the same pronoun is repeated three times: "granted to *us*", "called *us*", "granted to *us*"; although he may mean all Christians, it is more likely that he is referring only to the apostles.

The basis of Christian morality and of the practice of virtue (vv. 5–9) is God's initiative in calling the apostles (v. 3) and endowing them with graces (promises) sufficient to make all Christians "partakers of the divine nature".

"His divine power": usually in the Bible calling is attributed to God the Father (cf., e.g., 1 Pet 1:15; 2:9; 5:10); by emphasizing here that it is Jesus Christ who calls "by his own glory and excellence", the author is clearly acknowledging Jesus as God.

"His precious and very great promises": the promises made in the Old Testament, especially those to do with the coming of the Messiah and Saviour. Jesus Christ brought about the Redemption, whereby all men have access to the supernatural good things of which the prophets spoke.

"Partakers of the divine nature": this succinct phrase sums up the fruits that the good things (especially grace) produce in Christians. This sharing in God's own life is both the beginning and the final goal of Christian life. It is the beginning insofar as it is incorporation in Christ through Baptism, and brings with it (through grace and adoptive divine filiation) a sharing in God's own life. It is the final goal of the Christian life since this participation attains its fullness and enduring perfection in heaven, with the contemplation of God "as he is" (1 Jn 3:2 and note on same).

Of course, already in this life the Blessed Trinity dwells in the soul in grace (cf., e.g., Jn 14:17–23; 1 Cor 3:16; 6:19; and notes on same). "Our faith teaches us that man, in the state of grace, is divinized —filled with God" (St Josemaría Escrivá, *Christ Is Passing By*, 103).

Partaking of the divine nature is a basic feature of the Christian vocation. Pope Pius XII reminds us of this marvellous fact, which is closely linked to the mystery of the Incarnation: "If the Word 'emptied himself, taking the form of a servant' (Phil 2:7), he did so in order that his brethren according to the flesh might be made partakers of the divine nature (cf. 2 Pet 1:4), both during this earthly exile by sanctifying grace and in the heavenly home by the possession of eternal beatitude. For this reason the Only-begotten of the Father chose to become a son of man, that we might be made conformable to the image of the Son of God (cf. Rom 8:29) and be renewed according to the likeness of him who created us (cf. Col 3:10)" (*Mystici Corporis*, 20).

control, and self-control with steadfastness, and steadfastness with godliness, [7]and godliness with brotherly affection, and brotherly affection with love. [8]For if these things are yours and abound, they keep you from being ineffective or unfruitful in the knowledge of our Lord Jesus Christ. [9]For whoever lacks these things is blind and shortsighted and has forgotten that he was cleansed from his old sins. [10]Therefore, brethren, be the more zealous to confirm your call and election, for if you do this you will never fall; [11]so there will be richly provided for you an entrance into the eternal kingdom of our Lord and Saviour Jesus Christ.

Gal 6:10

1 Jn 2:9, 11

1 Thess 1:4

Jn 3:5f

On this subject, see also the notes on Rom 8:14–15 and Gal 4:6.

1:5–9. Lists of Christian virtues are also to be found in other parts of the New Testament (cf., e.g., Gal 5:22–23; 1 Tim 6:11; Rev 2:19). This passage provides a list which is well conceived from a pedagogical point of view—simple to remember, because each virtue is linked with the one before it; and the emphasis is on faith and charity, which mark the beginning and end of the list. St Ignatius of Antioch commented on the value of these two theological virtues: "Given an unswerving faith and love for Jesus Christ, there is nothing in all this that will not be obvious to you; for life begins and ends with those two qualities. Faith is the beginning, and love is the end; and the two together lead to God. All that makes for a soul's perfection follows in their train, for nobody who professes faith will commit sin, and nobody who possesses love can feel hatred" (*Letter to the Ephesians*, 14, 1–2).

For Christians, virtues are not an end in themselves but a means necessary for attaining knowledge of Christ (cf. note on 1:1); but union with the Lord calls for works, and if we failed to practise virtues we could not see Christ (v. 9). St Teresa of Avila constantly stresses the need to combine contemplation and action: "I

repeat that if you have this in view you must not build upon foundations of prayer and contemplation alone, for, unless you strive after the virtues and practise them, you will never grow to be more than dwarfs. God grant that nothing worse than this may happen—for, as you know, anyone who fails to go forward begins to go back" (*Interior Castle*, 8, 4,9).

1:10–11. Practice of the virtues not only assures one's vocation and election; it is essential for attaining entry to the eternal kingdom. Holy Scripture teaches that the ultimate prize is a gift from God; it conveys this idea by saying "there will be richly provided for you an entrance", which shows that it is God who bestows the prize—but he counts on man's free response. The Council of Trent solemnly taught that "eternal life should be set before those who persevere in good works to the end (cf. Mt 10:22) and who hope in God. It should be set before them as being the grace that God, through Jesus Christ, has mercifully promised his children, and 'as the reward' which, as God himself promised, must assuredly be given them for their good works and merits" (*De iustificatione*, 16).

"Lord and Saviour Jesus Christ": this expression, which occurs only in this letter (cf. 2:20; 3:2, 18), has become part of Christian tradition, because it is a

Spiritual testimony

Jude 5
2 Cor 5:1

Jn 21:18, 19

[12]Therefore I intend always to remind you of these things, though you know them and are established in the truth that you have. [13]I think it right, as long as I am in this body,[c] to arouse you by way of reminder, [14]since I know that the putting off of my body[c] will be soon, as our Lord Jesus Christ showed me. [15]And I will see to it that after my departure you may be able at any time to recall these things.

Mt 17:1–8
Mk 9:2–8
Lk 9:28–35
Jn 1:14

The Transfiguration, an earnest of the Second Coming

[16]For we did not follow cleverly devised myths when we made known to you the power and coming of our Lord Jesus Christ, but we were eyewitnesses of his majesty.* [17]For when he received honour and glory from God the Father and the voice was borne to him by the Majestic Glory, "This is my beloved Son,[d] with whom

---

perfect summary of faith in Jesus as God and Redeemer. It acknowledges who Jesus Christ is and what he has achieved.

1:12–15. This passage summarizes the purpose of the letter—to remind people about Christian truths and to encourage them to practise virtue.

The sacred author is moved to write by his apostolic zeal and the fact that he is soon to die. Both reasons accurately reflect the personality and spirit of St Peter the apostle.

As far as his foreknowledge of his death is concerned, we do not have much to go on: what he says may be a reference to what our Lord told him (cf. Jn 21:18ff); or it may refer to a later revelation, which certain traditions about the apostle's martyrdom report (for example, that of *Quo vadis?* given in an apocryphal book, *Acts of St Peter*, chap. 35).

The image of the tent ("body": v. 13; cf. Is 38:12) is very expressive of the ephemeral character of man's life on earth. St Paul also uses it (cf. 2 Cor 5:1 and note).

The letter is a kind of spiritual testimony (v. 15); hence its warning about staying true to the faith is a particularly solemn one.

1:16–18. The transfiguration of Jesus Christ, at which the voice of God the Father was heard (vv. 16–18), and the testimony of the Old Testament prophets (vv. 19–21) are a guarantee of the doctrine of Christ's second coming.

"The power and coming of our Lord Jesus Christ": this phrase sums up the purpose of apostolic preaching: "power" indicates that Jesus Christ is God and is almighty like the Father; the "coming" (literally "Parousia") means the same as his manifestation in glory at the end of time. This is not a matter of "myth"; it will be as real as his sojourn on this earth, of which the apostles are "eyewitnesses". When speaking of the Transfiguration, the sacred writer refers to the "majesty" of Jesus Christ (an attribute which he always possesses, because he is God) and the "voice" of the Father confirming Christ's divine nature (cf. Mt 17:5). The

---

c. Greek *tent*   d. Or *my son, my* (or *the*) *Beloved*

I am well pleased," [18]we heard this voice borne from heaven, for we were with him on the holy mountain.

Prophecy and the Second Coming

[19]And we have the prophetic word made more sure. You will do well to pay attention to this as to a lamp shining in a dark place, until the day dawns and the morning star rises in your hearts. [20]First of all you must understand this, that no prophecy of

Rev 2:28
Lk 1:78

---

simple line of argument is that if Jesus Christ allowed his divinity to be glimpsed just for a moment, he will also be able to manifest it in its fullness and forever at the end of time.

"On the holy mountain": this wording indicates that he is referring to the transfiguration and not to the baptism of our Lord (Mt 3:16–17). The mountain is described as "holy" because a theophany occurred there; similarly, in the Old Testament Zion is called a "holy mountain" because God revealed himself there (cf. Ps 2:6; Is 11:9).

1:19–21. "The prophetic word" finds its complete fulfilment in Jesus Christ (cf. Heb 1:1). This does not refer to a particular prophecy; at that time "the prophetic word" meant the messianic prophecies or (more usually) all the Old Testament insofar as it proclaims the enduring salvation to come.

These verses encapsulate the whole notion of biblical prophecy—its value, interpretation and divine origin. They also show the close connexion between the Old and the New Testaments. "The books of the Old Testament, all of them caught up into the Gospel message, attain and show forth their full meaning in the New Testament (cf. Mt 5:17; Lk 24:27; Rom 16:25–26; 2 Cor 3:14–16) and, in their turn, shed light on it and explain it" (Vatican II, *Dei Verbum*, 16).

By reaching their fulfilment in Jesus Christ, the Old Testament prophecies con-

firm the truthfulness of what Jesus said and did. Together with the Transfiguration they constitute a guarantee of the second coming of the Lord.

The comparison of prophecy to the morning star is a very good one, for that star is designed to bring light and announce the coming of day. Similarly, the fullness of Revelation which begins with the earthly life of Christ will reach its climax when he comes in glory.

1:20. Prophecy and Holy Scripture in general are not man-made; they are the word of God: there is nothing in the Bible that is not inspired by the Holy Spirit (v. 21). Therefore, against the false teachers of his time and of all eras, the sacred writer rejects any interpretation of Scripture based exclusively on human ingenuity; as the Second Vatican Council reminds us, it is "the Church which exercises the divinely conferred commission and ministry of watching over and interpreting the Word of God" (*Dei Verbum*, 12).

These words repeat the teaching of the Council of Trent: "No one should dare to rely on his own judgment in matters of faith and morals [...] to distort Holy Scripture to fit meanings of his own that are contrary to the meaning that holy Mother Church has held and now holds; for it is her office to decide on the true sense and interpretation of Holy Scripture" (*De libris sacris*; cf. Vatican I, *Dei Filius*, chap. 2).

2 Tim 3:16
Acts 3:21

scripture is a matter of one's own interpretation, ²¹because no prophecy ever came by the impulse of man, but men moved by the Holy Spirit spoke from God.ᵉ

2. FALSE TEACHERS DENOUNCED

Deut 13:2–6
Mt 24:24
1 Thess 4:1
Jude 4

The harm done by false teachers

2 ¹But false prophets also arose among the people, just as there will be false teachers among you, who will secretly bring in destructive heresies, even denying the Master who bought them,

1:21. This verse makes it clear that there is such a thing as biblical interpretation (cf. 2 Tim 3:13ff), and it specifies what it is. Scripture has been written under the inspiration of the Holy Spirit; God and the human author are involved in the writing of the sacred books in such a way that the end-product is, at one and the same time, entirely of God's making and entirely of man's.

"Holy Mother Church, relying on the faith of the apostolic age, accepts as sacred and canonical the books of the Old and the New Testaments, whole and entire, with all their parts, on the grounds that, written under the inspiration of the Holy Spirit (cf. Jn 20:31; 2 Tim 3:16; 2 Pet 1:19–21; 3:15–16), they have God as their author, and have been handed on as such to the Church herself. To compose the sacred books, God chose certain men who, all the while he employed them in this task, made full use of their powers and faculties so that, although he acted in them and by them, it was as true authors that they consigned to writing whatever he wanted written, and no more" (*Dei Verbum*, 11).

2:1–22. The sacred writer wants to expose the false teachers who are doing such damage among the Christians to whom he is writing. Before refuting their basic

error (denying the Parousia), he denounces their immoral conduct, particularly their greed (vv. 3, 14) and impurity.

The section begins by pointing out how evil the actions of these imposters are (vv. 1–3). He warns that eternal punishment awaits them (vv. 4–10); goes on to describe their corrupt conduct (vv. 10–19); and points out how seriously wrong it is for people who have become Christians to revert to their former life of sin (vv. 20–22).

The outspoken description of the false teachers, and the references to the punishment they will receive, must have made an impression on the original recipients of the letter and led them to distance themselves from the false teachers.

The parallel passage in the Letter of St Jude (vv. 4–16), from which the author of this letter seems to have drawn inspiration (cf. Introduction) fills out and illustrates the teaching contained in this chapter.

2:1–3. The Old Testament contains a good deal of warning and criticism of the false teachers who were sowing confusion among the people of Israel (cf., e.g., Deut 13:2–6; Jer 14:13–16; Ezek 13:1ff). Here similar warnings are given about people at work in the Christian communities;

e. Other authorities read *moved by the Holy Spirit holy men of God spoke*

bringing upon themselves swift destruction. ²And many will follow their licentiousness, and because of them the way of truth will be reviled. ³And in their greed they will exploit you with false words; from of old their condemnation has not been idle, and their destruction has not been asleep.*

Is 52:5
Acts 9:2

Rom 16:18
1 Thess 2:5

The punishment that awaits them
⁴For if God did not spare the angels when they sinned, but cast them into hell^f and committed them to pits of nether gloom to be

Gen 6:1–4
Mt 8:29
Jude 6

---

although the warning concerns events in the future (it is somewhat reminiscent of our Lord's prophecies about his coming again: cf. Mt 24:11), it is quite clear from things in the rest of the letter (cf. 2:12ff) that the false teachers were already at work. From the tone of these verses, it seems that they were Christians who had gone astray but still formed part of the community of the faithful.

The sacred writer bemoans the terrible damage they are doing: their bad example is leading many astray (St Jude says in the parallel passage that "they pervert the grace of our God into licentiousness": v. 4) and doing great harm to the Church by giving it a bad name: the "way of truth will be reviled" (literally: "blasphemed").

"The way of truth" (v. 2): as in Acts this word "way" is used to refer to the Christian way of life or the Gospel itself (cf. note on Acts 9:3).

2:4–10. To depict the eternal punishment awaiting the false teachers, he uses three well known biblical examples—the rebellious angels, the Flood, and the destruction of Sodom and Gomorrah. In the parallel passage in St Jude (vv. 5–10), instead of the Flood the example given is the punishment of the rebellious Israelites in the desert. Given that the examples here are more detailed and are in a chronological

order, commentators think that this letter is the later one (cf. Introduction).

Another feature of this passage is the stress it puts on the salvation of the godly (along with the punishment that awaits the wicked)—Noah in the midst of a perverse generation, and Lot, all alone in a wicked world. The Lord will judge each according to his merits.

2:4. Holy Scripture does not explain what kind of sin was committed by the angels who were cast into hell. Many saints (including St Augustine and St Thomas Aquinas) think it was a sin of pride. Christian religious instruction usually explains it in this way: "the angels were not all faithful to God; many of them through pride claimed to be equal to him and independent of him, and for this sin they were forever shut out from heaven and condemned to hell" (*St Pius X Catechism*, 39).

"Hell": the original has *tartarus*, the name given in Greek mythology to the place of torment kept for the enemies of the gods. "Pits of nether gloom": the Gospel also speaks of darkness when referring to the horrors of hell (cf. Mt 22:13; 25:30).

The fact that the angels were condemned should serve as a severe warning: even though they were privileged creatures they did not escape punishment. The nature of the punishment helps to show how evil sin is.

f. Greek *Tartarus*

Gen 8:18
1 Pet 3:6

Gen 19:24f
Jude 7

Gen 19:6f

Ezek 9:4

1 Cor 10:13
Jude 6
Rev 3:10

Jude 7, 8, 16

kept until the judgment; ⁵if he did not spare the ancient world, but preserved Noah, a herald of righteousness, with seven other persons, when he brought a flood upon the world of the ungodly; ⁶if by turning the cities of Sodom and Gomorrah to ashes he condemned them to extinction and made them an example to those who were to be ungodly; ⁷and if he rescued righteous Lot, greatly distressed by the licentiousness of the wicked ⁸(for by what that righteous man saw and heard as he lived among them, he was vexed in his righteous soul day after day with their lawless deeds), ⁹then the Lord knows how to rescue the godly from trial, and to keep the unrighteous under punishment until the day of judgment, ¹⁰and especially those who indulge in the lust of defiling passion and despise authority.

2:5. "A herald of righteousness": the Old Testament describes Noah as "righteous" (Gen 6:9); perhaps that is how the sacred writer deduces that he preached righteousness by his word and example. He may be evoking certain Jewish traditions (mentioned by Flavius Josephus) to the effect that, prior to the Flood, the patriarch preached to his contemporaries to try to convert them.

2:6–10. The destruction of Sodom and Gomorrah, cities proverbial for vice, is *the* biblical example of divine punishment of sinners; our Lord often reminded people about it (cf., e.g., Mt 10:15; 11:23–24; Lk 17:26–29). Despite harrassment, Lot stayed true to God in the midst of the corruption all round him (cf. Gen 18–19); that was why God saved him and his family when the two cities were wiped out. Similarly, when the Day of Judgment comes, God will save the godly and punish the ungodly. By mentioning Lot, the sacred writer seems to be saying that the ancient punishment is not just a warning to the wicked; it also helps the godly to persevere doing good, even in a hostile environment.

Apparently the main sin of the false teachers and the one to which the faithful were being drawn was that of lust (v. 10), as was the case in Sodom and Gomorrah.

This vice so clouds the mind that a person who becomes steeped in it ends up despising the "authority" of the Lord (literally, "lordship": cf. notes on Jude 8–10).

"Do not forget," St Josemaría Escrivá writes, "that when someone is corrupted by the concupiscence of the flesh he cannot make any spiritual progress. He cannot do good works. He is a cripple, cast aside like an old rag. Have you ever seen patients suffering from progressive paralysis and unable to help themselves or get up? Sometimes they cannot even move their heads. Well, in the supernatural order, the same thing happens to people who are not humble and have made a cowardly surrender to lust. They don't see, or hear, or understand anything. They are paralysed. They are like people gone mad. Each of us here ought to invoke our Lord, and his Blessed Mother, and pray that he will grant us humility and a determination to avail devoutly of the divine remedy of confession" (*Friends of God*, 181).

2:10–19. Without mincing his words, the sacred writer describes the perverse behaviour of the false prophets: they are arrogant and blasphemous (vv. 10–13); their lives are more suited to animals, for they let themselves be led by their passions, particularly lust and greed (vv. 13–16); despite their claims, they have no teaching

Their arrogance and immorality

Bold and wilful, they are not afraid to revile the glorious ones, [11]whereas angels, though greater in might and power, do not pronounce a reviling judgment upon them before the Lord. [12]But these, like irrational animals, creatures of instinct, born to be caught and killed, reviling in matters of which they are ignorant, will be destroyed in the same destruction with them, [13]suffering wrong for their wrongdoing. They count it pleasure to revel in the daytime. They are blots and blemishes, revelling in their dissipation,[g] carousing with you. [14]They have eyes full of adultery,

Jude 9

Ps 49:13
Jude 10

Jude 12

---

to offer (v. 17); with false promises of liberation they are leading the recent converts astray (vv. 18–19).

The parallel passage in St Jude (vv. 8–16) clarifies the meaning of some expressions here.

2:10–13. In their arrogance, these ungodly people "are not afraid to revile the glorious ones" (literally, "the glories", that is, the angels). It is not easy to say whether this is a reference to the angelic world in general or (as most commentators in fact think) to the fallen angels. In any event, it is clear that, blinded as they are by their pride, they are blaspheming creatures who are on a higher plane than they; the arrogance is all the greater when not even the angels themselves dare to revile the demons.

Nor can we say what form this blasphemy took: they may have been underestimating the power of the demons, judging them incapable of harming them —which would mean they felt they could continue their depraved lifestyle. Or they may have been invoking the fallen angels as patrons of their vices (cf. note on parallel passage in Jude: vv. 8–10).

2:13–16. Because these men were motivated exclusively by greed and a desire for sensual pleasure, they were really living like animals; their degraded conduct, which is denounced here very vigorously, should serve as a warning, because the

same thing can happen to people who let their passions get the better of them.

God inspired Balaam to bless the people of Israel on a number of occasions (cf. Num 22–24) but Balaam later led the Israelites into idolatry and fornication (cf. Num 31:16; Rev 2:14). In Jewish tradition he is the epitome of an evil and avaricious person; which is why the sacred writer refers to him when describing the greed and seductiveness of the false teachers. In the corresponding passage of St Jude (v. 11) Cain and Korah are also referred to (cf. note on Jude 11).

2:13–14. "Revelling in their dissipation [love feasts], carousing with you" (v. 13): from the letter of St Jude (v. 12) we can deduce that the false preachers used these occasions to indulge their greed and spread their errors. Intemperance (greed and lust, mainly) had made them slaves to their passions, unable to seek anything but sensual pleasure.

Christians should never let temporal things cloud their wisdom if they want to have a supernatural approach to life. Speaking of the value of the virtue of purity, the Church stresses "that everyone should have a high esteem for the virtue of chastity, its beauty and its power of attraction. This virtue increases the human person's dignity and enables him to love truly, disinterestedly, unselfishly and with

g. Other ancient authorities read *love feasts*

Num 22:5
Jude 11
Rev 2:14

Num 22:28f

Jude 12, 13

Jude 16

insatiable for sin. They entice unsteady souls. They have hearts trained in greed. Accursed children! [15]Forsaking the right way they have gone astray; they have followed the way of Balaam, the son of Beor, who loved gain from wrongdoing, [16]but was rebuked for his own transgression; a dumb ass spoke with human voice and restrained the prophet's madness.

[17]These are waterless springs and mists driven by a storm; for them the nether gloom of darkness has been reserved. [18]For, uttering

respect for others" (SCDF, *Declaration on Sexual Ethics*, 1). And, referring to the means to achieve this, it goes on to say: "the faithful of the present time, and indeed today more than ever, must use the means which have always been recommended by the Church for living a chaste life. These means are: discipline of the senses and the mind, watchfulness and prudence in avoiding occasions of sin, the observance of modesty, moderation in recreation, wholesome pursuits, assiduous prayer and frequent reception of the sacraments of Penance and the Eucharist. Young people especially should earnestly foster devotion to the Immaculate Mother of God" (ibid.).

2:17. The deceitfulness, emptiness and barrenness of these people's conduct is illustrated by two images ("waterless springs", "mists driven by a storm") which as it were summarizes those used by St Jude (vv. 12–13). "He calls them dry springs", St Augustine comments, "that is, springs insofar as they have been given knowledge of the Lord Christ; dry, on the other hand, because they do not live in keeping with that knowledge" (*De fide et operibus*, 1, 25). Vanity and hypocrisy are usually features of people who try to justify their doctrinal and moral deviations (cf. Mt 7:15–20).

2:18–19. These false teachers, sadly, have led some recent converts astray: those converts had only turned their back on sin and now they are being led astray

again, with promises of liberation, as if liberation could be found by following one's passions and instincts. What they are doing is becoming slaves to sin: "Every one who commits sin is a slave to sin" (Jn 8:34).

Christian freedom ("the glorious liberty of the children of God": Rom 8:21) has been gained for mankind by Christ through his death on the cross. From the beginning, some misinterpreted this freedom, and the apostles had to correct those who took it as "a pretext for evil" (1 Pet 2:16) or "as an opportunity for the flesh" (Gal 5:13), perverting "the grace of God into licentiousness" (Jude 4). Living in freedom does not mean ignoring the Law of God; in fact, the Law of Christ is "the perfect law, the law of liberty" (Jas 1:25; cf. note on same). "If you continue in my word, you are truly my disciples," the Master teaches, "and you will know the truth, and the truth will make you free" (Jn 8:31–32).

"Christ, our Liberator, has freed us from sin and from slavery to the Law and to the flesh, which is the mark of the condition of sinful mankind. Thus it is the new life of grace, fruit of justification, which makes us free. This means that the most radical form of slavery is slavery to sin. Other forms of slavery find their deepest root in slavery to sin. That is why freedom in the full Christian sense, characterized by the life of the Spirit, cannot be confused with a licence to give in to the desires of the flesh. Freedom is a new life in love" (SCDF, *Libertatis nuntius*, 4, 2).

loud boasts of folly, they entice with licentious passions of the flesh men who have barely escaped from those who live in error. [19]They promise them freedom, but they themselves are slaves of corruption; for whatever overcomes a man, to that he is enslaved.

Jn 8:34
Rom 6:16

Apostasy, a grave sin

[20]For if, after they have escaped the defilements of the world through the knowledge of our Lord and Saviour Jesus Christ, they are again entangled in them and overpowered, the last state has become worse for them than the first. [21]For it would have been better for them never to have known the way of righteousness than after knowing it to turn back from the holy commandment delivered to them. [22]It has happened to them according to the true proverb, The dog turns back to his own vomit, and the sow is washed only to wallow in the mire.

Mt 12–45
Lk 11:24

Lk 12:47, 48

Prov 26:11
Mt 7:6

3. THE SECOND COMING OF CHRIST

The teaching of Tradition

3 [1]This is now the second letter that I have written to you, beloved, and in both of them I have aroused your sincere mind

2 Pet 1:13

2:20–22. The sacred writer uses two popular proverbs (v. 22) to show the serious situation of those who return to a life of sin after knowing the saving teaching of Christ. These verses can apply to the false teachers themselves as well as to those they lead astray. "The last state has become worse for them than the first": our Lord said the same thing about someone who after having had a devil cast out of him fell under his sway once more: "the last state of that man becomes worse than the first" (Mt 12:45).

St Gregory the Great applies this passage to those who bewail their sins but do not give them up: "When the dog vomits, it is clearly throwing up food it cannot take; but when it returns to its vomit it once again burdens itself with a burden it had shed. So too, those who weep over the sins they have committed are undoubt-

edly casting away the iniquity with which they wrongly stuffed themselves and which oppressed their soul; an iniquity which they ingest once again when, after confession, they repeat it. A sow, for example, when she rolls in the mire to clean herself, comes out filthier than ever. So too, a person who weeps for his sin and yet does not give it up becomes guilty of a greater fault; because he scorns the forgiveness which he could obtain by weeping, and then wallows in the mire. When, despite his tears, he prevents his life being cleansed, then in the sight of God he causes those very tears to be stained" (*Regulae pastoralis liber*, 3, 30).

3:1–16. The truth most explicitly rejected by the false teachers was that of the second coming of the Lord (cf. v. 4); by rejecting it they were able to tone down

Jude 17

by way of reminder; [2]that you should remember the predictions of the holy prophets and the commandment of the Lord and Saviour through your apostles.

1 Tim 4:1

Mistaken notions

Jude 18

Is 5:19

[3]First of all you must understand this, that scoffers will come in the last days with scoffing, following their own passions [4]and

---

the moral demands of Christianity. The sacred writer now sets about refuting their arguments and outlining correct teaching on eschatology. Because we do not know exactly what kind of heresy is being refuted, some parts of the text are difficult to understand.

The whole passage is very well structured: a brief reference to the teaching of the prophets and apostles (vv. 1–2); fallacious ideas of the opponents (vv. 3–4); correct teaching about the second coming of our Lord (vv. 5–10); and an appeal for hope and vigilance, because we do not know the hour of the Lord's coming (vv. 11–16).

3:1–2. The letter referred to is probably 1 Peter, which also dealt with the subject of the Parousia (cf. 1 Pet 1:10–12; 5:12). Even if the author of the "second letter" was not St Peter but a disciple of his (cf. Introduction), the reference could still be to 1 Peter, which at that time would have already been well known to Christians generally.

"I have aroused your sincere mind by way of reminder", that is, I have given you a correct understanding of the true doctrine so that you can see where the false teachers have gone wrong. Having a sincere mind is not only a matter of holding on to the true doctrine, but also of detecting doctrinal or moral error.

The reference to the apostles alongside that of the prophets shows that from the beginning the apostles, as authorized messengers of Revelation, had a role

similar to that of the prophets in the Old Testament.

"The commandment of the Lord and Saviour" may mean the commandment of love (cf. Jn 13:34), insofar as it covers the whole Christian life, but here (cf. also 2:21) it seems to refer more to all the truths taught by Jesus, elsewhere these are described as the "gospel" (Gal 1:9; cf. Mk 1:14), "the word of the Lord" (Acts 8:25); "the mystery of God" (1 Cor 2:1) and "the faith" (Gal 1:23). As the Second Vatican Council teaches: "What was handed on by the apostles comprises everything that serves to make the People of God live their lives in holiness and increase their faith. In this way the Church, in her doctrine, life and worship, perpetuates and transmits to every generation all that she herself is, all that she believes" (*Dei Verbum*, 8).

3:3–4. Jesus had predicted that false teachers would appear and try to lead Christians astray (cf. Mt 24:24; Mk 13:22). The warnings which are often found in the New Testament about false ideas of one kind or another show how easy it is for us to wander away from the truth (cf., e.g., Acts 20:29–31; 1 Tim 4:1; 2 Tim 3:1–5; 1 Jn 2:19). St Jude uses almost the same words to unmask the scoffers of Christ, who let their passions gain the upper hand (cf. Jude 18 and note).

The false prophets referred to in the letter deny the second coming of Christ on the grounds that things are still the same, none of the catastrophes they

saying, "Where is the promise of his coming? For ever since the
fathers fell asleep, all things have continued as they were from the
beginning of creation."

Ezek 12:22
Mt 24:48

True teaching about the End

⁵They deliberately ignore this fact, that by the word of God heavens
existed long ago, and an earth formed out of water and by means
of water, ⁶through which the world that then existed was deluged
with water and perished. ⁷But by the same word the heavens and

Gen 1:2, 6, 9

Gen 7:21
2 Pet 2:5

expected have occurred (they may have misinterpreted what our Lord said about the signs of the second coming and of the end of the world: cf. Mk 13:21ff).

"The fathers": some take this as meaning the first generation of Christians, most of whom had already died; the false teachers would have argued that the second coming should have happened during the lifetime of that generation. It could also be a reference to Old Testament forebears, especially, the ancestors of the entire human race; in which case the scoffers referred to may have been influenced by a current of Greek culture and philosophy which held that the world was eternal and unchanging; they would argue that no substantial change had occurred from the beginning up to now— which was a good indication that nothing was going to happen in the future, either.

3:5–7. These errors are replied to with information familiar to all: the world is not unchangeable, for creation and the Flood shows that its being and continued existence depend on the word of God. Besides, the delay in the second coming is understandable if one remembers that time does not count in the eternity of God (v. 8), and, moreover, by leaving this interval, divine mercy is giving men an opportunity to mend their ways (vv. 9–10).

Creation and the Flood, therefore, show that changes in the cosmos are a

function of the will of God: with a mere word he caused a mass of earth and water to appear, later to be separated out into dry land and sea (cf. Gen 1:6–10); in the Flood, God's word caused the waters once again to drown the earth in punishment of men's sins, returning things to the original state of chaos in some way, until dry land appeared again (cf. Gen 8:3–14).

The sacred writer does not mean to provide any kind of scientific explanation of the origin of the world. He limits himself to recalling what the first chapters of the Bible say in a simple, figurative language suited to a more primitive mind (cf. Gen 1–11)—ideas his readers accepted unquestioningly, as we know from the rabbinical writings of the time. However, the conclusions he draws are perfectly valid: if the word of God caused Creation and the Flood, that same word can bring about a final day of conflagration.

It is interesting how much the sacred writer stresses the cosmic role of "fire" in the final upheaval (cf. 3:7, 10, 12). It may be that he is picking up a biblical tradition which uses fire as an image for the presence of God (cf., e.g., Ex 3:1–4; 13:21–22; Deut 4:24; Mic 1:3–4, 6), for the punishment he inflicts (e.g., Deut 32:22; Is 5:24–25; 66:15–16; Zeph 1:15–18) and for when he intervenes to purify man (e.g., Is 6:7; 30:27–28; 66:18–22; Mal 4:1–3). Therefore, it is likely that the writer wants in this way to stress that the end of

2 Pet 3:10   earth that now exist have been stored up for fire, being kept until the day of judgment and destruction of ungodly men.

Ps 90:4   [8]But do not ignore this one fact, beloved, that with the Lord one

Hab 2:3; 1 Pet day is as a thousand years, and a thousand years as one day. [9]The
3:20; 1 Tim 2:4 Lord is not slow about his promise as some count slowness, but is
Rom 2:4   forbearing toward you,[h] not wishing that any should perish, but

Mt 24:29, 35 that all should reach repentance. [10]But the day of the Lord will
1 Thess 5:2 come like a thief, and then the heavens will pass away with a loud
Rev 20:11

---

the world will involve a special kind of divine intervention, similar to that which took place at Creation and at the Flood; that one of its effects will be the punishment of the ungodly; and that it will also involve a special kind of purification through a profound transfiguration: "new heavens and a new earth" (v. 13). It is possible (in what way we cannot say) that fire may be used by God to bring these events about.

There is therefore no basis here for the theory which sees this cosmic fire as a reflection of Persian or Stoic philosophical notions. In Persian philosophy the end of the world is seen in terms of a last battle between good and evil; the Stoics had a theory that the cosmos evolved in a cyclical way; every time it is destroyed a new cycle starts, just like the previous one.

3:8. This passage from v. 4 of Psalm 90 was often cited by Jewish rabbis in their calculations about how long the messianic times would last and when the end of the world would be; later on, milleniarists would use it as a basis for their far-fetched theories about Christ and his saints bearing temporal rule for a thousand years over an earthly kingdom prior to the End. The author of the letter cites the psalm as an authority for the view that time is a function of Creation and has no

connexion with the eternity of God: the fact that the Parousia has not happened is no reason to deny that it will happen.

3:9–10. In this passage we are reminded that God, in his great mercy, does not seek our condemnation but, rather, wants all men to be saved (cf. 1 Tim 2:4; Rom 11:22) and shows wonderful patience towards them. The fact that the Parousia has not yet come about is quite compatible with the certainty that it will happen, and happen all of a sudden; therefore, far from being an excuse for making Christian life less demanding, the Parousia is a spur to stay vigilant (the Master himself used the simile of the thief: cf. Mt 24:43–44; Lk 12:39). "Since we know neither the day nor the hour, we should follow the advice of the Lord and watch constantly so that, when the single course of our earthly life is completed (cf. Heb 9:27), we may merit to enter with him into the marriage feast and be numbered among the blessed (cf. Mt 25:31–46) and not, like the wicked and slothful servants (cf. Mt 25:26), be ordered to depart into the eternal fire (cf. Mt 25:41)" (Vatican II, *Lumen gentium*, 48).

"The earth and the works that are upon it": there are so many variants in the Greek manuscripts that it is almost impossible to reconstruct the original text: but they all convey the idea that the earth will be affected by this universal cataclysm.

---

h. Other ancient authorities read *on your account*

noise, and the elements will be dissolved with fire, and the earth and the works that are upon it will be burned up.

Moral lessons to be drawn
[11]Since all these things are thus to be dissolved, what sort of persons ought you to be in lives of holiness and godliness, [12]waiting for and hastening[i] the coming of the day of God, because of which

Is 34:4

3:11–16. The writer now follows up these considerations with a moral exhortation, based on the conviction that the old world will disappear (v. 12), producing new heavens and a new earth (v. 13), and that men living in the period prior to this cataclysm will not know when it is going to happen (v. 15).

All this should not make Christians afraid; in fact, it should bolster their hope (vv. 12–14). God will keep his promise to grant heaven to those who persevere in good; but this hope of future reward should not lead one to neglect temporal affairs: "Far from diminishing our concern to develop this earth, the expectancy of a new earth should spur us on, for it is here that the body of a new human family grows, foreshadowing in some way the age which is to come" (Vatican II, *Gaudium et spes*, 39).

Hope opens the way to upright conduct (v. 11) of an even higher standard (v. 14). Christians should realize that they have a pressing duty to grow in virtue as long as they live in this world (v. 15): "God may have given us just one more year in which to serve him. Don't think of five, or even two. Just concentrate on this one year, that has just started. Give it to God, don't bury it! This is the resolution we ought to make" (St Josemaría Escrivá, *Friends of God*, 47).

The practice of virtue leads to holiness and enduring union with God (v. 14; cf. 1 Thess 3:13). "'While we are at home in the body we are away from the Lord' (2 Cor 5:6) and, although we have the first fruits of the Spirit (cf. Rom 8:23) we groan inwardly in our anxiety to be with Christ (cf. Phil 1:23). The same love urges us to live more for Him who died for us and who rose again (cf. 2 Cor 5:15). We make it our aim, then, to please the Lord in all things (cf. 2 Cor 5:9) and we put on the armour of God that we may be able to stand against the wiles of the devil and resist the evil day (cf. Eph 6:11–13)" (*Lumen gentium*, 48).

3:12. "Waiting for and hastening": these two verbs convey the idea that Christian hope is something dynamic; it is in no way passive. Contrary to a view quite widespread among the Jews of the time, it does not mean that the Parousia will come sooner, the more meritorious men are; what it means is that the more closely united to Christ they are, the nearer they are to his glory. Therefore, it is urgent that all should embrace faith in Christ. We who have this faith pray in the Our Father, "Thy kingdom come." The first Christians made the same petition in their ejaculatory prayer, "Marana tha", "Come, Lord" (1 Cor 16:22; Rev 22:20), referring to the second coming of the Lord.

"The day of God": the usual expression in the New Testament is "the day of the Lord" (1 Cor 1:8; 5:5; 1 Thess 5:2; 2 Thess 2:2; 2 Pet 3:10); both expressions refer to the point at which Christ will come to judge the living and the dead.

i. Or *earnestly desiring*

Is 65:17; 66:22
Rev 21:1, 27

the heavens will be kindled and dissolved, and the elements will melt with fire! [13]But according to his promise we wait for new heavens and a new earth in which righteousness dwells.

Jude 24

[14]Therefore, beloved, since you wait for these, be zealous to be found by him without spot or blemish, and at peace. [15]And count

Rom 2:4
1 Tim 1:15, 16

the forbearance of our Lord as salvation. So also our beloved brother Paul wrote to you according to the wisdom given him, [16]speaking of this* as he does in all his letters. There are some things in them hard to understand, which the ignorant and unstable twist to their own destruction, as they do the other scriptures.

3:13. "New heavens and a new earth": one of things promised for the End is that creation will be renewed, re-fashioned: the prophets proclaimed this (cf. Is 65:17), and the New Testament speaks of drinking new wine at the heavenly banquet (cf. Mt 14:25), being given a new name (cf. Rev 2:17), singing a new song (cf. Rev 5:9), living in a new Jerusalem (Rev 21:3). All this imagery conveys the idea that the whole universe will be transformed, man included (cf. Rom 8:19–22). "We know neither the moment of the consummation of the earth and of man (cf. Acts 1:7) nor the way the universe will be transformed. The form of this world, distorted by sin, is passing away (cf. 1 Cor 7:31), and we are taught that God is preparing a new dwelling and a new earth in which righteousness dwells (cf. 2 Cor 5:2; 2 Pet 3:13), whose happiness will fill and surpass all the desires of peace arising in the hearts of men" (*Gaudium et spes*, 39).

3:15–16. The reference to the writing of St Paul is clear evidence of the fact that from the very beginning of Christianity unity in faith was considered essential. It is difficult to say whether the sacred writer is thinking of some specific passage, for themes and even wording found in this letter are to be found in many Pauline letters—for example, on the subject of

God's forbearance in waiting for men to mend their ways (cf. Rom 2:4–11; 1 Tim 1:16); or that of holiness as the Christian goal (cf. 1 Cor 1:7–8; Col 1:21–22; Eph 1:5–14).

The "wisdom" of St Paul may be a reference to the special endowments the Apostle had for the spread of the Gospel; or it may refer to the charism of divine inspiration, thereby acknowledging that the Letters of St Paul are sacred scripture, because it would mean putting them on the level of the other sacred books (v. 16).

"Some things ... difficult to understand": he does not mention any specific subject; the point he is making is that the false teachers can do damage if they base their errors on arbitrary misinterpretations of Pauline texts. In his time St Augustine warned about the fact that "the heresies and perverse dogmas which entrap souls and hurl them into the abyss originate simply in a bad understanding of good scriptures, and the rashness and audacity with which people put forward their misinterpretations" (*In Ioann. Evang.*, 18, 1).

That is why the Church, while at the same time giving people every encouragement to read Scripture, has established precise rules to avoid erroneous interpretations and to obtain the maximum possible fruit from assiduous reading. "It is for the bishops, 'with whom the apostolic doctrine resides' [St Irenaeus]

Final exhortation and doxology

[17]You therefore, beloved, knowing this beforehand, beware lest you be carried away with the error of lawless men and lose your own stability. [18]But grow in the grace and knowledge of our Lord and Saviour Jesus Christ. To him be the glory both now and to the day of eternity. Amen.

Mk 13:5

Rom 16:27
Jude 25

---

suitably to instruct the faithful entrusted to them in the correct use of the divine books, especially of the New Testament, and in particular of the Gospels. They do this by giving them translations of the sacred texts which are equipped with necessary and really adequate explanations. Thus the children of the Church can familiarize themselves safely and profitably with the Sacred Scriptures, and become steeped in their spirit" (Vatican II, *Dei Verbum*, 25).

3:17–18. The letter ends with a very succinct summary of some of its main points —pastoral concern, ways to defend oneself against false teachers, and faith in the divinity of Christ.

"Beloved": the faithful are referred to in this solicitous way elsewhere in the letter (3:1, 8, 14). The warnings and threats made by the sacred writer are born of his pastoral zeal to establish them in the truth (1:12) and remind them what the true teaching is (3:1).

When he encourages them not to lose their "own strength", he is reminding them that firmness in the faith is an essential weapon for protecting themselves against deceitful teachers who are causing their faith and morals to waver (cf. 2; 3:16). Understanding and love should be shown towards those who are in error, but this should not "make us indifferent to truth and goodness. Love, in fact, impels the followers of Christ to proclaim to all men the truth which saves" (*Gaudium et spes*, 28).

"To him be the glory": most of the doxologies which appear in the New Testament are in praise of God the Father (cf. Jude 25; Rom 16:27); this one is addressed to Christ, whose divinity, as in other passages of the letter, is openly confessed. He has the same glory as the Father: the doxology is not simply expressing a desire but stating a fact. The eternal love of Jesus Christ is the basis of the Christian's hope. "While she slowly grows to maturity, the Church longs for the completed Kingdom and, with all her strength, hopes and desires to be united in glory with her King" (*Lumen gentium*, 5).

Introduction to the First Letter of St John

According to a tradition which goes back to the second century, the apostle St John wrote his three letters in Ephesus, on his return from exile on Patmos around the years 95–96. The authenticity of the first letter is well documented from early on; its internal structure confirms that it was written by the same person as wrote the Fourth Gospel.

The first explicit testimony comes from St Irenaeus, bishop of Lyons. Born around the year 140 in Smyrna (Asia Minor), Irenaeus had there known St Polycarp, a direct disciple of St John.[1] In his book *Against Heresies*[2] Irenaeus makes use of New Testament texts dealing with the Incarnation of the Word of God, including a series of quotations from St John ("the disciple of the Lord"), deriving both from the Fourth Gospel and from 1 John.[3]

Clement of Alexandria (150–214), in addition to writing a commentary on this letter, only fragments of which have come down to us, frequently quotes it in his work, attributing it explicitly to the apostle John.[4] The same is true of Tertullian (d. 222),[5] and Origen (d. 253), who makes a point of underlining the relationship between the Fourth Gospel and 1 John.[6]

This epistle is included in all the early catalogues or canons of inspired books, with St John named by its author. For example, the famous Muratorian Fragment, containing a canon composed in Rome around the year 180, expressly mentions the prologue of the letter, attributing it to St John.

Detailed analysis of the text confirms that it was written by the same person as wrote the Fourth Gospel. There are very obvious similarities of style; structure; phrases; vocabulary; and ideas. Typical Johannine expressions occur in both texts—for example, being born of God, being of God, abiding in God, abiding in the truth, walking in the light, etc. In both, too, we find the frequent use of certain contrasts, much favoured by Semites—light/darkness, truth/lies, love/hate, death/life, God/the devil, righteousness/sin.

There is also evidence in the two texts of interest in certain doctrinal themes. Thus, Christ is described as the Word (Logos: 1 Jn 1:1 and Jn 1:1), the only Son (1 Jn 4:9 and Jn 1:18), and the Saviour of the world (1 Jn 4:14 and Jn 4:42). St John also puts stress on the reality of the Incarnation (cf. the

---

1. St Polycarp (d. probably 22 February 156) actually refers to 1 John 4:2–3 in his *Letter to the Philippians* (chap. 7). 2. 3, 16, 5, 8. 3. E.g., 1 Jn 2:18, 19, 21; 4:1–3; 5:1. 4. Cf. *Stromata*, 2, 15, 66; 3, 4, 32; 5, 44; 6:45. 5. Cf. *Adversus Praxeam*, 15; *Scorpiace*, 12; *Adversus Marcionem*, 5, 16. 6. Cf. Eusebius of Caesarea, *Ecclesiastical History*, 6, 25, 8.

prologues of the letter and the Gospel) and points to its redemptive value "to take away sins" (1 Jn 3:5; cf. Jn 1:29).

The beginning of the Christian life is seen as passing "out of death into life" (e.g., 1 Jn 3:14 and Jn 5:24), or as being "born of God" (1 Jn 3:9; 4:7; 5:1, 4; and Jn 1:13; 3:3), so that the Christian becomes a "child of God" (1 Jn 3:1–2 and Jn 1:12) and comes "to have life" (cf. 1 Jn 5:12 and Jn 3:36). Similarly, the true disciple of Christ should be recognized by the fact that he keeps the commandments, God's "word" (1 Jn 2:5 and Jn 14:21, 23). And following Christ's example (1 Jn 2:6 and Jn 13:15), he should particularly practise brotherly love (1 Jn 3:11 and Jn 13:34), which is called the "new commandment" (1 Jn 2:7–8 and Jn 13:34).

There has never been any real doubt about the canonicity of the letter. As we here said, it has figured in all the early lists of inspired books; and from the second century onwards it is cited by many Greek and Latin Fathers. It appears on the lists of secred books compiled by all the earliest councils which dealt with this subject—Laodicea (c.360), Rome (382), Hippo (393), the third Council of Carthage (397), etc.

In his *Ecclesiastical History*[7] Eusebius of Caesarea echoes this constant tradition by classifying 1 John among these writings which everyone always accepted as sacred and canonical (*homologúmena*). And St Jerome states that it was accepted the world over as canonical "by all competent men of the Church".[8]

In its fourth session[9] the Council of Trent solemnly declared this letter, along with all the other books in the two Testaments, to be canonical.

IMMEDIATE READERSHIP

The First Letter of St John carries no heading, unlike the other New Testament epistles (with the exception of Hebrews) and ordinary secular correspondence of the time. In fact, it makes no mention of the writer's name or the addressees' names, and contains none of the usual opening greeting(s) and no special words of farewell.

The fact that the addressees are not named suggests that this is a kind of circular letter sent to all the Christian communities of some region.

According to a tradition passed down by St Irenaeus,[10] the apostle John, on his return from exile on the island of Patmos, spent the last years of his life in Ephesus, at that time the capital of the Roman province of Asia. From there he ruled over the various churches of Asia Minor whose names are given in the book of Revelation (Rev 2–3). It is quite likely therefore that the faithful of those communities were the people to whom this letter was originally sent.

---

7. Cf. 3, 24, 17.   **8.** *On Famous Men*, 9, 18.   **9.** *De librir sacris.*   **10.** *Against Heresies*, 3, 1, 1.

Introduction to the First Letter of St John

The letter must have been written after the year 95/96 when, during Nerva's reign, St John returned from Patmos. Although the question is still open, most experts are inclined to the view that this letter is later than the Fourth Gospel, since it seems to presuppose the teachings contained therein. Finally, of the three New Testament letters which bear St John's name, this one is probably chronogically the latest, having been written towards the end of the first century of the Christian era.

THE REASON FOR THE LETTER

As is obvious from its content, some false teachers (antichrists, deceivers, children of the devil, as St John calls them: cf. 2:18, 26; 3:7, 10; 4:1) had appeared in these young churches and, although they probably no longer had any links with them (cf. 2:19), they still were a threat to purity of faith and Christian morality. The apostle is writing to denounce their errors and stress then the faith of believers.

We do not know exactly who these heretics were. From the tenor of the letter, it appears that they were spreading both doctrinal and moral errors to do with the person and salvific work of Christ, denying that Jesus was the Messiah, the Son of God (cf. 2:22; 4:3, 14f). Also, St John's insistence of the fact that Jesus Christ "has come in the flesh" (4:2) suggests that they denied the Incarnation;[11] the rather mysterious reference to Jesus Christ having come "by water and blood, ... not with the water only but with the water and the blood" (5:6) also seems to be directed against the same errors.

All this points to the Gnostic heresy of Cerinthus, according to which Jesus was not born of a virgin but was the son of Joseph and Mary, and his birth had been like that of anyone else. Therefore, he was not the true Son of God; the divine Word merely dwelt in him for a period of time, from his baptism in the Jordan up to the time of his passion—which meant that the blood of Christ shed on the cross had no redemptive value. St John asserts, to the contrary, that Christ's blood "cleanses us from all sin" (1:7), that Christ "is the expiation for our sins" and "for the sins of the whole world" (2:2).

Along with these Christological errors, errors on questions of morals were being spread—an erroneous concept of the Christian life: they thought they were without sin (cf. 1:8); they claimed to have acquired a special knowledge of God which exempted them from keeping his commandments (cf. 2:4–6). Practical errors of this type confirm the influence of these heretics of Gnostic ideas, which had begun to spread towards the end of the first century.

---

11. Cf. also the prologue of the letter: 1:1–4.

CONTENT

In the structure of the letter it is fairly easy to identify a *prologue* (1:1–4) and a brief *epilogue* (5:13) followed by an appendix (5:14–21). The prologue, which is very like that of the Fourth Gospel, states the basic idea of the letter—the communion or union of the Christian with God, which manifests itself in faith in Jesus Christ, and in the practice of brotherly love. This communion results in the life which the Christian receives in and through Jesus Christ, the incarnate Son of God. This idea is summed up in the epilogue: "I write this to you who believe in the name of the Son of God, that you may know that you have eternal life" (5:13).

However, it is not easy to find any clear breaks in the central part of the letter, because its thought does not develop linearly but, rather, in a spiral way: again and again the same basic ideas occur, focused on from different angles. Therefore, the division we have chosen is not meant to indicate that the text has any rigid structure; it is merely designed to highlight the main themes so as to facilitate reading.

The first part (1:5—2:29), which begins with the message that "God is light", outlines the demands implied by the Christian life, which is depicted as "walking in the light". The light/darkness (cf. 1:5, 7; 2:8–11) and truth/lies (cf. 1:6, 8; 2:4, 21–27) antithesis are repeatedly referred to.

This holy life of the Christian is made possible by the fact that the blood of Jesus "cleanses us from all sin" (1:7), for he is our "advocate with the Father" (2:1). To stay in communion with God one needs to recognize oneself as a sinner (3:2) and to strive not to sin (1:8—2:2), keep the commandments (especially that of brotherly love: 2:3–11), not love the world (2:12–17), and not listen to the "antichrists" (2:18–29).

The second part (3:1–24), which begins with a statement about the Christian's divine filiation, puts further stress on the same demands, viewed from the perspective of the fact that Christians are children of God. Divine filiation will attain its fullness when we shall be gloriously transfigured at the second coming of the Lord so as to "see him as he is" (3:2). It is this hope that sustains and encourages Christians on the road to holiness, and that brings them to struggle against sin (3:3–10) and practise brotherly love and the other commandments of the Lord (3:11–24).

The third part (4:1—5:12) develops still further in breadth and depth the main ideas of the letter, arranging them in a kind of literary triptych—faith in Jesus Christ (4:1–6), love (4:7–21) and, again, faith in our Lord (5:1–12). Believers, unlike the false prophets, are "of God" (4:2, 4, 6); and "God is love" (4:8, 16) and all genuine love comes from God (cf. 4:7); our union with God is founded on this love. At the same time, this divine love poured into our hearts equips us and obliges us to love others, who are our brothers (cf. 4:11–16). In sum, love of God and love of neighbour are inseparable (cf. 4:17–21).

Once again the decisive role of faith in Christ is underlined (cf. 5:1)—a living faith which expresses itself in deeds (cf. 5:1–5) and is grounded on the witness borne by God the Father and the Holy Spirit about the Son (cf. 5:6–12).

After a short conclusion (cf. 5:13) which summarizes the central theme of the letter, St John adds, as a kind of appendix, some final counsels (cf. 5:14–21).

TEACHING

1. *Communion with God.* St John gives a full outline of the doctrine of the communion or union of the Christian with God. He does so partly because the false teachers were claiming that they had a higher understanding of God, a *gnosis*, unconnected with traditional Christian teaching, and an enduring union with him, thanks to which they did not feel obliged to keep the commandments, particularly that of fraternal charity.

To counter these errors, St John stresses that only those who stay in communion with the apostles and accept their message can attain union with the Father and the Son (cf. 1:3). To describe this communion he uses clear, bold language: knowing God (cf. 2:3, 13, 14; 3:1, 6; 4:6–8; 5:20), being in God (cf. 2:5; 5:20) or in the light (cf. 2:9); having the Father (cf. 2:23) or the Son (cf. 5:12) and therefore eternal life (cf. 3:15; 5:12); and, above all, the expression "abiding" in God (cf. 2:6, 24, 26; 3:6, 24), articulated most strongly when he says that "all who keep his commandments abide in him, and he in them" (3:4; cf. 4:13–16).

The basic requirement for being in communion with God is confessing true faith in Christ as the Son of God (cf. 2:23; 4:15), since it is he who has brought us the revelation of the Father and he who gives us divine life (cf. 5:12). To guarantee this orthodox faith, Christians receive interior instruction from the Holy Spirit (through the "anointing" given at Baptism: cf. 2:20, 27) and external teaching from apostolic tradition (cf. 2:24).

As usual in the language of the Bible, knowledge of God is not something purely speculative, for a person only really knows God when he is united to him by charity, which is love of God and love of neighbour for God. In this way faith and love build each other up: knowing God better leads to brotherly love, and brotherly love enables one the bettter to love God: "he who loves ... knows God. He who does not love does not know God; for God is love" (4:7–8). A love-impregnated knowledge of God expresses itself in keeping his commandments (cf. 2:3–6), for "he who loves ... knows God. He who does not love does not know God; for God is love" (3:24); love of God is particularly visible when you keep the commandment of brotherly love (cf.

2:9–11; 3:14–17; 4:12). In a word, "he who abides in love abides in God, and God abides in him" (4:16); whereas, as St Augustine will later say, "acting against charity is acting against God".[12]

2. *Faith in Jesus Christ.* From start (cf. 1:1–3) to finish (cf. 5:13, 20) the letter keeps stressing faith in the person and redemptive work of the Son of God, Jesus Christ. Both to expose demons and to fortify Christians in the faith they have had from the beginning, the apostle places the emphasis on the divinity of Jesus Christ, on his redemptive Incarnation, and on his role as the only Mediator betweed God and man.

The very prologue summarizes important dogmatic truths about Christ:[13] he is the Word (1:1), that is, the second person of the Blessed Trinity, the Son of God (1:3); he exists eternally alongside the Father (cf. 1:1–2); he took on a true human nature (ibid.). He is that imperishable Life, which through him is communicated to believers.

These statements are developed in the course of the letter. Thus, the title of "Son" of God is mentioned repeatedly:[14] the Greek word *hyiós* is used; it is never used when speaking of the divine filiation of the Christian, but only for the "only Son" (4:9), who is "true God" (5:20). So, against the "antichrists" who denied that Jesus was the Christ (cf. 2:22), Christian faith professes that "Jesus is the Christ" (5:1), "Jesus is the Son of God" (5:5). God the Father has borne witness concerning his Son (cf. 5:9–11) and has commanded us to believe in the name of his Son Jesus Christ (3:25); only if we obey shall we be united to the Father (2:26; 4:15) and have eternal life (5:11–13). On the other hand, those who deny the Son are making God out to be a liar (5:10).

In addition to denying Christ's divinity, the heretics also denied his redemptive incarnation. St John answers them by categorically stating that Christ is true man, that the Incarnation did take place: "the life was made manifest" (1:2); Jesus Christ "has come in the flesh" (4:2). He stresses the redemptive value of Christ's life and death: he came to take away sins (3:5) and to destroy the works of the devil (3:8); "he is the expiation for our sins, and not for ours only but also for the sins of the whole world" (2:2). Christians have their sins forgiven "for his sake" (2:12) and in his blood are cleansed from all sin (1:7). In a word: God sent him as the Saviour of the world (4:14).

Finally, Jesus Christ is the Mediator between God and man: he reveals the Father to us, unites us to him and gives us divine life. Because he is the Word of God, the very fact that he has become man is revelation itself. He came to make the true God known to us (5:20); his redemptive incarnation is the supreme proof of the Father's love for men (cf. 3:16; 4:9–10).

By confessing belief in Jesus Christ, we become united to the Father (cf. 2:23; 4:15). This union is not just something external; it is fellowship with the

---

12. *In Epist. Ioann. ad Parthos,* 7, 5.   **13.** 1:1–4. Cf. the prologue of St John's Gospel (Jn 1:1ff) with which it is so closely related.   **14.** 1:3, 7; 2:22–23; 3:8, 23; 4:9, 14, 15; 5:5, 9–13.

Father (1:3), because through Jesus Christ and in him we are in the true God (5:20), really sharing in the eternal life of God (cf. 5:11–13). In other words, we are children of God in Christ and through Christ.

In order to abide in communion with God, the Christian should live as Christ lived (2:6), by keeping the commandments. Since Christ is pure (3:3) and without sin (3:5), the Christian who should strive to purify himself (3:3); since Christ is righteous, so too the Christian should be righteous (3:7), that is, live a holy life. Above all, Jesus is the model of love: by dying for us he has shown us what true love means (3:16).

3. *Charity*. This is the central theme of the letter. St John uses both the noun "love"[15] and the verb "to love".[16] Twice he develops the theme to the point where he says, "God is love" (4:8, 16). As St Augustine comments, in this letter the apostle "said many things, practically all of them about charity".[17]

God is love because in himself, in life within the Trinity, he is a living community of love. St John arrives at this understanding through deep meditation (under the inspiration of the Holy Spirit) on the way God works in the history of salvation and, particularly, in effecting the redemptive Incarnation: "In this the love of God was made manifest among us, that God sent his only Son into the world, so that we might live through him" (4:9).

To understand this wonderful proof of God's love for men, we need to reflect on the fact that the Father *sent his only Son*, the Beloved, with whom he is well pleased (cf. Mt 3:17 and par.); he sent him *to the world*, that is, sinful mankind, the enemy of God (cf. Jn 3:16), as *expiation for our sins*, dying on the cross (4:10) to communicate divine life to us, *making us his children* by means of grace (cf. 3:1). The fullness of love is found in God. We are made to partake of that fullness, through Christ: we become God's children. It is Christ who, by his incarnation and his redemptive death (3:16), reveals to us and bestows on us this love of the Father.

Divine love is bestowed on us by supernatural rebirth in Baptism. The Christian, as St John frequently puts it, "is born of God" (3:9; 4:7; 5:1, 2, 4); he receives as a gift the infused virtue of charity which equips him (and at the same time obliges him) to love both God and his neighbour.

In line with this double precept of charity, as Jesus taught it (cf. Mt 22:37–40 and par.), the Christian's response to the love which the Father has shown him in Christ should embrace both love of God and love of neighbour.

Love for God (cf. 4:19–21; 5:2) should manifest itself in keeping his commandments (5:3; cf. 3:3–5, 24), in not loving the world insofar as it is the enemy of God (cf. 2:15–16) and in striving to cleanse oneself of all sin (cf. 3:3, 4, 6; 2:8–9)—in a word, living in a holy way (cf. 3:7). Above all, God's

---

15. 18 times. In the original Greek the word used is always the same (*ágape*), but in translation it is sometimes given as "love" and sometimes as "charity". **16.** 28 times. **17.** *In Epist. Ioann. ad Parthos*, prologue.

commandment is that "we should believe in the name of his Son Jesus Christ and love one another" (3:23).

St John presents brotherly love as the new commandment, although it is also an old commandment (2:7; cf. Jn 13:34–35), a message which was passed on and heard from the beginning (3:11; cf. 3:23); and as a debt we have contracted, a required response to the love of the Father and of the Son. God the Father loved us so much that he sent his own Son; therefore, "we also *ought* to love one another" (4:11). Jesus Christ "laid down his life for us; and we ought to lay down our lives for the brethren" (3:16). Since this love of the Father and of the Son is a love expressed in deeds, the apostle exhorts us "not (to) love in word or speech but in deed and in truth" (3:18).

Love for our neighbour is also a logical consequence of divine filiation, for "every one who loves the parent [God] loves the child" (5:1), that is, his brothers. Therefore, brotherly love is one of the best criteria for identifying the children of God: "for he who does not love his brother whom he has seen, cannot love God whom he has not seen" (4:20); rather, he is a liar and belongs to the devil's faction (cf. 3:10). Finally, brotherly love is the way to God, the way to be in communion with him: "if we love one another, God abides in us and his love is perfected in us" (4:12; cf. 2:10; 3:14).

4. *Divine filiation.* Communion with God, and the life of grace received from Jesus Christ, make the Christian a child of God: "see what love the Father has given us, that we should be called children of God; and so we are" (3:1).

Although different from Christ's natural filiation to God,[18] the Christian's divine filiation is a marvellous supernatural fact. God, through Christ, gives men his Life, making them partakers of his own divine nature (cf. 2 Pet 1:4); and so St John often refers to Christians as "born of God" (cf. 2:29; 3:9; 4:7; 5:1, 4). It is not a matter, therefore, of just an extrinsic relationship (like a title of honour, or adoption human-style): we *are really* children of God (cf. 3:1). In this life, divine filiation brings with it a mysterious identification with Christ, but the seed of divine life will not attain its full growth until eternal life, when we shall see him "as he is" (3:2).

The third chapter further spells out the demands made on us as children of God—avoiding sin (cf. 3:3–10) and practising fraternal love (cf. 3:11–24). However, in other parts of the letter there are also many references to the way those born of God, those who belong to God, live: they do right (2:29); they overcome the evil one (4:4) and the world (5:4); and, especially, they believe in Jesus Christ and keep the commandments, practising brotherly love (cf. 5:1–2).

St John goes so far as to say that "no one born of God commits sin; ... he cannot sin" (3:9; cf. 5:18 and note); he does not mean an impeccability based

---

18. St John even uses different words in Greek to refer to the Son of God (*hyiós*) and to Christians as children of God (*tekna*). When addressing his disciples, affectionately calling them "little children", he uses other terms—*teknía, paidía.*

on one's own efforts, or something natural to man, which was what the Gnostics thought, for in the same letter he speaks of the need to recognize that we are sinners (cf. 1:8–10). What the apostle is saying, rather, is that the Christian counts on the guarantee and strength he has been given to overcome sin—grace, divine filiation, Jesus Christ himself (cf. 3:9).

Finally, and by way of contrast, St John counterposes the children of God and "the children of the devil",[19] telling us how to distinguish between them: the children of the devil sin (cf. 3:8); they do not do right; nor do they practise charity (cf. 3:10).

---

19. 3:10. Not to be taken in a literal sense; in a typical Semitic circumlocution, St John uses the term to describe those whose actions indicate they are on the devil's side, that is, they are people who through sin have broken with God and gone over to the Enemy (cf. notes on 3:6–9; 3:10).

THE FIRST LETTER OF JOHN

The Revised Standard Version, with notes

Prologue

Jn 1:1–18; 20–20, 25, 27 1 Jn 2:13 Lk 24:39 Jn 1:4, 14; 14:6; 15:27

1 [1]*That which was from the beginning, which we have heard, which we have seen with our eyes, which we have looked upon and touched with our hands, concerning the word of life—[2]the life

---

1:1–4. Since the time of the Fathers, these verses have been described as the "prologue", like the prologue of the Fourth Gospel (Jn 1:1–18). In fact, there are many similarities in doctrine, style and even language between the two.

Both passages sing the praises of the mystery of the Incarnation: the Word of God who existed from all eternity, "from the beginning", became man (has been seen, heard, looked upon and touched) so that men might partake of divine life— might have "fellowship", communion, with the Father and the Son. Like the Gospel prologue, this one is written in a rhythmical way—"That which was ..., which we have heard ..., which we have seen ...". And many of the ideas are the same—for example, the reference to "the beginning" (cf. Jn 1:1); the term "the Word" to refer to the second Person of the Blessed Trinity; the reference to "life" (cf. Jn 1:4).

As St Bede points out, "from the very start of the epistle we are being taught the divinity and, at the same time, the humanity of our God and Lord Jesus Christ" (*In I Epist. S. Ioannis*, ad loc.).

1:1. "That which was from the beginning": although the pronoun used is neuter—as if to indicate the ineffable character of the mystery of Christ—the whole phrase refers not to a thing or an abstract teaching, but to the divine Person of the Son, who in the fullness of time was made manifest (v. 2), assuming a human nature. In other words, St John, as in his Gospel, is teaching that Jesus, a historical person (the apostles have lived with him, have seen him, have heard him speak) is the

eternal Word of God (cf. Jn 1:1 and note).

"That which we have heard, ... seen ..., touched ... ": all those references to perception by the senses show the apostle's desire to make it clear that God really did become man. This may be because heretics were denying the Incarnation, or it may simply be that he thought it necessary to spell out this fundamental truth of our faith. He did so in the Gospel (cf., e.g., Jn 20:30–31); and in this letter we frequently find phrases like "Jesus Christ has come in the flesh" (4:2); "Jesus is the Christ" (2:22; cf. 5:1); "Jesus is the Son of God" (4:15; cf. 5:1, 12, 20).

We have recently been reminded that "the Church reverently preserved the mystery of the Son of God, who was made man, and in the course of the ages and of the centuries has propounded it for belief in a more explicit way"; moreover, what the Church teaches "concerning the one and the same Christ the Son of God, begotten before the ages in his divine nature and in time in his human nature, and also concerning the eternal persons of the Most Holy Trinity, belongs to the immutable truth of the Catholic faith" (SCDF, *Mysterium Filii Dei*, 2 and 6).

1:2. St John introduces this verse by way of parenthesis to explain what he means by "the word of life". In the Gospel he had written, "In him [the Word] was life" (Jn 1:4) and elsewhere he records Jesus' statement, "I am the bread of life" (Jn 6:35, 48). These expressions declare that the Son of God has life in all its fullness, that is, divine life, the source of all life, natural and supernatural. Jesus in fact identified himself with Life (cf. Jn 11:25;

131

was made manifest, and we saw it, and testify to it, and proclaim to you the eternal life which was with the Father and was made manifest to us—³that which we have seen and heard we proclaim also to you, so that you may have fellowship* with us; and our fellowship is with the Father and with his Son Jesus Christ. ⁴And we are writing this that our joyᵃ may be complete.

Mt 13:17
Acts 4:20
1 Cor 1:9
Jn 15:11
2 Jn 12

14:6). By the Incarnation, the Word of God *manifests* true life and at the same time makes it possible for that life to be communicated to men—imperfectly, by means of grace, while they are in this world, and perfectly in heaven, by means of the beatific vision (cf. 1 Jn 5:11–12).

"And we testify to it": the testimony of the apostles is something unique in the history of the Church, because (unlike those who succeed them) they know our Lord personally, they have been "witnesses" of his life, death and resurrection (cf. Lk 24:48; Acts 1:8).

"With the Father": the Greek implies closeness, difference, and the mutual relationship between Father and Son, so providing a glimpse of the mystery of the Blessed Trinity (cf. note on Jn 1:1).

1:3–4. This testimony about Christ is designed to lead to fellowship and complete joy.

Fellowship with the apostles (the Greek word is *koinonía*) means, firstly, having the same faith as those who lived with Jesus: "They saw our Lord in the body," St Augustine reminds us, "and they heard words from his lips and have proclaimed them to us; we also have heard them, but we have not seen him […]. They saw him, we do not see him, and yet we have fellowship with them, because we have the same faith" (*In Epist. Ioann. ad Parthos*, 1, 3).

To have fellowship with the Father and the Son we need to have the same faith as the apostles: "St John openly teaches that those who desire to partake of union with God must first partake of union with the Church, learn the same faith and benefit from the same sacraments as the apostles received from the fullness of Truth made flesh" (St Bede, *In I Epist. S. Ioannis*, ad loc.). The Church, the Second Vatican Council teaches, is not simply a collection of people who think the same way; it is the people of God "whom Christ established as a communion of life, love and truth" (*Lumen gentium*, 9).

Fellowship, communion, with the apostles, with the Church, has as its purpose to bring about union with God ("with the Father and with his Son Jesus Christ"); this is a subject St John develops over the course of this letter, as he previously did in his Gospel (cf., e.g., Jn 17:20ff). Here he uses expressions such as "to have the Son", and, in respect of the Son, "to have the Father" (2:23; 5:11ff); "to be in God" (2:5; 5:20); "to abide in God" (2:6, 24; 3:24; 4:13, 15, 16). This deep, intimate communion means that, without losing his personality, man shares in a wonderful and real way in the life of God himself. If Holy Scripture uses many different expressions in this connexion, it is due to the fact that the human mind, because it is so limited, cannot fully grasp the marvellous truth of communion with God.

Complete joy is the outcome of this communion. Most manuscripts say "our joy"; others, including the Vulgate, say "your joy". The difference is not important, because "our" involves the apostles and the faithful, particularly in view of

a. Other ancient authorities read *your*

1. UNION WITH GOD

God is light

⁵This is the message we have heard from him and proclaim to you, that God is light and in him is no darkness* at all.

1 Tim 6:16
Jas 1:17

the mutual fellowship previously mentioned (cf. Jn 15:11; 17:13). This joy, which will reach its fullness in the next life, is already in this life in some sense complete, insofar as knowledge of Jesus is the only thing that can satisfy man's aspirations.

1:5—2:29. This section describes what communion with God is, and the demands it makes on us. We can say there are two parts in the section: the first (1:5—2:11) teaches that communion with God means walking in the light and, therefore, rejecting sin and keeping the commandments. The second (2:12–19) warns the readers to guard against worldly concupiscence and not trust false teachers.

St John is writing as a pastor of souls who has lived the life of the Lord and reflected deeply upon it. His teaching interweaves truths of faith with moral and ascetical demands because he wants Christians to live in a way consistent with their faith. Therefore, the text does not really divide into a doctrinal section and a moral section.

1:5. "God is light": the imagery of light/darkness was much employed in ancient times—sometimes to promote the notion that the world had two principles, one good and the other evil. In St John the image clearly has a different meaning, one connected with biblical teaching on light. When God reveals himself to men, in one way or another light usually plays a part: examples range from the burning bush (cf. Ex 3:1ff) to the coming of the Holy Spirit in the form of tongues of fire

(cf. Acts 2:1ff). This imagery is used to show God's sublimity—as we find also in St Paul: "the Lord of Lords, ... who dwells in unapproachable light, whom no man has ever seen or can see" (1 Tim 6:15–16).

The image of light also helps to show what revelation involves: God has made himself known to us, enlightening our hearts (cf. 2 Cor 4:6). Thus, we can say that God is light, Jesus Christ has made him known to us, and Christian revelation is the splendour of that light. In St John's Gospel the idea of Christ as the light which enlightens the world occurs very often (cf., e.g., Jn 1:4, 9; 8:12; 9:5). St Thomas Aquinas explains, in this connexion, that philosophers prior to Christ had a certain light which allowed them to attain some knowledge of God through reason; the people of Israel had much more light, through divine revelation in the Old Testament; angels and saints, because they have greater knowledge of God by virtue of grace have divine light to a special degree; but only the Word of God is the true light, because he is by his very essence the light which enlightens (cf. *Commentary on St John*, 1, 9).

The expression "God is light" has also a moral dimension: in God there is no darkness because there is no sin; he is sovereign good and all perfection. The light/darkness imagery, therefore, helps to underline the gravity of sin: "the light has come into the world, and men loved darkness rather than light, because their deeds were evil" (Jn 3:19). Those who lead a holy life are called children of light (Jn 12:36; Lk 16:8; Eph 5:8; 1 Thess 5:5); whereas those who do evil

Jn 3:19
Lk 25:53
1 Thess 5:4
Mt 26:28
Heb 9:12, 14
Rev 1:5; Ps 51
Prov 20:9
Rom 3:10

Walking in the light. Rejecting sin

[6]If we say we have fellowship with him while we walk in darkness, we lie and do not live according to the truth; [7]but if we walk in the light, as he is in the light, we have fellowship with one another, and the blood of Jesus his Son cleanses us from all sin. [8]If we say we

---

live in darkness (1 Thess 5:4), which is the symbol of sin (Lk 22:53).

St John uses the statement that "God is light" to encourage Christians to live in an upright way; as does St Augustine, who comments that we must be united to God and "darkness should be cast away from us so as to allow light to enter, because darkness is incompatible with light" (*In Epist. Ioann. ad Parthos*, 1, 5).

1:6–10. The clause "if we say" introduces three suppositions—very probably claims made by some early heretics, especially Gnostics (who boasted of having attained fullness of knowledge and thought they were incapable of sinning).

St John is using the literary technique of parallelism, much employed by Semitic writers: the first sentence states an idea which is repeated and filled out in the later ones. Here, the first statement ("we lie") is later extended to "we deceive ourselves" (v. 8) ..., and then to "we make him [God] a liar" (v. 10). This literary device shows that the author of the letter was familiar with this style of writing, very common in the Old Testament.

1:6–7. Walking in darkness/walking in the light—a graphic description of sinful conduct and upright conduct. St John insists that one cannot justify a life of sin by claiming to have communion with God: "mere confession of faith is in no sense sufficient", St Bede declares, "if that faith is not confirmed by good works" (*In I Epist. S. Ioannis*, ad loc.).

"Fellowship with one another": If there were an exact parallelism between the parts of the passage, we would expect it to read "fellowship with him", which is how some Fathers read it. If the text reads differently, it is because mutual communion, the fellowship with the Church to which St John is referring, is a pledge and sign of fellowship with God: "the Church, in Christ, is in the nature of a sacrament—a sign and instrument, that is, of communion with God and of unity among all men" (Vatican II, *Lumen gentium*, 1).

"The blood of his Son Jesus cleanses us from all sin": this idea is often found in the book of Revelation when it says that the blood of Christ sets us free (cf. Rev 1:5), cleanses souls and makes them white (cf. Rev 7:14), ransoms them for God (cf. Rev 5:9) and defeats the enemies of salvation (cf. Rev 12:11). It is made quite clear that the blood of Christ purifies all types of sin, past and present, mortal and venial. (On the blood of Christ as atonement for all sins, see the notes on Heb 9:12, 14.)

1:8. "If we say we have no sin": the Old Testament often says that all men are sinners (cf. 7:70; Job 9:2; 14:4; 15:14; 25:4; Prov 20:9; Ps 14:1–4; 51; etc.) and this is also clear from the New Testament (cf. especially Rom 3:10–18). The Council of Trent condemns anyone who says "that a man once justified cannot sin again and cannot lose grace" (*De iustificatione*, can. 23).

Loss of the sense of sin is a danger that threatens man in all epochs. The apostle's warning (to his contemporaries in the first instance) has particular rele-

have no sin, we deceive ourselves, and the truth is not in us. ⁹If we confess our sins, he is faithful and just, and will forgive our sins and cleanse us from all unrighteousness. ¹⁰If we say we have not sinned, we make him a liar, and his word is not in us.

Prov 28:13
Jas 5:16

2 ¹My little children, I am writing this to you so that you may not sin; but if any one does sin, we have an advocate with the Father, Jesus Christ the righteous; ²and he is the expiation for our sins, and not for ours only but also for the sins of the whole world.

Jn 14:16; Rom 8:34; Heb 7:25
Acts 3:14

1 Jn 4:10
Jn 11:51f
Rom 3:25

---

vance in our own time. "Deceived by the loss of the sense of sin," John Paul II reminds us, "and at times by an illusion of sinlessness which is not at all Christian, the people of today also need to listen again to St John's admonition, as addressed to each one of them personally: 'If we say we have no sin, we deceive ourselves, and the truth is not in us', and indeed 'the whole world is in the power of the evil one' (1 Jn 5:19). Every individual therefore is invited by the voice of divine truth to examine realistically his or her conscience, and to confess that he or she has been brought forth in iniquity, as we say in the *Miserere* Psalm (cf. Ps 51:7)" (*Reconciliatio et paenitentia*, 22).

1:9–10. "If we confess our sins": the Council of Trent quotes this text (without intending to define its exact meaning) when it teaches that confession of sins is of divine institution: "The Catholic Church has always understood that integral confession of sins was also instituted by the Lord (Jas 5:16; 1 Jn 1:9; Lk 17:14) and is by divine law necessary for all falls after Baptism" (*De Sacramento paenitentia*, chap. 5).

The sacred writer puts emphasis on the interior disposition of the Christian: he should humbly admit that he is a sinner; and St Augustine explains: "If you confess yourself to be a sinner, the truth is in you: the truth is light. Your life

does not yet shine as brightly as it might, because there are sins in you; but now you are beginning to be enlightened, because you confess your iniquities" (*In Epist. Ioann. ad Parthos*, 1, 6).

"Faithful and just": a translation of two Hebrew words which literally have to do with love and faithfulness. The Old Testament uses this expression to stress that God's faithful love is always ready to forgive.

2:1–2. To make sure that no one makes a wrong appeal to divine mercy so as to justify their continuing to sin, St John exhorts all to avoid sin. It is one thing to acknowledge that we are sinners and to be conscious of our frailty; it is a very different matter to become completely passive or pessimistic, as if it were not possible to avoid offending God. "Jesus understands our weakness and draws us to himself on an inclined plane," St Josemaría Escrivá explains. "He wants us to make an effort to climb a little each day. He seeks us out, just as he did the disciples of Emmaus, whom he went out to meet. He sought Thomas, showed himself to him and made him touch with his fingers the open wounds in his hands and side. Jesus Christ is always waiting for us to return to him; he knows our weakness" (*Christ Is Passing By*, 75).

"My little children": it is difficult to translate this and other similar expres-

Keeping the commandments

[1 Jn 4:20]
[1 Jn 5:3]
[Jn 14:21, 23]

[3]And by this we may be sure that we know him, if we keep his commandments.* [4]He who says "I know him" but disobeys his commandments is a liar, and the truth is not in him; [5]but whoever keeps his word, in him truly love for God is perfected. By this we

sions in St John, charged as they are with tenderness and a sense of pastoral responsibility. They express a deep, strong love, like that of Jesus at the Last Supper (cf. Jn 13:33). This same Greek term appears six more times in this letter (2:12, 28; 3:7, 18; 4:4; 5:21); at other times he uses words equivalent to our "my little ones" (cf. 2:14, 18) or "dearly beloved" (2:7; 3:2, 21; 4:1, 7, 11; 3 Jn 2, 5, 11). All these expressions reflect how very close St John was to the faithful.

"We have an advocate with the Father": Jesus Christ, who is the only Mediator (cf. 1 Tim 2:5), intercedes for us. He, who has died for our sins (he is "the expiation"), presents his infinite merits to God the Father, by virtue of which the Father pardons us always. The Holy Spirit is also called Paraclete or Advocate insofar as he accompanies, consoles and guides each Christian, and the whole Church, on its earthly pilgrimage (cf. note on Jn 14:16–17).

"St John the apostle exhorts us to avoid sin", St Alphonsus says, "but because he is afraid we will lose heart when we remember our past faults, he encourages us to hope for forgiveness provided we are firmly resolved not to fall again; he tells us that we have to put our affairs in order with Christ, who died not only to forgive us but also (after dying) to become our advocate with the heavenly father" (*Reflections on the Passion*, chap. 9, 2).

2:3–6. "By this we may be sure": a phrase that occurs often in this letter (cf., e.g., 2:5, 18; 3:19, 24), usually to preface

clear criteria for distinguishing doctrinal and moral truth from error. In this instance, it has to do with keeping the commandments being a sign of true knowledge of God.

For St John, knowing God is not a merely intellectual exercise nor does he mean that the immensity of God can be grasped by man's limited understanding. It refers to something much simpler and more important: knowing God means being united to him by faith and love— by grace. If this letter puts so much emphasis on knowing God (cf., e.g., 2:14; 3:1; 4:6–8; 5:20) or knowing Jesus Christ (cf. 2:13–14; 3:6), it may be because the heretics (particularly the Gnostics) were boasting of having attained special knowledge of God, superior to that of ordinary faithful. And so the apostle describes what true knowledge of God consists in, using expressions which complement one another—knowing him (v. 4); in him who knows God "truly love for God is perfected" (v. 5); abiding in him (v. 6).

"Keeping his commandments" (vv. 3 and 4), "Keeping his word" (v. 5), "walking in the same way in which he walked" (v. 6): keeping the commandments is absolutely necessary, because there is no room for faith without works (cf. 1 Jn 3:17–18; Jas 2:14ff; Gal 5:6). Similarly, one must keep the word of God, that is, accept all revelation docilely (an idea found very often in John: cf., e.g., Jn 5:38; 8:31, 51; 1 Jn 2:14). But, above all, Christians must identify their life with Christ's; St Prosper comments: "Walk as he walked: does that not mean

may be sure that we are in him: ⁶he who says he abides in him   Jn 13:15, 34
ought to walk in the same way in which he walked.

⁷Beloved, I am writing you no new commandment, but an old   Deut 6:5
commandment which you had from the beginning; the old   Mt 22:37–40
commandment is the word which you have heard. ⁸Yet I am
writing you a new commandment, which is true in him and in you,   Jn 13:34
because[b] the darkness is passing away and the true light is already   Rom 13:12
shining. ⁹He who says he is in the light and hates his brother is in   Jn 8:12
the darkness still. ¹⁰He who loves his brother abides in the light,   Jn 11:10
and in it[c] there is no cause for stumbling. ¹¹But he who hates his   Jn 12:35–36
brother is in the darkness and walks in the darkness, and does not

---

giving up the comforts he gave up, not being afraid of the kind of trials he bore, teaching what he taught [...], persevering in helping even those who show no appreciation, praying for one's enemies, being kind to evildoers, serenely tolerating the proud?" (*De vita contemplativa*, 2, 21).

2:7–8. In a play on words, St John draws his readers' attention to the commandment of brotherly love, which he goes on to describe in vv. 9–11. It is, he says, an old commandment (v. 7) and at the same time a new one (v. 8). Old, because Christianity and charity are inseparable and that is something the faithful have known "from the beginning", that is, since they first received instruction; in some way, it can be said that it is even pre-Christian, because it is impressed on the heart of man. Yet it is new, because it is not out of date and has become a reality in Christ and in Christians. The novelty lies not in the precept (which is to be found in the Old Testament: cf. Lev 19:18) but in the standard which Jesus sets ("even as I have loved you": Jn 13:34) and in the fact that it covers everyone: we must love everyone, friends and enemies, without distinction of race, or ideology, or social status (cf. note on Jn 13:34–35).

Moreover, Christian love is not limited to seeking the earthly happiness of others, but tries to lead all to faith and holiness: "What is perfection in love?" St Augustine asks. "Loving our enemies and loving them so that they may be converted into brothers. Our love should not be a material one. Wishing someone temporal well-being is good; but, even if he does not have that, his soul should be secured [...]. It is uncertain whether this life is useful or useless to someone; whereas life in God is always useful. Therefore, love your enemies in such a way that they become your brothers; love them in such a way that you attract them to fellowship with yourself in the Church" (*In Epist. Ioann. ad Parthos*, 1, 9).

2:9–11. In the special style of this letter, an application is made of the new commandment, possibly to counter false teachers, who despised the ordinary faithful and were sowing discord among the Christians. The rhythm of the language—hate, love, hate—in which the positive idea is placed between two opposed ideas, highlights the importance of brotherly love.

"The principal apostolate we Christians must carry out in the world," St Josemaría Escrivá writes, "and the best witness we can give of our faith, is to

b. Or *that* **c.** Or *him*

know where he is going, because the darkness has blinded his eyes.

The apostle's confidence in the faithful

1 Jn 1:7; 2:2
1 Cor 6:11

1 Jn 1:1
Jn 1:1

Jn 5:38

[12]I am writing to you, little children, because your sins are forgiven for his sake. [13]I am writing to you, fathers, because you know him who is from the beginning. I am writing to you, young men, because you have overcome the evil one. I write to you, children, because you know the Father. [14]I write to you, fathers,

---

help bring about a climate of genuine charity within the Church. For who indeed could feel attracted to the Gospel if those who say they preach the Good News do not really love one another, but spend their time attacking one another, spreading slander and quarrelling? It is all too easy, and very fashionable, to say that you love everyone, Christians and non-Christians alike. But if those who maintain this ill-treat their brothers in the faith, I don't see how their behaviour can be anything but 'pious hypocrisy'. By contrast, when in the Heart of Christ we love those 'who are children of the same Father, and with us share the same faith and are heirs to the same hope' (Minucius Felix, *Octavius*, 31), then our hearts expand and become fired with a longing to bring everyone closer to our Lord" (*Friends of God*, 226).

Light/darkness: the section which began at 1:5 ("God is light") ends with the repetition of this contrasting imagery.

2:12–14. These verses, which are a kind of aside, are not easy to translate. The main difficulty has to do with the meaning of the expression, "I am writing (or I insist) *because*". The Greek conjunction may have an explanatory meaning (as the New Vulgate translates it): "I am writing to you *that* your sins have been forgiven ..."; in which case the apostle would be trying to build up the Christians' resis-

tance to the arguments of the heretics; as if he were saying, "You can be sure that your sins have been forgiven ...", that is, that it is you, not they, who are Christians.

However, it is also correct in the context to understand it as being the causal. In this way the apostle is invoking his authority over these Christians, confident that they will listen to him; it is as if he were saying, "I can tell you, and you have the duty and the right to pay heed to me, because your sins have been forgiven ...".

The way he addresses his readers, calling them little children, children, fathers, young men, is also open to various interpretations. The first two (little children, children) are usually taken to mean all Christians, without distinction of age or the length of time they have been in the Church; whereas the other two (fathers, young men) would be addressed to those particular groups. However, it is possible that these are simply rhetorical devices, in which case what is said to young people is perfectly applicable to older people, and vice versa; this is the way St Augustine understood it: "Remember that you are fathers; if you forget Him who is from the beginning, you will have lost your paternity. Also see yourselves over and over again as young men: strive to win; win so as to be crowned; be humble in order not to succumb in the struggle" (*In Epist. Ioann. ad Parthos*, 2, 7).

because you know him who is from the beginning. I write to you, young men, because you are strong, and the word of God abides in you, and you have overcome the evil one.

Detachment from the world

[15]Do not love the world or the things in the world. If any one loves the world, love for the Father is not in him. [16]For all that is in the world, the lust of the flesh and the lust of the eyes and the pride of life, is not of the Father but is of the world. [17]And the world passes away, and the lust of it; but he who does the will of God abides for ever.

Jn 5:42; Jas 4:4
Prov 27:20
Tit 2:12
Jas 4:16
Mt 7:21
1 Pet 4:2

"Because you know him who is from the beginning": a reference to Jesus Christ, as distinct from the Father, who appears at the start of v. 14. St John puts emphasis on *knowing*, which covers not just theoretical knowledge but more particularly a knowledge that comes from faith and love (cf. note on 2:3–6).

2:13. "The evil one": the devil is explicitly mentioned several times in this letter; he is the enemy of the children of God (2:14; 5:18); a sinner from the beginning (3:8); and has the world in his power (5:18–19; cf. Jn 16:11).

"The apostle writes: '*You have overcome the evil one*'! And so it is. It is necessary to keep going back to *the origin of evil and of sin* in the history of mankind and the universe, just as Christ went back to these same roots in the Paschal Mystery of his Cross and Resurrection. There is no need to be afraid to call *the first agent of evil* by his name—*the Evil One*. The strategy which he used and continues to use is that of not revealing himself, so that the evil implanted by him from the beginning may receive its development from man himself, from systems and from relationships between individuals, from classes and nations—so as also to become ever more a '*structural*' *sin*, ever less identifiable as '*personal sin*'. In other words, so that man may feel in a certain sense

'freed' from sin but at the same time be ever more deeply immersed in it" (John Paul II, *Letter to Young People*, 31 March 1985, 15).

2:15–17. The term "world" has a number of meanings in Holy Scripture (cf. note on Jn 17:14–16). Here it has the pejorative sense of enemy of God and man (cf. also note on Jas 1:26–27), and includes everything that is opposed to God—the kingdom of sin. Following Christ involves a radical choice: "No one can serve two masters" (Mt 6:24); "friendship with the world is enmity with God" (Jas 4:4).

"The pride of life": this is the usual translation in Latin. The original Greek says more or less "the arrogance of earthly things"; the two translations are compatible because reliance on material things leads to pride.

The list St John gives here of the signs of a worldly life summarizes everything opposed to fidelity to the love of God. "Lust of the flesh is not limited to disordered sensuality. It also means softness, laziness bent on the easiest, most pleasurable, way, any apparent shortcut, even at the expense of fidelity to God [...]. We can and ought to fight always to overcome the lust of the flesh, because, if we are humble, we will always be granted the grace of our Lord.

"St John tells us that the other enemy is the lust of the eyes, a deep-seated

Not listening to heretics

1 Jn 2:22
2 Jn 7
1 Tim 4:1

¹⁸Children, it is the last hour;* and as you have heard that antichrist is coming, so now many antichrists have come;

---

avariciousness that leads us to appreciate only what we can touch. Such eyes are glued to earthly things and, consequently, they are blind to supernatural realities. We can, then, use this expression of Sacred Scripture to mean that disordered desire for material things, as well as that deformation which views everything around us—other people, the circumstances of our life and of our age—in a merely human way.

"Then the eyes of our soul grow dull. Reason proclaims itself capable of understanding everything, without the aid of God. This is a subtle temptation, which hides behind the power of our intellect, given by our Father God to man so that he might know and love him freely. Seduced by this temptation, the human mind appoints itself the centre of the universe, being thrilled with the prospect that 'you will be like God' (Gen 3:5). So filled with love for itself, it turns its back on the love of God.

"In this way does our existence fall prey unconditionally to the third enemy: pride of life. It's not merely a question of passing thoughts of vanity or self-love, it's a state of general conceit. Let's not deceive ourselves, for this is the worst of all evils, the root of every false step. The fight against pride has to be a constant battle, to such an extent that someone once said that pride only disappears twenty-four hours after each of us has died. It is the arrogance of the Pharisee whom God cannot transform because he finds in him the obstacle of self-sufficiency. It is the haughtiness which leads to despising others, to lording it over them, to mistreating them. For 'when pride comes, then comes disgrace' (Prov 11:2)" (St Josemaría Escrivá, *Christ Is Passing By*, 5–6).

2:18–27. This passage covers one of the main themes in St John's letters—the fidelity of Christians being tested by the heretics. The style, replete with contrasts and parallelisms, makes what he has to say very lively.

First he describes the circumstances these Christians find themselves in: the presence of heretics leads one to think that the antichrist predicted by our Lord (cf. Mt 24:5–24 and par.) has come already and the "last hour" (v. 18) has begun.

He goes on to unmask those who are cast in the role of antichrist, and contrasts them with true believers: 1) they are not of us (v. 19), whereas you know the truth (vv. 20–21); 2) the heretics are imposters who deny the basic truth that Jesus is the Christ (vv. 22–23), whereas you *abide* in the Father and in the Son (vv. 24–25); 3) they arrogantly present themselves as teachers, but the anointing *abides* in you and you have no need of spurious teachers (vv. 26–27).

The repetition of the word *abide* stresses the need to keep the teaching of the Church intact. The faithful have a right to practise their faith in peace, and it is part of the mission of pastors to strengthen them in the faith, as St John is doing here. When introducing his *Creed of the People of God*, Pope Paul VI said: "It is true that the Church always has a duty to try to obtain a deeper understanding of the unfathomable mysteries of God (which are so rich in their saving effects) and to present them in ways even more suited to the successive generations. However, in fulfilling this inescapable duty of study and research, it must do everything it can to ensure that Christian

therefore we know that it is the last hour. [19]They went out from us, but they were not of us; for if they had been of us, they would have continued with us; but they went out, that it might be plain

Acts 20:30
1 Cor 11:18

---

teaching is not damaged. For if that happened, many devout souls would become confused and perplexed—which unfortunately is what is happening at present" (*Homily*, 30 June 1968).

2:18. "The last hour": this expression was probably familiar to the early Christians, who had a lively desire to see the second coming of Christ. As many passages in the New Testament indicate, the fullness of time already began with the Incarnation and the Redemption brought about by Christ (cf. Gal 4:4; Eph 1:10; Heb 9:26). From that point onwards, until the end of the world, we are in the last times, the last earthly stage of salvation history: hence the urgency Christians should feel about their own holiness and the spread of the Gospel. "To prevent anyone dragging his feet," St Augustine urges, "listen: 'children, it is the last hour', go on, run, grow; it is the last hour. It may be an extended one, but it is the last hour" (*In Epist. Ioann. ad Parthos*, 3, 3). This eschatological sense of the last times, which the prophets announced long before (cf. Is 2:2; Jer 23:20; 49:26), is also to be found in the Fourth Gospel (cf., e.g., Jn 2:4; 5:28; 17:1).

"The antichrist": a sign of "the last hour" foretold by our Lord and the apostles is the feverish activity of false prophets (cf. Mt 24:11–24; Acts 20:29–30; 2 Thess 2:2ff; 2 Tim 4:1ff; 2 Pet 3:3). Although this term is only to be found in the letters of St John (1 Jn 2:18, 22; 4:3; 2 Jn 7), the "antichrist's" features are similar to those of the "man of lawlessness", "the enemy" St Paul speaks about (cf. 2 Thess 2:1–12) and the "beasts"

of the Apocalypse (cf., e.g., Rev 11:7; 13:1ff); the distinguishing mark they all share is their brutal opposition to Christ, his teaching and his followers. It is difficult to say whether the antichrist is an individual or a group. In St John's letters, the latter seems to be the case: it is a reference to all those who oppose Christ (the "many antichrists") who have been active since the start of Christianity and will continue to be so until the end of time.

2:19. "They were not of us": St John unmasks the antichrists; they could not have led the faithful astray had they not come from the community; but they were only pretending to be Christians—wolves in sheep's clothing (cf. Mt 7:15), "false brethren" (Gal 2:4)—and that is how they are able to sow confusion. Our Lord himself warned that both wheat and cockle would grow side by side in the Kingdom of God (cf. Mt 13:24–30); the sad fact that this is happening should not cause Christians to doubt the holiness of the Church. As St Augustine explains: "Many who are not of us receive, along with us, the sacraments; they receive Baptism with us, they receive with us what they know the faithful receive—the blessing, the Eucharist and the other holy sacraments; they receive communion from the same altar as we do, but they are not of us. Temptation reveals this to be so; when temptation overtakes them, they flee as if borne away by the wind, because they are not wheat. When winnowing begins on the threshing floor of the Lord on the day of judgment, they will all fly away; remember that" (*In Epist. Ioann. ad Parthos*, 3, 5).

1 Jn 2:27
2 Cor 1:21
2 Pet 1:12

1 Jn 4:3

that they all are not of us. [20]But you have been anointed by the Holy One, and you all know.[d] [21]I write to you, not because you do not know the truth, but because you know it, and know that no lie is of the truth. [22]Who is the liar but he who denies that Jesus is the

---

2:20. "Anointed by the Holy One": it is difficult to say exactly what this means (cf. also v. 27); St John says that this anointing has the effect of countering the work of the antichrist. He may be referring to the sacrament of Baptism or that of Confirmation, or both, where anointing with chrism is part of the sacramental rite. In any case he is referring to the action of the Father and of the Son through the Holy Spirit on the soul of the Christian who has received these sacraments: this explains why the anointing "instructs" Christians "to know everything" (v. 27; RSV alternate reading).

"The Holy One": St John uses this expression to describe God the Father (cf., e.g., Rev 6:10; Jn 17:11), God the Son (cf. Jn 6:69; Rev 3:7), or simply God, without specifying which Person. The last-mentioned use was very common among Jews of the time, to refer to the one true God.

"You all know": not only about the anointing but about Christian teaching in general. Some important manuscripts, which the Sistine-Clementine Vulgate follows, read: "You know all" (cf. RSV alternate reading). Both readings are complementary, for the apostle is stressing that Christians do not need to listen to teachings other than those of the Church: they are being guided by the Holy Spirit, who gives them sureness of faith. The Second Vatican Council quotes this text when teaching about the "supernatural appreciation of the faith [*sensus fidei*] of all the faithful": "The whole body of the faithful, who have an anointing that comes from the Holy One (cf. 1 Jn 2:20 and 27), cannot err in matters of belief. This characteristic is shown in the supernatural appreciation of the faith of the whole people, when, 'from the bishops to the last of the faithful' they manifest a universal consent in matters of faith and morals" (*Lumen gentium*, 12).

2:22. "Jesus is the Christ": this is a basic truth of Christian faith. As in most of St John's writings, this wording means not only that Jesus is the Messiah but also that he is the Son of God (cf. Jn 20:31). From the earliest days of Christianity, faith in Jesus, which included both his messiahship and his divinity, could be expressed by applying to him the titles of "Messiah" and "Son of God", or simply one or other of those titles. Over the course of the centuries the Church has been developing and deepening its understanding of revealed truths about Christ—partly in reaction to heresies attacking that truth. In recent years also the Magisterium has taken issue with erroneous ideas: "The opinions according to which it has not been revealed and made known to us that the Son of God subsists from all eternity in the mystery of the Godhead, distinct from the Father and the Holy Spirit, are in open conflict with this belief; likewise the opinions according to which the notion is to be abandoned of the one person of Jesus Christ begotten in his divinity of the Father before all the ages and begotten in his humanity of the Virgin Mary in time; and lastly the assertion that the humanity of Christ existed not as being assumed into the eternal person of the Son of God but

---

d. Other ancient authorities read *you know everything*

Christ? This is the antichrist, he who denies the Father and the 1 Jn 4:15
Son. ²³No one who denies the Son has the Father. He who Jn 5:23; 14:7, 9
confesses the Son has the Father also. ²⁴Let what you heard from 1 Jn 1:3; 2:7
the beginning abide in you. If what you heard from the beginning
abides in you, then you will abide in the Son and in the Father.
²⁵And this is what he has promised us,ᵉ eternal life. Jn 5:24

²⁶I write this to you about those who would deceive you; ²⁷but 1 Jn 2:20; Jn
the anointing which you received from him abides in you, and you 14:26; Jer 31:34

---

existed rather of itself as a person, and therefore that the mystery of Jesus Christ consists only in the fact that God, in revealing himself, was present in the highest degree in the human person Jesus.

"Those who think in this way are far removed from the true belief in Christ, even when they maintain that the special presence of God in Jesus results in his being the supreme and final expression of divine Revelation. Nor do they come back to the true belief in the divinity of Christ by adding that Jesus can be called God by reason of the fact that in what they call his human person God is supremely present" (SCDF, *Mysterium Filii Dei*, 3).

2:23. "Has the Father": a very graphic way of referring to union with God (cf. 2 Jn 9). St John, who has other ways of saying the same thing—for example, "knowing him" (1 Jn 2:3f; Jn 14:7); "seeing him" (Jn 14:7, 9)—may have had in mind the errors of the Gnostics, who held that union with God was attained through a special kind of knowledge (*gnosis*), available only to initiates of their sect. The apostle repeats the teaching given in his Gospel: only through Christ, through faith in him, can one attain union with and knowledge of the Father (cf. Jn 1:18; 14:9–10); Jesus and the Father are one, only God (Jn 14:11). So, faith in Christ is inseparable from faith in the Blessed Trinity; so, too, denial of the Son's

divinity involves rejection of the Father. "Once the mystery of the divine and eternal person of Christ the Son of God is abandoned, the truth respecting the Most Holy Trinity is also undermined" (SCDF, *Mysterium Filii Dei*, 4).

2:27. The anointing (cf. note on 2:20) refers to the Holy Spirit, who acts on the faithful by instructing them "about everything". Our Lord had said this would be so: "the Counsellor, the Holy Spirit, whom the Father will send in my name, he will teach you all things" (Jn 14:26).

The apostle does not mean that the faithful have no need of the Magisterium of the Church (the very fact that he is writing to them shows otherwise); what he wants to make quite clear is that their true teacher is the Holy Spirit (he it is who guides the Magisterium in its teaching, and he also acts in the soul of the Christian, helping him or her to accept that teaching). "If his anointing teaches you everything, it seems that we [pastors] are toiling to no purpose; why so much shouting on our part [...]? This is the marvellous thing. The sound of our words is striking your ears, but the Master is within. Do not think that it is a question of somebody learning from a man; we can attract your attention by the power of our voice, but if he who does the teaching is not within, all our sermons will be in vain" (St Augustine, *In Epist. Ioann. ad Parthos*, 3, 13).

e. Other ancient authorities read *you*

have no need that any one should teach you; as his anointing teaches you about everything, and is true, and is no lie, just as it has taught you, abide in him.

1 Jn 4:17
2 Thess 1:9

1 Jn 3:7, 10

²⁸And now, little children, abide in him, so that when he appears we may have confidence and not shrink from him in shame at his coming. ²⁹If you know that he is righteous, you may be sure that every one who does right is born of him.

2. LIVING AS GOD'S CHILDREN

We are children of God

Rom 8:14–17
Eph 1:5
Jn 15:21; 17:25

Col 3:4

3 ¹See what love the Father has given us, that we should be called children of God; and so we are. The reason why the world does not know us is that it did not know him. ²Beloved, we

---

2:28–29. These two verses sum up what has gone before and also act as an introduction to a passage on divine filiation. The central idea which St John has been repeating—"abide in him"—now opens out on to the prospect of the Last Judgment: Jesus Christ, who will be our Judge, is the same person as gave us revelation and life. This is one of the foundations of Christian hope.

"We may have confidence": the sacred writer changes to the plural, to include himself: we all have to give an account of our actions and we should have confidence in Christ our Judge. The word translated as "confidence" is much richer in Greek than in English; it is the equivalent of freedom, frankness, confident audacity. "It will be a great thing at the hour of death", St Teresa of Avila writes, "to realize that we shall be judged by One whom we have loved above all things [...]. Once our debts have been paid we shall be able to walk in safety. We shall not be going into a foreign land, but into our own country, for it belongs to him whom we have loved so truly and who himself loves us" (*Way of Perfection*, 40, 8).

3:1–24. This entire chapter shows how moved the apostle is when he contemplates the marvellous gift of divine filiation. The Spirit, who is the author of all Holy Scripture, has desired John to pass on to us this unique revelation: we are children of God (v. 1).

It is not easy to divide the chapter into sections, because the style is very cyclic and colloquial and includes many repetitions and further thoughts which make for great vividness and freshness. However, we can distinguish an opening proclamation of the central message (vv. 1–2) and emphasis on two requirements of divine filiation—rejection of sin in any shape or form (vv. 3–10), and brotherly love lived to the full (vv. 11–24).

3:1. "We should be called children of God": the original Hebrew expression, which reads "we are called ...", is also used by our Lord in the Beatitudes (cf. Mt 5:9): "to be called" means the same as "to be called by God"; and in the language of the Bible, when God gives someone a name he is not simply conferring a title but is causing the thing that the name indicates (cf., e.g., Gen 17:5), for the

are God's children now; it does not yet appear what we shall be, but we know that when he appears we shall be like him, for we shall see him as he is.

Rom 8:29
Phil 3:21
1 Cor 13:12

---

word of God is efficacious, it does what it says it will do. Hence St John's adding: "and so we are".

Therefore, it is not just a matter of a metaphorical title, or a legal fiction, or adoption human-style: divine filiation is an essential feature of a Christian's life, a marvellous fact whereby God gratuitously gives men a strictly supernatural dignity, an intimacy with God whereby they are *domestici Dei*, "members of the household of God" (Eph 2:19). This explains the tone of amazement and joy with which St John passes on this revelation.

This sense of divine filiation is one of the central points in the spirituality of Opus Dei. Its founder wrote: "We do not exist in order to pursue just any happiness. We have been called to penetrate the intimacy of God's own life, to know and love God the Father, God the Son, and God the Holy Spirit, and to love also—in that same love of the one God in three divine Persons—the angels and all men.

"This is the great boldness of the Christian faith—to proclaim the value and dignity of human nature and to affirm that we have been created to obtain the dignity of children of God, through the grace that raises us up to a supernatural level. An incredible boldness it would be, were it not founded on the promise of salvation given us by God the Father, confirmed by the blood of Christ, and reaffirmed and made possible by the constant action of the Holy Spirit" (*Christ Is Passing By*, 133).

"The world does not know us, (because) it did not know him": these words are reminiscent of our Lord's at the Last Supper: "the hour is coming when whoever kills you will think he is

offering service to God. And they will do this because they have not known the Father, nor me" (Jn 16:2–3). Divine filiation brings with it communion and a mysterious identification between Christ and the Christian.

3:2. The indescribable gift of divine filiation, which the world does not know (v. 1), is not fully experienced by Christians, because the seeds of divine life which it contains will only reach their full growth in eternal life, when we see him "as he is", "face to face" (1 Cor 13:12); "this is eternal life, that they know thee the only true God, and Jesus Christ whom thou hast sent" (Jn 17:3). In that direct sight of God as he is, and of all things in God, the life of grace and divine filiation achieve their full growth. Man is not naturally able to see God face to face; he needs to be enlightened by a special light, which is given the technical theological name of *lumen gloriae*, light of glory. This does not allow him to "take in" all of God (no created thing could do that), but it does allow him to look at God directly.

Commenting on this verse, the *St Pius V Catechism* explains that "beatitude consists of two things—that we shall behold God such as he is in his own nature and substance; and that we ourselves shall become, as it were, gods. For those who enjoy God while they retain their own nature, assume a certain admirable and almost divine form, so as to seem gods rather than men" (1, 13, 7).

"When he appears": two interpretations are possible, given that in Greek the verb has no subject: "when (what we shall be) is revealed we shall be as he is"; or, as the New Vulgate translates it,

145

A child of God does not sin

Mt 5:48
Lev 19:2

³And every one who thus hopes in him purifies himself as he is pure.

Jn 1:29
Is 53:5
1 Pet 2:24

⁴Every one who commits sin is guilty of lawlessness; sin is lawlessness. ⁵You know that he appeared to take away sins, and in

---

"when he (Christ) is revealed we will be like him (Christ)". The second interpretation is the more likely.

3:3. "Purifies himself": Christian hope, which is grounded on Christ, is something active and it moves the Christian to "purify himself". This verb is evocative of the ritual purifications required of priests in the Old Testament prior to engaging in divine service (cf. Ex 19:10; Num 8:21; Acts 21:24); here, and in other places in the New Testament, it means interior purification from sins, that is, righteousness, holiness (1 Pet 1:22; Jas 4:8). Our model is Jesus Christ, "as he is pure"; he is the One who has never had sin, the Righteous One (1 Jn 2:29; 3:7); a Christian has no other model of holiness, as Jesus himself said: "Learn from me" (Mt 11:29; cf. Jn 14:6). "We have to learn from him, from Jesus, who is our only model. If you want to go forward without stumbling or wandering off the path, then all you have to do is walk the road he walked, placing your feet in his footprints and entering into his humble and patient Heart, there to drink from the wellsprings of his commandments and of his love. In a word, you must identify yourself with Jesus Christ and try to become really and truly another Christ among your fellow men" (St Josemaría Escrivá, *Friends of God*, 128).

3:4–5. "Sin is lawlessness": although this is not strictly speaking a definition, it does convey a basic idea: every sin is more than a transgression of a precept of the moral law; it is above all, an offence

against God, the author of that law, a despising and a rejection of his will.

To understand the scope of this assertion, one needs to start from the fact that man has been created by God and is ever-dependent on him. So, every sin involves a pretentious desire to be like God (cf. Gen 3:5), to build one's life without reference to, or even in opposition to, God. Everyone who sins severs his allegiance to God and takes the devil's side. In this the mystery and "lawlessness" of sin consists. "This expression," Pope John Paul II explains, "which echoes what St Paul writes concerning the *mystery of evil* (cf. 2 Thess 2:7), helps us to grasp the obscure and intangible element hidden in sin. Clearly, sin is a product of man's freedom. But deep within its human reality there are factors at work which place it beyond the merely human, in the border-area where man's conscience, will and sensitivity are in contact with the dark forces which, according to St Paul, are active in the world almost to the point of ruling it (cf. Rom 7:7–24; Eph 2:2; 6:12)" (*Reconciliatio et paenitentiae*, 14).

Moreover, now that Christ has brought about our Redemption, every sin implies an offence to our Redeemer; it means crucifying again the Son of God (cf. Heb 6:6). So, St John reminds us about the main purpose of the Incarnation: "he appeared to take away sins" (v. 5). There is an echo here of the words the apostle heard the Baptist say: "Behold the Lamb of God, who takes away the sins of the world!" (Jn 1:29).

Thus, as we profess in the Creed at Mass, "for us men and for our salvation

him there is no sin. [6]No one who abides in him sins;* no one who sins has either seen him or known him. [7]Little children, let no one deceive you. He who does right is righteous, as he is righteous. [8]He who commits sin is of the devil; for the devil has sinned from the beginning. The reason the Son of God appeared was to destroy the works of the devil. [9]No one born of God commits sin; for God's[f] nature abides in him, and he cannot sin because he is[g] born

Rom 6:14
1 Jn 2:29
Jn 8:44
Gen 3:15
1 Jn 3:6
5:18

---

he (the Word) came down from heaven". Being true God and therefore completely exempt from sin (v. 5), he took on our human nature, to burden himself with our sins and nail them to the cross. Therefore, the Christian, ransomed from the power of the devil by the precious blood of Christ, and intimately united to him by the life of grace, has broken with sin once for all.

3:6–9. This passage acts as a preface to v. 10, where the apostle spells out the criteria for distinguishing the children of God from the children of the devil—the practice of Christian virtues and the keeping of the commandments of God, especially that of brotherly love.

To understand correctly what St John is saying here, it is useful to remember his controversy with the false teachers (the Gnostics): these were trying to deceive the faithful (v. 7) and claimed to have a special knowledge of God (*gnosis*), which put them above good and evil, so that what the Church regarded as sin they saw as morally indifferent and as incapable of undermining the union with God they claimed they had.

To identify these heretics, the apostle has recourse to words of our Lord: "the tree is known by its fruit" (Mt 12:33). Thus, the genuine Christian is recognized by deeds of righteousness (v. 7), that is, by keeping the commandments of God and leading a holy life. And the qualities essential to the Christian life are incom-

patible with sin; these qualities are— divine filiation ("he is born of God": v. 9), intimate union with Christ ("who abides in him": v. 6), and sanctifying grace, together with the infused virtues and the gifts of the Holy Spirit (this seems to be what the expression "God's nature abides in him" means: v. 9). Thus it is understandable that "No one who abides in him (Christ) sins" (v. 6).

In fact, as long as "God's nature abides in him … he cannot sin" (v. 9). Clearly St John does not mean that a Christian is incapable of sinning; at the start of the letter he said, "If we say we have no sin, we deceive ourselves" (1:8). What he wants to make quite clear is that no one can justify his own sin by the device of claiming to be a child of God: the righteousness of the children of God reflects itself in their actions, whereas "he who commits sin is of the devil" (v. 8), for sin cuts one off from God and means one has submitted to the slavery of the devil.

The ancient heresy has grown up again, in a way, in our own time: there are those who claim that union with God is not broken by transgression of his commandments, even in grave matter, provided one does not withdraw one's "fundamental option" for God. Against this error, the Magisterium of the Church reminds us that "care must be taken not to reduce mortal sin to an act of 'fundamental option'—as is commonly said today—against God, intending thereby an explicit and formal contempt for God

---

f. Greek *his*   **g.** Or *for the offspring of God abide in him, and they cannot sin because they are*

of God. [10]By this it may be seen who are the children of God, and who are the children of the devil: whoever does not do right is not of God, nor he who does not love his brother.

---

or neighbour. For mortal sin exists also when a person knowingly and willingly, for whatever reason, chooses something gravely disordered. In fact, such a choice already includes contempt for the divine law, a rejection of God's love for humanity and the whole of creation: the person turns away from God and loses charity" (*Reconciliatio et paenitentia*, 17).

3:10. "Children of the devil": this is a common Semitic way of speaking, meaning "the devil's supporters". In St John's writings we find references to "children of the devil" (cf. Jn 8:44; Acts 13:10) and to people who are "of the devil" (v. 8), and Judas is even called a "devil" (Jn 6:70; but he never uses an expression like "born of the devil". Therefore, the expressions "children of the devil" and "children of God" cannot be put on the same plane.

Also, "children of God" refers here primarily to the moral dimension of Christian life, as a description (the opposite of "the children of the devil") of those whose actions show they are on God's side. However, being children of God has a radically different meaning from being children of the devil, because it derives from something transcendental —God's causing the Christian to partake of his own divine nature through the life of grace (cf. 1 Jn 3:1–2 and notes on same).

The criteria for distinguishing the two groups mentioned are: the practice of righteousness, that is, striving for holiness and fighting against sin, reviewed in the previous section (vv. 3–9), and the practice of brotherly love, as we shall see in the next section (vv. 11–24).

3:11–22. St John begins this important passage on the subject of brotherly love with the same elevated tone as in 1:5. As usual with his style, it is difficult to discern any rigid arrangement of concepts, but there is a clear connexion of ideas, expressed in paradoxes and contrasts. 1) Statement of the central theme —the commandment of love (v. 11). 2) Its counterpoint is the sin of Cain (v. 12); those who do not practise brotherly love are as much murderers as he was (vv. 13–15). 3) Our model (a new contrast) is Christ, who gave his life for us (v. 16); brotherly love, following our Lord's example, must go beyond mere talk; it must show itself in deed and in truth (vv. 17–18). 4) The consequence of brotherly love is total confidence in God, who knows everything (vv. 19–22).

This passage of St John has led to many beautiful, touching commentaries by the Fathers of the Church. "I believe this is the pearl the merchant in the Gospel was looking for, which when he found it led him to sell everything he had and buy it (Mt 13:46). This is the precious pearl—charity; unless you have it, everything else you have is of no use to you; and if you have it alone, you need nothing else. Now you see with faith; later on you will see with intuitive vision; if we love now, when we do not see, what degree of love shall we not attain when we do see! And, meanwhile, what should we be doing? We should be loving the brethren. You may be able to say, I have not seen God; but can you say, I have not seen man? Love your brother. If you love your brother whom you see, you will also see God, because you will see charity, and God dwells within it" (St Augustine, *In Epist. Ioann. ad Parthos*, 5, 7).

Loving one another

[11]For this is the message which you have heard from the beginning, that we should love one another, [12]and not be like Cain who was of the evil one and murdered his brother. And why did he murder him? Because his own deeds were evil and his brother's righteous. [13]Do not wonder, brethren, that the world hates you. [14]We know that we have passed out of death into life, because we love the brethren. He who does not love abides in death. [15]Any one who hates his brother is a murderer, and you know that no

1 Jn 2:7
Jn 13:34

Gen 4:8

Jn 15:18
Jn 5:24
Mt 5:21f

3:11. The new commandment of brotherly love, which Jesus expressly taught at the Last Supper (cf. Jn 13:34–35 and note) is the "message" which Christians have learned from the beginning (cf. 1 Jn 2:7). There is no more sublime commandment, and all the commandments are summed up in it. As St Augustine explains, "Everyone can make the sign of the cross of Christ; everyone can answer, Amen; everyone can sing Alleluia; everyone can have himself baptized, can enter churches, can build the walls of basilicas. But charity is the only thing by which the children of God can be told from the children of the devil. Those who practise charity are born of God; those who do not practise it are not born of God. An important mark, an essential difference! You may have whatever you like, but if you lack this, just this, everything else is of no use whatsoever; and if you lack everything and have nothing but this, you have fulfilled the law!" (*In Epist. Ioann. ad Parthos*, 5, 7).

3:12. Cain is the prototype of those who belong to the devil; not only because he took his brother's life by violence, but because the hatred nestling in his heart prevented him from recognizing his brother's goodness. The same reaction can happen today: "Because you don't know, or don't want to know, how to imitate that man's upright manner of acting, your secret envy makes you seek to ridicule him" (St Josemaría Escrivá, *Furrow*, 911).

3:13. In this verse, an aside breaking the flow of the argument, St John seeks to encourage all Christians, particularly his immediate readers who were probably experiencing persecution (perhaps that ordered by the emperor Domitian). Jesus clearly predicted that his disciples would be persecuted as he was (cf. Jn 15:18–22).

For a Christian, difficulties should provide an opportunity to show firmness in the faith and not be sad or discouraged (cf. Jn 16:1–4): "If you are reproached for the name of Christ, you are blessed, because the spirit of glory and of God rests upon you" (1 Pet 4:14).

3:14–15. The Christian life involves passing from death to life, from sin to grace. Anyone who does not practise the commandment of love "remains in death [sin]".

"Anyone who hates his brother is a murderer." This unambiguous statement echoes the teaching of Jesus in the Sermon on the Mount: "every one who is angry with his brother shall be liable to judgment" (Mt 5:22). The internal sin of hatred has the same malicious root as the external act of murder.

By speaking in this way, St John makes it crystal clear that hatred of one's neighbour is incompatible with the Christian faith.

Jn 15:13

Jas 2:16

Deut 15:7

Mt 7:21

Jas 1:22; 2:15f

2 Jn 4

3 Jn 3–4

1 Jn 4:17

Heb 4:16

Mt 7:7

murderer has eternal life abiding in him. [16]By this we know love, that he laid down his life for us; and we ought to lay down our lives for the brethren. [17]But if any one has the world's goods and sees his brother in need, yet closes his heart against him, how does God's love abide in him? [18]Little children, let us not love in word or speech but in deed and in truth.

[19]By this we shall know that we are of the truth, and reassure our hearts before him [20]whenever our hearts condemn us; for God is greater than our hearts, and he knows everything. [21]Beloved, if our hearts do not condemn us, we have confidence before God;

3:16–18. From Jesus the Christian learns what love is and what demands it makes —not only through his teaching (like that about the Good Shepherd in John 10:1ff or his discourse at the Last Supper) but above all by his example: "he laid down his life for us", by dying on the cross. We "ought" to do the same; the Greek word St John uses implies a duty. That is, the precept of brotherly love imposes an obligation for two reasons—by the very nature of things, since all men are brothers and children of God; and because we are indebted to Christ and must respond to the infinite love he showed by giving his life for us.

Using an example very like that in the Letter of St James (cf. Jas 2:15–16), he shows that true love expresses itself in actions: anyone who "closes his heart" when he sees others in need does not truly love. The saints have constantly reminded us of St John's teaching: "what the Lord desires is works. If you see a sick woman to whom you can give some help, never be affected by the fear that your devotion will suffer, but take pity on her: if she is in pain, you should feel pain too; if necessary, fast so that she may have your food, not so much for her sake as because you know it to be your Lord's will. That is true union with his will. Again, if you hear someone being highly praised, be much more pleased than if

they were praising you" (St Teresa of Avila, *Interior Castle*, 5, 3, 11).

3:19–22. The apostle reassures us: God knows everything; not only does he know our sins and our frailties, he also knows our repentance and our good desires, and he understands and forgives us (St Peter, on the Lake of Tiberias, made the same confession to Jesus: "Lord, you know everything, you know that I love you": Jn 21:17).

St John's teaching on divine mercy is very clear: if our conscience tells us we have done wrong, we can seek forgiveness and strengthen our hope in God; if our conscience does not accuse us, our confidence in God is ardent and bold, like that of a child who has loving experience of his Father's tenderness. The love of God is mightier than our sins, Pope John Paul II reminds us: "When we realize that God's love for us does not cease in the face of our sin or recoil before our offences, but becomes even more attentive and generous; when we realize that this love went so far as to cause the Passion and Death of the Word made flesh who consented to redeem us at the price of his own blood, then we exclaim in gratitude: 'Yes, the Lord is rich in mercy', and even: 'The Lord *is* mercy'" (*Reconciliatio et paenitentia*, 22).

This confidence in God makes for confidence in prayer: "If you abide in me,

²²and we receive from him whatever we ask, because we keep his commandments and do what pleases him. ²³And this is his commandment, that we should believe in the name of his Son Jesus Christ and love one another, just as he has commanded us. ²⁴All who keep his commandments abide in him, and he in them. And by this we know that he abides in us, by the Spirit which he has given us.

Jn 14:13–15
Jn 6:28; 13:34
Jn 15:10
1 Jn 4:13
Rom 8:9

3. FAITH IN CHRIST. BROTHERLY LOVE

Faith in Christ, not in false prophets

4 ¹Beloved, do not believe every spirit, but test the spirits* to see whether they are of God; for many false prophets have gone

1Jn 2:18
2 Jn 7
Mt 24:24
1 Tim 4:1

---

and my words abide in you, ask whatever you will, and it shall be done for you" (Jn 15:7; cf. 14:13f; 16:23, 26–27).

3:23–24. The commandments of God are summed up here in terms of love for Jesus and love for the brethren. "We cannot rightly love one another unless we believe in Christ; nor can we truly believe in the name of Jesus Christ without brotherly love" (St Bede, *In I Epist. S. Ioannis*, ad loc.). Faith and love cannot be separated (cf. Gal 5:6); our Lord himself told us what would mark his disciples out—their love for one another (Jn 13:34–35).

Keeping the commandments confirms to the Christian that he is abiding in God: "If you keep my commandments, you will abide in my love" (Jn 15:10). Moreover, it ensures that God abides in his soul, by the indwelling of the Holy Spirit: "If you love me you will keep my commandments. And I will pray the Father, and he will give you another Counsellor, to be with you for ever" (Jn 14:15–16).

"May God be your house and you God's; dwell in God that God may dwell in you. God dwells in you to support you;

you dwell in God in order not to fall. Keep the commandments, have charity" (*In I Epist. S. Ioannis*, ad loc.).

4:1–6. In the third part of the letter (4:1–5:12), the sacred writer expands further on the two things which sum up God's commandments (3:23)—faith in Jesus (4:1–6; 5:1–12) and brotherly love (4:7–21).

He begins by giving criteria for recognizing the true spirit of God and for identifying false teachers (4:1–6), clearly echoing what he said in the second chapter (cf. 2:18–29). There the heretics were called "antichrists", here "false prophets". There he underlined the indwelling of the Blessed Trinity in believers ("you will abide in the Son and in the Father": 2:24), the anointing "abides in you" (2:27); here he emphasizes rather the fact of belonging to God or not. This idea is developed in three points: 1) he who confesses Jesus Christ "is of God"; 2) he who does not confess him "is not of God" (vv. 2–3); you "are of God", they "are of the world" (vv. 4–5); 3) we (he must surely mean the apostles) "are of God", and therefore apostolic teaching merits attention and must be listened to (v. 6).

1 Cor 12:3 out into the world. ²By this you know the Spirit of God: every spirit which confesses that Jesus Christ has come in the flesh is of 1 Jn 2:22 God, ³and every spirit which does not confess Jesus is not of God. This is the spirit of antichrist, of which you heard that it was 1 Jn 2:13–14 coming, and now it is in the world already. ⁴Little children, you are of God, and have overcome them; for he who is in you is Jn 15:19 greater than he who is in the world. ⁵They are of the world, therefore what they say is of the world, and the world listens to Jn 8:47; 14:17 them. ⁶We are of God. Whoever knows God listens to us, and he

---

"Being of God", in St John's language, does not refer to originating from God, because in fact everyone, good and bad, faithful or not, comes from God. It means, rather, belonging to a group ("to my sheep": Jn 10:26) and it also means a mode of existence: "he who is from the earth ... of the earth speaks" (Jn 3:31); "you are from below, I am from above" (Jn 8:23); "Everyone who is of the truth hears my voice" (Jn 18:37). Faith, therefore, is not a superficial thing, something that affects us on the outside only: it actually changes a person's inner life; belonging to the community of the children of God involves a new way of being, which can be seen from the fact that we live in accordance with the faith we profess.

4:2–3. "Every spirit which confesses that Jesus Christ has come in the flesh ...": according to this translation (which fits certain Greek manuscripts) the Apostle would be emphasizing the fact that the Incarnation really happened, as if the false prophets opposed to the faith were saying that Christ's human nature was not real but only apparent (that was the position of the Docetists).

In the context, the alternate reading— "every spirit which confesses Jesus Christ come in the flesh"—may fit in better, since St John often insists that the Christian's faith centres on the person of Jesus Christ,

who, being God, became man (cf. 2:22; 4:15; 5:1–5). By emphasizing this he is taking issue with the Gnostics particularly, who were saying that Jesus was the Son of God only from his Baptism onwards (cf. note on 1 Jn 5:6).

On the antichrist, see the note on 2:18.

4:4. St John repeats his conviction that Christians are assured of victory in their battle against the evil one (cf. 2:13; 5:4, 18). But what makes them victorious is the power of Christ working in them; so, while bolstering their faith he is also calling on them to be humble: "Do not become proud; recognize who has conquered in you. Why did you win? 'Because he who is in you is more powerful than he who is in the world.' Be humble; carry your Lord; be a little donkey for your rider. It is in your best interest to have him guide and direct you; because if you do not have him as your rider, you will be inclined to toss your head and kick out; but woe to you if you have no guide! That freedom would mean your ending up as prey for wild beasts" (St Augustine, *In Epist. Ioann. ad Parthos*, 7, 2).

4:6. "Whoever knows God listens to us": as elsewhere in the letter, there is a change from "you" to "we" (cf. 2:18, 28; 3:13–14). One could argue that the apostle is simply including himself in the Christian community as a whole, as if to

who is not of God does not listen to us. By this we know the spirit of truth and the spirit of error.

God is love. Brotherly love, the mark of Christians

⁷Beloved, let us love one another; for love is of God, and he who loves is born of God and knows God. ⁸He who does not love does

1 Jn 4:16

---

say "Whoever knows God listens to the Christians." However, the obvious interpretation is that the "us" refers to those in authority in the Church, bringing it perfectly into line with what Jesus says: "He who hears you hears me" (Lk 10:16). Obedience to the living Magisterium of the Church is, therefore, the rule for distinguishing the spirit of truth from the spirit of error. It could not be otherwise, for it is the Holy Spirit himself who guides the Church in its teaching and leads the faithful to accept that teaching: "the assent of the Church can never be lacking to such definitions [of the Supreme Magisterium] on account of the same Holy Spirit's influence, through which Christ's whole flock is maintained in the unity of the faith and makes progress in it" (Vatican II, *Lumen gentium*, 25).

4:7–21. St John now expands on the second aspect of the divine command-ment (cf. 1 Jn 3:23)—brotherly love. The argument is along these lines: God is love and it was he who loved us to begin with (vv. 7–10); brotherly love is the response which God's love calls for (vv. 11–16); when our love is perfect, we feel no fear (vv. 17–18); brotherly love is an expres-sion of love of God (vv. 19–21).

This is not tiresome repetition of the ideas already discussed (2:7–11; 3:11–18): contrary to the false teaching which is beginning to be spread, charity is the sure mark, the way to recognize the genuine disciple.

St Jerome hands down a tradition concerning the last years of St John's life:

when he was already a very old man, he used always say the same thing to the faithful: "My children, love one another!" On one occasion, he was asked why he insisted on this: "to which he replied with these words worthy of John: 'Because it is the Lord's commandment, and if you keep just this commandment, it will suffice'" (*Commentary on Gal.*, 3, 6, 10).

4:7. The divine attributes, God's perfec-tions, which he has to the highest degree, are the cause of our virtues: for example, because God is holy, we have been given a capacity to be holy. Similarly, because God is love, we can love. True love, true charity, comes from God.

4:8. "God is love": without being strictly speaking a definition (in 1:5 he says "God is light"), this statement reveals to us one of the most consoling attributes of God: "Even if nothing more were to be said in praise of love in all the pages of this epistle", St Augustine explains, "even if nothing more were to be said in all the pages of Holy Scripture, and all we heard from the mouth of the Holy Spirit were that 'God is love', there would be nothing else we would need to look for" (*In Epist. Ioann. ad Parthos*, 7, 5).

God's love for men was revealed in Creation and in the preternatural and supernatural gifts he gave man prior to sin; after man's sin, God's love is to be seen, above all, in forgiveness and redemp-tion (as St John goes on to say: v. 9), for the work of salvation is the product of God's mercy: "It is precisely because sin

Jn 3:16

not know God; for God is love. ⁹In this the love of God was made manifest among us, that God sent his only Son into the world, so 1 Jn 2:2 that we might live through him. ¹⁰In this is love, not that we loved Rom 3:25; 5:8 God but that he loved us and sent his Son to be the expiation for

---

exists in the world, which 'God so loved … that he gave his only Son' (Jn 3:16), that God, who 'is love' (1 Jn 4:8), *cannot reveal himself other than as mercy*. This corresponds not only to the most profound truth of that love which God is, but also to the whole interior truth of man and of the world which is man's temporary homeland" (John Paul II, *Dives in misercordia*, 13).

4:9. God has revealed his love to men by sending his own Son; that is, it is not only Christ's teachings which speak to us of God's love, but, above all, his presence among us: Christ himself is the fullness of revelation of God (cf. Jn 1:18; Heb 1:1) and of his love for men. "The source of all grace is God's love for us, and he has revealed this not just in words but also in deeds. It was divine love which led the second Person of the most holy Trinity, the Word, the Son of God the Father, to take on our flesh, our human condition, everything except sin. And the Word, the Word of God, is the Word from which Love proceeds (cf. *Summa theologiae*, 1, 43, 5, quoting St Augustine, *De Trinitate*, 9, 10).

"Love is revealed to us in the incarnation, the redemptive journey which Jesus Christ made on our earth, culminating in the supreme sacrifice of the cross. And on the cross it showed itself through a new sign: 'One of the soldiers pierced his side with a spear, and at once there came out blood and water' (Jn 19:34). This water and blood of Jesus speaks to us of a self-sacrifice brought to the last extreme: 'It is finished' (Jn 19:30) —everything is achieved, for the sake of

love" (St Josemaría Escrivá, *Christ Is Passing By*, 162).

"Among us": it is difficult to convey in English everything the Greek contains. The Greek expression means that the love of God was shown *to* those who witnessed our Lord's life (the apostles) and to all other Christians, who participate in this apostolic witness (cf. note on 1 Jn 1:1–3; this idea is repeated in vv. 14 and 16). But it also means "*within* us", inside us, in our hearts, insofar as we partake of God's own life by means of sanctifying grace: every Christian is a witness to the fact that Christ has come so that men "may have life, and have it abundantly" (Jn 10:10).

4:10. Given that love is an attribute of God (v. 8), men have a capacity to love insofar as they share in God's qualities. So, the initiative always lies with God.

When explaining in what love consists, St John points to its highest form of expression: "he sent (his Son) to be the expiation of our sins" (cf. 2:2). Similar turns of phrase occur throughout the letter: the Son of God manifested himself "to destroy the works of the devil" (3:8); "he laid down his life for us" (3:16). All these statements show that: 1) Christ's death is a *sacrifice* in the strict sense of the word, the most sublime act of recognition of God's sovereignty; 2) it is an atoning sacrifice, because it obtains God's pardon for the sins of men; 3) it is the supreme act of God's love, so much so that St John actually says, "in this is love."

What is amazing, St Alphonsus teaches, "is that he could have saved us without suffering or dying and yet he

our sins. ¹¹Beloved, if God so loved us, we also ought to love one
another. ¹²No man has ever seen God; if we love one another, God
abides in us and his love is perfected in us.

¹³By this we know that we abide in him and he in us, because
he has given us of his own Spirit. ¹⁴And we have seen and testify
that the Father has sent his Son as the Saviour of the world.
¹⁵Whoever confesses that Jesus is the Son of God, God abides in

Mt 18:33

Jn 1:18

1 Jn 3:24
Rom 5:5

Jn 3:17; 4:42

1 Jn 5:5

---

chose a life of toil and humiliation, and a bitter and ignominious death, even death on a cross, something reserved for the very worst offenders. And why was it that, when he could have redeemed us without suffering, he chose to embrace death on the cross? To show us how much he loved us" (*The Love of Jesus Christ*, chap. 1).

4:11–12. The apostle underlines here the theological basis of brotherly love: the love which God has shown us by the incarnation and redemptive death of his Son, places us in his debt: we have to respond in kind; so we "ought" to love our neighbour with the kind of gratitude and disinterest that God showed by taking the initiative in loving us.

Moreover, by loving one another we are in communion with God. The deepest desire of the human heart, which is to see and to possess God, cannot be satisfied in this life, because "no man has ever seen God" (v. 12); our neighbour, on the other hand, we do see. So, in this life, the way to be in communion with God is by brotherly love. "Love of God is the first thing in the order of commands", St Augustine explains, "and love of neighbour is the first thing in the order of practice [...]. You, who do not yet see God, will, by loving your neighbour, merit to see him. Love of neighbour cleanses our eyes to see God, as John clearly says, If you do not love your neighbour, whom you see, how can you love God, whom you do not see? (cf. 1 Jn 4:20)" (*In Ioann. Evang.*, 17, 8).

4:13. Having the gift of the Holy Spirit is the sure sign of being in communion with God. Since the Holy Spirit is the love of the Father and of the Son, his presence in the soul in grace is necessarily something dynamic, that is, it moves the person to keep all the commandments (cf. 3:24), particularly that of brotherly love. This impulse shows that the third Person of the Blessed Trinity is at work within us; it is a sign of union with God.

The Spirit's action on the soul is a marvellous and deep mystery. "This breathing of the Holy Spirit in the soul," says St John of the Cross, "whereby God transforms it into himself, is so sublime and delicate and profound a delight to it that it cannot be described by mortal tongue, nor can human understanding, as such, attain to any conception of it" (*Spiritual Canticle*, stanza 39).

4:14–15. Once more (cf. v. 1:4) John vividly reminds his readers that he and the other apostles have seen with their own eyes the Son of God, made man out of love for us. They were eyewitnesses of his redemptive life and death. And in the Son, sent by the Father as Saviour of the world, the unfathomable mystery of God is revealed—that his very being is Love.

"It is 'God, who is rich in mercy' (Eph 2:4) whom Jesus Christ has revealed to us as Father: it is his very Son who, in himself, has manifested him and made him known to us (cf. Jn 1:18; Heb 1:1f)" (John Paul II, *Dives in misericordia*, 1).

him, and he in God. [16]So we know and believe the love God has for us. God is love, and he who abides in love abides in God, and God abides in him. [17]In this is love perfected with us, that we may have confidence for the day of judgment, because as he is so are we in this world. [18]There is no fear in love, but perfect love casts out fear. For fear has to do with punishment, and he who fears is not perfected in love. [19]We love, because he first loved us. [20]If any

1 Jn 4:8

1 Jn 2:28

Rom 8:15

1 Jn 4:10
1 Jn 2:4

4:16. "Knowing" and "believing" are not theoretical knowledge but intimate, experienced attachment (cf. notes on 2:3–6; 4:1–6; Jn 6:69; 17:8). Therefore, when St John says that they knew and believed "the love God has for us" he is not referring to an abstract truth but to the historical fact of the incarnation and death of Christ (v. 14), the supreme manifestation of the Father's love.

"He who abides in love abides in God, and God abides in him": St Thomas Aquinas explains "that in some way the loved one is to be found in the lover. And so, he who loves God in some way possesses him, as St John says (1 Jn 4:16) [...]. Also, it is a property of love that the lover becomes transformed into the loved one; so, if we love vile and perishable things, we become vile and perishable, like those who 'became detestable like the things they loved' (Hos 9:10). Whereas, if we love God, we are made divine, for the Apostle says, 'He who is united to the Lord becomes one spirit with him' (1 Cor 6:17)" (*On the Two Commandments of Love*, prol., 3).

4:17–18. The perfection of charity shows itself in serene confidence in God and consequent absence of fear. Love is perfected "*in* us", as a gratuitous gift from God, but it can also be said that it grows *with* us, thanks to our free response to grace.

Confidence for the day of judgment (cf. also the note on 2:28) is something we should have also in this life; a basis for it is to be found in the daring statement, "... because as he is so are we in this world". This is not just a reference to imitating Christ's virtues or qualities: it means the profound identification with Christ which the Christian should attain: "it is no longer I who live, but Christ who lives in me" (Gal 2:20).

The fear which is incompatible with charity is servile fear, which sees God only as one who punishes those who transgress his commandments. But filial fear, which *is* compatible with charity, is what gives a Christian a deep horror of sin because it is something which cuts him off from the love of God his Father. In the early stages of the Christian life, fear of God is very helpful (cf., e.g., Ps 111:10; Sir 1:27): the Council of Trent teaches that sinners "by turning from a salutary fear of divine justice to a consideration of God's mercy, are encouraged to hope, confident that God will be well-disposed to them for Christ's sake" (*De iustificatione*, 6).

4:18. "The solution is to love", St J. Escrivá says. "St John the Apostle wrote some words which really move me: 'qui autem timet, non est perfectus in caritate.' I like to translate them as follows, almost word for word: the fearful man doesn't know how to love. You, therefore, who do love and know how to show it, you mustn't be afraid of anything. So, on you go!" (*The Forge*, 260).

one says, "I love God," and hates his brother, he is a liar; for he who does not love his brother whom he has seen, cannot[h] love God whom he has not seen. [21]And this commandment we have from him, that he who loves God should love his brother also.

Mt 22:37–40
Jn 15:17

Everyone who believes in Jesus overcomes the world

5 [1]Every one who believes that Jesus is the Christ is a child of God, and every one who loves the parent loves the child. [2]By this we know that we love the children of God, when we love God

1 Jn 2:22
Mt 16:16

4:19. Commenting on this passage, St Augustine exclaims: "How could we have loved him if he had not first loved us? By loving him, we become his friends; but he loved us when we were his enemies, in order to make us his friends. He loved us first and gave us the boon of loving him. We did not yet love him, but on loving him we become beautiful. What is a misshapen and deformed man doing, loving a beautiful woman? […] Can he, by loving, change and become beautiful? […]. Our soul, my brethren, is ugly due to iniquity; loving God makes it beautiful. What kind of love is this which makes the lover beautiful? God is always beautiful, never deformed, never changeable. He, who is ever beautiful, first loved us" (*In Epist. Ioann. ad Parthos*, 9, 9).

"We love": this can also be translated as "we should love one another", repeating 4:11. But here it seems to have an emphatic meaning: we are capable of loving.

4:20–21. "He is a liar": this is a very harsh statement (cf. 1:6–10; 2:4): being a liar means being on the devil's side, for the devil is the father of lies (cf. Jn 8:44). Loving God means keeping all the commandments (cf. Jn 14:15; 15:10), and the principal commandment is that of charity; therefore, it is not possible to love God without loving one's neighbour. Clement of Alexandria records a beau-

tiful phrase of Christian tradition on this point when he says, "Seeing your brother is seeing God" (*Stromata*, 1, 19; 2, 15).

St John concludes this exhortation to charity by giving a new format to Christ's commandment, which makes it quite clear that love of neighbour is inseparable from love of God: true charity is a current that runs from God to the Christian and from the Christian to his fellow men. "The true disciple of Christ is marked by love both of God and of his neighbour" (Vatican II, *Lumen gentium*, 42).

5:1–5. The fifth chapter is a summary of the entire letter, focusing on faith in Jesus Christ (vv. 6–12) and the confidence that faith gives (vv. 13–21).

In the opening verses (vv. 1–5) St John points to some consequences of faith: he who believes in Christ is a child of God (v. 1); he loves God and men, his brothers (v. 2); he keeps the commandments (v. 3) and shares in Christ's victory over the world (vv. 4–5).

5:1. "He who loves the parent ...": it is axiomatic that one who loves his father also loves his brothers and sisters, because they share the same parent. The New Vulgate clarifies the scope of this maxim in this letter by adding the word *Deum*: "He who loves God his father ..." loves him who is born of God; Christian fraternity is a consequence of divine filiation.

h. Other ancient authorities read *how can he*

Jn 14:25
Mt 11:30
1 Jn 2:13, 14
Jn 16:33

1 Jn 4:4

Jn 19:34

and obey his commandments. ³For this is the love of God, that we keep his commandments. And his commandments are not burdensome. ⁴For whatever is born of God overcomes the world; and this is the victory that overcomes the world, our faith. ⁵Who is it that overcomes the world but he who believes that Jesus is the Son of God?

Testimony borne to Christ

⁶This is he who came by water and blood, Jesus Christ, not with the water only but with the water and the blood. ⁷And the Spirit is

---

5:4. "This is the victory that overcomes the world, our faith": faith in Jesus Christ is of crucial importance because through it every baptized person is given a share in Christ's victory. Jesus has overcome the world (cf. Jn 16:33) by his death and resurrection, and the Christian (who through faith becomes a member of Christ) has access to all the graces necessary for coping with temptations and sharing in Christ's own glory. In this passage the word "world" has the pejorative meaning of everything opposed to the redemptive work of Christ and the salvation of man that flows from it.

5:6. The "water" and the "blood" have been interpreted in different ways, depending on whether they apply (following the more literal meaning) to events in the life of Christ, or are regarded as symbols of particular sacraments. The water, if referred to the life of Christ, would be an allusion to our Lord's baptism (cf. Mt 3:13–17 and par.), where the Father and the Holy Spirit bore witness to Christ's divinity; the blood would refer to the cross, where Christ, God and true man, shed his blood to bring Redemption. According to this interpretation, St John is answering the Gnostics, who said that Jesus of Nazareth became the Son of God through baptism and ceased to be the Son of God prior to his passion: therefore, only the man Jesus, devoid of divinity,

died on the cross; which would be a denial of the redemptive value of Christ's death.

Understood as symbols of the sacraments, the water would refer to Baptism (cf. Jn 3:5), where we receive the Holy Spirit and the life of grace (cf. Jn 7:37–39); the blood would apply to the Eucharist, where we partake of the blood of Christ in order to have life in us (cf. Jn 6:53, 55, 56). Jesus came on earth to give his life for men (cf. Jn 10:10); we obtain that life in the first instance by means of the living water of Baptism (cf. Jn 4:14; 7:37ff); and also by the application of the blood of Christ, which cleanses us from all sin (cf. 1 Jn 1:7; 2:2; 4:10).

The two interpretations are compatible with one another, given that sacraments are sensible signs of the supernatural effects of Christ's redemptive death. Referring to Baptism, Tertullian wrote: "We have also a second laving, and it too is unique—the baptism with blood. The Lord spoke of this when he said, 'I have a baptism to be baptized with' (Lk 12:50), having had already been baptized once. So, he did come 'by water and blood' (1 Jn 5:6), as John writes, in order to be bathed by the water and glorified by the blood, in order to make us (who are called by water) chosen ones through blood. These two baptisms spring from the wound in his pierced side; so it is that those who believed in his blood would be washed by the water; those who were

the witness, because the Spirit is the truth. [8]There are three witnesses,* the Spirit, the water, and the blood; and these three agree. [9]If we receive the testimony of men, the testimony of God is greater; for this is the testimony of God that he has borne witness to his Son. [10]He who believes in the Son of God has the testimony in himself. He who does not believe God has made him a liar, because he has not believed in the testimony that God has borne to his Son. [11]And this is the testimony, that God gave us eternal life, and this life is in his Son. [12]He who has the Son has life; he who has not the Son of God has not life.

Jn 5:32, 37; 8:18

Jn 3:33
Rom 8:16

1 Jn 1;2; 5:20

Jn 3:36

---

washed in the water would also drink of the blood" (*De baptismo*, 6).

5:7–8. The Sistine-Clementine edition of the Vulgate included an addition which left the text reading as follows: "There are three who give witness *in heaven: the Father, the Word, and the Holy Spirit; and these three are one. And there are three who give witness on earth:* the Spirit, the water, and the blood; and these three agree." The words shown in italics (known as the Johannine "comma" or addition) were the subject of heated debate (around the end of the nineteenth century) as to their authenticity. The Holy Office (as it was then called) left theologians free to research the matter (cf. *Declaration*, 2 June 1927) and in fact it has been shown that the "comma" was introduced in Spain around the fourth century AD in a text attributed to Priscillian, and therefore does not belong to the original inspired text. The "comma" makes express mention of the Blessed Trinity; however, even without it the text proclaims that mystery of faith fairly clearly: it makes mention of Jesus Christ, the Son of God (vv. 5–6), and of the Holy Spirit (v. 7) and of the Father, both of whom bear witness to the Son (v. 9).

According to the legal prescriptions of the Old Testament, the testimony of one witness was insufficient at trials (Deut 17:6; cf. Jn 8:17). St John points to three witnesses (the Holy Spirit, water and blood), thereby refuting the Gnostic teaching; he is saying that the water and the blood, that is, Christ's baptism and his death on the cross, are a manifestation of his divinity. Clearly the word "witness" is used here in a broad sense: namely, in the sense that at those two important moments in his life, Christ makes known to us that he is true God.

The Fathers who interpreted these words as referring to the sacraments usually comment on the fact that in the sacraments the grace of God is communicated internally and is signalled externally. St Bede writes along those lines: "The Holy Spirit makes us adoptive sons of God; the water of the sacred fount cleanses us; the blood of the Lord redeems us: the spiritual sacrament gives us a dual witness, one visible, one invisible" (*In I Epist. S. Ioannis*, ad loc.).

5:9–12. In his characteristic style St John strings together a series of short phrases (and their opposites, as contrasts) which are full of meaning. In a very few words, he enunciates three important truths, which he expects Christians to be very familiar with: 1) God the Father has borne witness to his Son (v. 9); 2) this witness brings an obligation with it; if one does not believe one is making God out to be a liar (v. 10); 3) God has given us life in Christ (vv. 11–12).

4. CONCLUSION

Jn 1:12; 20:31 ¹³I write this to you who believe in the name of the Son of God, that you may know that you have eternal life.

Prayer for sinners

1 Jn 3:21f
Mt 7:7
Jn 14:13 ¹⁴And this is the confidence which we have in him, that if we ask anything according to his will he hears us. ¹⁵And if we know that

---

Earlier the apostle pointed out that faith in Jesus can be the object of reason because it is based on external proofs, and that its fruit is supernatural life (cf. 1 Jn 1:1–5). Now he adds that in addition to the aforementioned witnesses—the Spirit, the water and the blood (vv. 6–8) —God the Father bears witness. Although John does not expressly say so, it is clear that God bore witness to Jesus throughout his earthly life: Jesus' words, miracles, passion and death, and his resurrection are evidence God has supplied of Christ's divinity. The believer "has the testimony [of God] in him" (v. 10), within him, insofar as he accepts and makes the Christian message (Revelation) his own, convinced that it comes from God, who cannot deceive or be deceived. In his turn, he who believes in Jesus Christ manifests his faith to others, passing on to them the conviction that Jesus is true God.

Faith produces the fruit of supernatural life, which is the seed and firstfruit of eternal life (cf. 11–12); that life can be given us only by Jesus Christ, our Saviour. "To those of us who are still making our pilgrim way in this life has been given the hope of eternal life, which we shall only receive in its full form in heaven when we reach Him" (St Bede, *In I Epist. S. Ioannis*, ad loc.).

5:13–21. St John's words in v. 13 are evocative of the first epilogue to his Gospel, where he explains why he wrote that book: "that you may believe that

Jesus is the Christ, the Son of God, and that believing you may have life in his name" (Jn 20:31). In this verse of the letter, the apostle stresses the efficacy of faith, which is already an anticipation of eternal life (cf. notes on 1 Jn 3:2; 5:9–12).

His final counsels are designed to strengthen our confidence in prayer and to urge the need for prayer on behalf of sinners (vv. 14–17); they also stress the conviction and confidence that faith in the Son of God gives the believer (vv. 18–21).

5:14–15. Earlier, the apostle referred to confidence in prayer and to how we can be sure of receiving what we pray for: that confidence comes from the fact that "we keep his commandments and do what pleases him" (1 Jn 3:22). Now he stresses that God always listens to us, if we ask "according to his will". This condition can be taken in two ways, as St Bede briefly explains: "insofar as we ask for the things he desires, and insofar as those of us who approach him are as he desires us to be" (*In I Epist. S. Ioannis*, ad loc.). The asker therefore needs to strive to live in accordance with God's will, and to identify himself in advance with God's plans. If one does not try to live in keeping with God's commandments, one cannot expect him to listen to one's prayers.

When prayer meets those requirements, "we know that we have obtained the requests made of him", as our Lord

he hears us in whatever we ask, we know that we have obtained the requests made of him. [16]If any one sees his brother committing what is not a mortal sin, he will ask, and God[i] will give him life for those whose sin is not mortal. There is sin which is mortal; I do not say that one is to pray for that. [17]All wrongdoing is sin, but there is sin which is not mortal.

Mt 12:31
Heb 6:4–6

himself assured us: "if you ask anything in my name, I will do it" (Jn 14:14). "It is not surprising, then," the Curé of Ars teaches, "that the devil should do everything possible to influence us to give up prayer or to pray badly, because he knows better than we do how much hell fears prayers and how impossible it is that God should refuse us what we ask him for in prayer. How many sinners would get out of sin if they managed to have recourse to prayer!" (*Selected Sermons*, 5th Sunday after Easter).

5:16–17. "Mortal sin": the meaning of the original text is "sin which leads to death". The gravity of this sin (St John does not specify its exact nature) recalls the gravity of blasphemy against the Holy Spirit (cf. Mt 12:31–32) and of the sin of apostasy which Hebrews speaks of (Heb 6:4–8).

The Fathers have interpreted this expression in various ways, referring to different grave sins. In the context of the letter (in the previous chapters St John often speaks about the antichrists and false prophets who "went out" from the community: 2:19) the best interpretation seems to be that of St Bede and St Augustine, who apply it to the sin of the apostate who, in addition, attacks the faith of other Christians. "My view is", St Augustine says, "that the sin unto death is the sin of the brother who, after knowing God by the grace of our Lord Jesus Christ, attacks brotherly union and in a passion of envy reacts against that very

grace by which he was reconciled to God" (*De Sermo Dom. in monte*, 1, 22, 73).

If St John does not expressly command his readers to pray for these sinners, it does not mean that they are beyond recovery, or that it is useless to pray for them. Pope St Gelasius I teaches: "There is a sin of death for those who persist in that same sin; there is a sin not of death for those who desist from sin. There is, certainly, no sin for the pardon of which the Church does not pray or from which, by the power which was divinely granted to it, it cannot absolve those who desist from it" (*Ne forte*).

Referring to this passage of St John, Pope John Paul II says: "Obviously, the concept of *death* here is a spiritual death. It is a question of the loss of the true life or 'eternal life', which for John is knowledge of the Father and the Son (cf. Jn 17:3), and communion and intimacy with them. In that passage the sin *that leads to death* seems to be the denial of the Son (cf. 1 Jn 2:22), or the worship of false gods (cf. 1 Jn 5:21). At any rate, by this distinction of concepts John seems to wish to emphasize the incalculable seriousness of what constitutes the very essence of sin, namely the rejection of God. This is manifested above all in *apostasy* and *idolatry*: repudiating faith in revealed truth and making certain created realities equal to God, raising them to the status of idols and false gods (cf. 1 Jn 5:16–21)." And after referring to blasphemy against the Holy Spirit (cf. Mt 12:31–32) he adds: "Here of course it is a

i. Greek *he*

The Christian's confidence as a child of God

1 Jn 3:9
Jn 17:15

Gal 1:4

¹⁸We know that any one born of God does not sin, but He who was born of God keeps him, and the evil one does not touch him.

¹⁹We know that we are of God, and the whole world is in the power of the evil one.

question of extreme and radical manifestations—rejection of God, rejection of his grace, and therefore opposition to the very source of salvation (cf. St Thomas, *Summa theologiae* 2–2, 14, 1–3)—these are manifestations whereby a person seems to exclude himself voluntarily from the path of forgiveness. It is to be hoped that very few persist to the end in this attitude of rebellion or even defiance of God. Moreover, God in his merciful love is greater than our hearts, as St John further teaches us (cf. 1 Jn 3:20), and can overcome all our psychological and spiritual resistance. So that, as St Thomas writes, 'considering the omnipotence and mercy of God, no one should despair of the salvation of anyone in this life' (ibid., ad 1)" (*Reconciliatio et paenitentia*, 17).

5:18–20. "We know": each of these verses begins this way. He does not mean theoretical knowledge but that understanding that comes from living faith. St John is once again stressing the Christian's joyful confidence, which he has been expounding throughout the letter (cf. 2:3–6 and note). This confidence is grounded on three basic truths: 1) he who is born of God does not sin (cf. 1 Jn 3:6–9 and note); 2) "we are of God", and therefore we are particularly free of the world, which is still in the power of the evil one (cf. 4:4; 5:12); 3) the Son of God has become man (cf. 4:2; 5:1). The incarnation of the Word is the central truth which sheds light on the two previous ones, because our supernatural insight is the effect of the Incarnation (v. 20): Jesus Christ, true

God and true man, is also eternal life, for only in him can we attain that life.

5:18. "In this Johannine affirmation", Pope John Paul II teaches, "there is an indication of hope, based on the divine promises: the Christian has received the guarantee and the necessary strength not to sin. It is not a question therefore of a sinlessness acquired through one's own virtue or even inherent in man, as the Gnostics thought. It is a result of God's action. In order not to sin the Christian has knowledge of God, as St John reminds us in this same passage. But a little earlier he had written: 'No one born of God commits sin; for God's seed [RSV: "nature"] abides in him' (1 Jn 3:9). If by 'God's seed' we understand, as some commentators suggest, Jesus the Son of God, then we can say that in order not to sin, or in order to gain freedom from sin, the Christian has within himself the presence of Christ and the mystery of Christ, which is the mystery of God's loving kindness" (*Reconciliatio et paentientia*, 20).

5:19. "The whole world is in the power of the evil one": although the Greek term may be neuter and would allow a more abstract translation ("in the power of evil"), it is more consistent with the context to take it in a personal sense. St John is pointing up the contrast between Christ's followers and those of the evil one: whereas the world (in the pejorative sense) is like a slave in the power of the devil, true Christians are *in* Christ, as free people, with a share in Christ's own life.

Jn 17:3
Rom 9:5

1 Cor 10:14

[20]And we know that the Son of God has come and has given us understanding, to know him who is true; and we are in him who is true, in his Son Jesus Christ. This is the true God and eternal life. [21]Little children, keep yourselves from idols.

"We have been born of God through grace and have been reborn in Baptism through faith. On the other hand, those who love the world are in the power of the enemy, be it because they have not yet been liberated from him by the waters of regeneration or because, after their rebirth, they have once more submitted to his rule through sinning" (*In I Epist. S. Ioannis*, ad loc.).

5:20. "Him who is true": that is, the only true God as distinct from false gods; the Jews used to refer to God as "the True", without naming him. When St John goes on to say that "we are in him, who is true, in his Son Jesus Christ", he is confessing the divinity of Christ and the fact that he is the only mediator between the Father and mankind.

5:21. Although at first sight, this final exhortation may seem surprising, it was appropriate in its time, because these first Christians were living in the midst of a pagan world, and were exposed to the danger of idolatry.

However, St John may be speaking metaphorically: the true danger facing Christians, then and now, is that of following the idols of the heart—that is, sin; in which case he is giving this final counsel: Keep away from sin, be on your guard against those whose fallacious arguments could lead you to sin.

Introduction to the
Second and Third Letters of St John

These two letters of St John, which on account of their brevity are also called the "lesser epistles", conform to the style of letters of the period in the Greco-Roman world: they begin in the usual formal way (with the sender's name, then that of the addressee, and the greeting) and end with a concluding salutation.

The author introduces himself in both as "the elder" (cf. 2 Jn 1; 3 Jn 1). The Second Letter is addressed "to the elect lady and her children" (2 Jn 1), a symbolic way of referring to a local church, very probably one in Asia Minor. The Third is addressed to a Christian called Gaius (3 Jn 1), and perhaps through him to a group of faithful.

THE AUTHOR

In neither letter does the sacred writer give his name. However, the wide circulation they received from the very beginning (despite their slightness) is an implicit testimony to the authority of the writer. To this must be added the many testimonies which, from earliest times, attribute these letters to St John the apostle.

Thus, St Polycarp (d. 156), a disciple of the apostle, in his *Letter to the Philippians*[1] seems to use the text of 2 John 7. St Irenaeus (d. 202), a disciple, in turn, of St Polycarp quotes 2 John 7 and 11, expressly attributing that letter to St John.[2] Also, Tertullian (d. *c.*222), a witness to tradition in north Africa, refers to 2 John 7.[3] An indirect testimony is to be found in Clement of Alexandria (d. 214), who, to introduce a quotation from 1 John, uses this form of words: "John in his longer epistle", implying that he knew of at least one other, shorter, letter by the same writer.[4] Explicit quotations from the two letters are to be found in many different writers of the third to fifth centuries— St Dionysius of Alexandria,[5] St Athanasius,[6] St Cyril of Jerusalem,[7] St Gregory Nazianzen,[8] St Augustine[9] etc.

Both letters, along with 1 John, figure as works of St John the apostle in the earliest lists or canons of inspired books. The Muratorian Canon, written

---

1. Cf. 7:1. **2.** Cf. *Against Heresies*, 1, 16, 3; 3, 16, 8. **3.** Cf. *De carne Christi*, 24. **4.** Cf. *Stromata*, 2, 16, 76. **5.** Cf. Eusebius of Caesarea, *Ecclesiastical History*, 7, 25, 11. **6.** *Epist.* 39. **7.** *Catechesis*, 4, 36. **8.** *Poems*, 1, 12, 37. **9.** *De doctrina christiana*, 2, chap. 8, 12.

around the year 180, which reflects the tradition of the Roman church, speaks of the letters (plural) of St John. The provincial Council of Laodicea (*c*.360), a witness to the tradition of Asia Minor, includes in its canon 60 a list of inspired books in which the three letters figure. The same is true of various African councils—Hippo (393) and the third and fourth councils of Carthage (397 and 419). Finally, we might mention a letter from Pope St Innocent I (20 February 405) to Exuperius, bishop of Toulouse, where in reply to a question from the bishop as to which books are inspired, he sends him the well-known list with St John's three letters among the New Testament writings.

Alongside this broad consensus, which reflects so many testimonies from different parts of the Church, there were, in the early centuries, some doubts as to whether St John was the author of these two letters.

Very early on, Origen (d. 253) mentions the doubts current at his time.[10] Eusebius places both letters among the "disputed writings" of the New Testament, that is, the books not accepted by all as canonical;[11] he himself did accept them.[12] The same has to be said of St Jerome, who regarded them as authentic Johannine texts but noted the doubts obtaining in his time.[13]

These doubts originate from the text by Papias of Hierapolis (written around the year 130) which rationalist criticism has also used to deny the authenticity of the Fourth Gospel.[14] In the passage from Papias, recorded by Eusebius it says: "If ever anyone came who had carefully followed the presbyters, I inquired as to the words of the presbyters or what Thomas or James or what John or Matthew or any other of the disciples of the Lord, and what Aristion and the presbyter [elder] John, the Lord's disciple, were saying."[15]

If some modern critics have chosen to attribute the Gospel to "John the elder", taking him to be a different person from the apostle, they are naturally ever more inclined to do this in regard to these two letters signed by "the elder". However, even in the case of these letters the arguments offered are not convincing because, as against this one ambiguous testimony from Tradition, which does not even mention the Johannine writings, there is almost complete unanimity from the second century onwards as regards their Johannine authenticity. Official church documents have always attributed both letters to St John the apostle.

In addition to the testimonies from Tradition, there are also similarities of language and content between these letters and the Fourth Gospel which speak in favour of St John as author.

There is certainly no doubt about both letters being by the same author: it is enough to compare the initial greetings and endings, which are almost identical in wording.[16] Also, both letters, especially the Second, contain a

---

10. Cf. *In Ioann. comm.*, 6, 3; see *Ecclesiastical History*, 6, 27, 7–10.   **11.** Cf. *Ecclesiastical History*, 3, 25, 3.   **12.** Cf. *Demonstration Evangelica*, 3, 5, 88.   **13.** Cf. *Epist. ad Paulinum*, 53, 8; *On Famous Men*, 9, 18.   **14.** Cf. *The Navarre Bible: St John* (2005), p. 13.   **15.** *Ecclesiastical History*, 3, 39, 4.
16. Compare 2 Jn 1 with 3 Jn 1; 2 Jn 4 with 3 Jn 3, 4; 2 Jn 12 with 3 Jn 13, 14.

series of expressions and ideas characteristic of St John. The typical turns of phrase are: "love in the truth" (1 Jn 3:18; 2 Jn 1: 3 Jn 1); "know the truth" (1 Jn 2:21; 2 Jn 1); "abiding in Christ" or "in the doctrine of Christ" (1 Jn 2:28; 2 Jn 9); "having the Father and the Son" (1 Jn 2:23; 2 Jn 9); reference to traditional Christian teaching by the phrase "as you have heard from the beginning" (1 Jn 2:24; 3:11; 2 Jn 6); insistence on brotherly love ("that we love one another": 1 Jn 3:11, 23; 4:7; 2 Jn 5), a commandment which is not new, but which we have had from the beginning (cf. 1 Jn 2:7; 2 Jn 5); love for God consists in keeping the commandments (cf. 1 Jn 5:3; 2 Jn 6); he who does right "is of God" (1 Jn 3:10; 3 Jn 11), whereas he who does evil "has not seen God" (1 Jn 3:6; 3 Jn 11).

The first two letters speak of "many antichrists", "false prophets" or "deceivers (who) have gone into the world" (1 Jn 2:18; 4:1; 2 Jn 7); they are people who do not confess "that Jesus Christ has come in the flesh" (1 Jn 4:2; 2 Jn 7). Also, in 1 and 2 John the apostle expresses the wish that "our joy may be complete" (1 Jn 1:4; 2 Jn 12).

As can be seen, there is scarcely a verse of 2 John that does not have its parallel in 1 John. In fact, the second is usually regarded as a first draft (or else a resume) of the first.

To conclude: both the testimony of Tradition and analysis of the texts agree in pointing to St John the apostle as the author.

As regards canonicity the doubts which arose in the second to fourth centuries had no great importance, and, as we have indicated, from the fourth century onwards these letters appear in all the lists of inspired books. In the Councils of Trent[17] and Vatican I,[18] the Church has solemnly declared them to be canonical.

---

17. Cf. *De libris sacris.*   18. Cf. *Dei Filius*, chap. 2.

Special Introduction to the Second Letter of St John

This letter is addressed to "the elect lady and her children" (v. 1), probably not a noble Christian woman and her family, but a local church; at the end of the letter, in similar phrasing, the apostle describes as "your elect sister" (v. 13) the Christian community from which he is writing—probably Ephesus.

The counsels the writer gives have to do with the same subjects as are covered more extensively in 1 John—brotherly love and observance of the commandments (vv. 4–6), and the need to be on guard against deceivers (vv. 7–11). Since the latter do "not acknowledge the coming of Jesus Christ in the flesh" (v. 7), the apostle exhorts the faithful to abide in the doctrine of Christ (v. 9), who is the Son of the Father (v. 3), so as to live in communion with the Father and the Son (v. 9).

In the absence of other information in the Tradition of the Church, it is reasonable to suppose that this letter was written in the last years of the first century, as a warning at a time when danger from heretics was not yet as serious as that revealed in 1 John (1 John being a later letter).

THE SECOND LETTER OF JOHN

The Revised Standard Version, with notes

Greeting

¹The elder* to the elect lady* and her children, whom I love in the truth, and not only I but also all who know the truth, ²because of the truth which abides in us and will be with us for ever:

³Grace, mercy, and peace will be with us, from God the Father and from Jesus Christ the Father's Son, in truth and love.

3 Jn 1
1 Pet 5:13
Jn 14:17

1 Tim 1:2
2 Tim 1:2

1:1–3. The normal heading of a letter in the Greco-Roman world (cf. note on 1 Cor 1:1) included the name of the sender ("the elder"), that of the addressee ("the elect lady and her children"), and the greeting (v. 3).

Like St Paul, St John uses this format but gives it his personal, Christian seal, especially in the greeting. Thus, whereas normally the greeting sent good wishes, St Paul usually says "grace and peace" (cf. the note on Rom 1:7); St John adds "mercy" (cf. also 1 Tim 1:2; 2 Tim 1:2). This is a way of stressing his supernatural conviction that they are receivers of divine favours.

The letter is addressed to the elect lady and her children, a metaphor meaning a particular church of Asia Minor: this allows one to suppose that it may have been a circular letter, addressed in the first instance to one community, but meant to be read later in many other communities, at least in Asia Minor.

"The truth": this word is used four times in this short section. In New Testament language, especially in the writings of St John, "truth" means the revelation of God which reaches its climax in Jesus Christ ("I am the truth": Jn 14:6) and includes all the truths in which we have to believe (cf. Jn 17:17, 19); but it is above all an interior principle of supernatural life and activity (cf. 1 Jn 2:24). Therefore, "to love in the truth" is much more than "to love sincerely"; it means "loving in Christ", the formula which St Paul uses (cf., e.g., Rom 16:8) and which is equivalent to "loving with

the same love as that with which Christ loves". Of course, this is presented as a goal which the Christian should aim at though he will never fully achieve it.

1:1. "The elder": this is the literal translation. Among the Jews, elders were the most prominent people in the communities and formed one of the "estates" in the Sanhedrin (cf. note on Mt 2:4). In the New Testament and in the first era of Christianity, the titles of "elder" and "bishop" were used indiscriminately to refer to pastors of local communities, pastors appointed by the apostles (cf. note on Acts 20:28; and also Acts 11:30; 14:23; 20:17; 1 Tim 4:14; 5:17–19; Tit 1:5, 7). Even St Peter describes himself as "a fellow elder" (1 Pet 5:1). Only much later did the terminology we now have become fixed, reserving the title of "bishop" to bishops, and that of "elder" to ordinary priests.

Here the definite article—*the* elder—indicates that the writer is a person well known to those he is addressing and one who has authority over them. That elder *par excellence* is none other than St John himself.

1:3. "From the Father and from Jesus Christ, the Father's Son": this phrase is one of many supportive of the dogma of the consubstantiality between the Father and the Son, that is, that the two have the same substance, are one, only God. St John attests here, St Bede teaches, "that the grace, mercy and peace that are given to the faithful also come from Christ, as

The law of love

3 Jn 3

1 Jn 2:7

1 Jn 5:3

[4]I rejoiced greatly to find some of your children following the truth, just as we have been commanded by the Father. [5]And now I beg you, lady, not as though I were writing you a new commandment, but the one we have had from the beginning, that we love one another. [6]And this is love, that we follow his commandments; this is the commandment, as you have heard from the beginning, that you follow love.

Precautions against heretics

1 Jn 2:18;
4:1, 3

Gal 4:11

[7]For many deceivers have gone out into the world, men who will not acknowledge the coming of Jesus Christ in the flesh; such a one is the deceiver and the antichrist. [8]Look to yourselves, that

---

well as from God the Father; and in order to show that he is equal to the Father and coeternal with him he says that the gifts of the Son are the same as those of the Father" (*In II Epist. S. Ioannis*, ad loc.). Jesus, speaking about his consubstantiality with the Father, says, "whatever he [God the Father] does, that the Son does likewise" (Jn 5:19).

1:4–6. Among all similarities of language and content between the Second and Third Letters, this passage is a particularly significant one.

The apostle's joy (v. 4) is based on the fact that the Christians have learned that walking in the truth entails keeping the commandment of brotherly love, which they have had from the beginning. The verses sum up one of the main themes of the First Letter, where St John expounds these teachings at greater length (cf. 1 Jn 2:7–11; 3:11–24; 4:7–21 and notes on same).

"That you follow love": the Greek is ambiguous and literally says "that you follow it"; "it" could refer to the commandment (that is how the New Vulgate reads it) or to love. The sense is not very different, if one remembers that in St John's teaching the commandments reduce

to love of God and love of neighbour: "Listen carefully to a brief precept", St Augustine exhorts, "love and do what you like" (*In Epist. Ioann ad Parthos*, 7, 8).

St John also emphasizes that this is a commandment they have had "from the beginning" (vv. 5 and 6); that is, Tradition is so definite on this point that anyone who teaches otherwise is a liar and a deceiver. This helps to explain the connexion between these verses and the ones which follow. In fact the false teachers were causing harm in two ways—by corrupting the faith and by destroying unity and mutual love.

1:7–11. These warnings are a summary of things said in the First Letter (cf. 2:18–29; 4:1–6; 5:1–5; and notes on same). St John shows how to recognize these heretics—by the fact that they do not acknowledge the divinity of Jesus Christ incarnate (cf. 1 Jn 4:2–3 and note); and he warns that anyone who turns his back on sound teaching is abandoning the Father and the Son (cf. 1 Jn 2:22–25 and notes). The passage ends with instructions on precautions to take in dealings with those people (vv. 10–11).

On the "antichrist" (v. 7), see the note on 1 Jn 2:18.

you may not lose what you[a] have worked for, but may win a full
reward. [9]Any one who goes ahead and does not abide in the
doctrine of Christ does not have God; he who abides in the
doctrine has both the Father and the Son. [10]If any one comes to
you and does not bring this doctrine, do not receive him into the
house or give him any greeting; [11]for he who greets him shares his
wicked work.

1 Jn 2:23

Conclusion and greetings
[12]Though I have much to write to you, I would rather not use
paper and ink, but I hope to come to see you and talk with you

3 Jn 13f

1:8. "That you may not lose what you
have worked for": many important codexes
read "what we have worked for", referring to the efforts of the apostles. Both
readings have equal support in the Greek
codexes; both make sense and show that
in order to persevere in the faith (and
obtain the reward for doing so) care and
effort are needed, on the part of both
pastors and other faithful.

St Cyril of Jerusalem exhorted:
"Keep careful watch, to ensure that the
enemy does not make off with any who
are off guard or remiss; and that no
heretic may pervert part of what you have
been given. Accepting the faith is like
putting into the bank the money we have
given you; God will ask you for an
account of this deposit" (*Catechesis V,
De fide et symbolo*).

1:10–11. John does not mince his words:
faith, a most precious gift from God,
needs to be protected from harm. The
letter has to do with certain errors which
were spreading at the time, but its
teaching applies to all periods of history.

In the Middle East hospitality and
greeting were not, as they are sometimes
among us, mere marks of courtesy or
good manners; they involved a real sense

of solidarity and affinity. Hence the
warning that reception of these people
implied complicity in their evil deeds (v.
11), and the consequent danger of giving
scandal to others.

Instructions of a similar kind are to
be found in Mt 18:17; 1 Cor 5:9–13; Tit
3:10–11. The Church has a duty to safe-
guard the faith—and to try to get those
who undermine it to mend their ways. In
exceptional cases it may have recourse to
disciplinary measures if "neither by
fraternal correction or reproof, nor by any
methods of pastoral care, can the scandal
be sufficiently repaired, justice restored
and the offender reformed" (*Code of
Canon Law*, can. 1341).

St Vincent of Lerins warned: "If you
were to tolerate, even just once, a
doctrinal error, I shudder to describe the
grave danger to religion that would
result; once you give way in any area of
catholic dogma you will give way in
another and another, as something quite
lawful and required by custom"
(*Commonitorium*, 23).

1:12–13. The ending shows St John's
great warmth and affection. Like St Paul
(cf. Rom 1:11–12) he longs to visit those
Christians as soon as possible to confirm

---

a. Other ancient authorities read *we*

face to face, so that our joy may be complete.

[13]The children* of your elect sister greet you.

them in the faith and for the sheer pleasure a meeting will give both him and them.

The greeting sent in v. 13 comes from the members of the church from which he is writing, probably that of Ephesus.

Special Introduction to the Third Letter of St John

Addressed to a Christian named Gaius (v. 1), this letter must have been written at a time of strife in some Christian community. All we know about Gaius is what can be gleaned from the letter; St John praises him for being a true Christian (vv. 3–4), as he showed by the welcome he gave the apostle's envoys (vv. 5–8). That welcome also revealed his respect for the person of St John. His attitude contrasts with that of Diotrephes, who must have been the man in charge of that community (v. 9); Diotrephes does not accept the apostle's authority, nor did he receive his envoys; he even dared to excommunicate those who did welcome them (vv. 9–10). That explains why a previous letter the apostle sent to the church (v. 9) has not had any effect.

A man called Demetrius is also mentioned, probably the bearer of the letter; "everyone" has good things to say about him (v. 12). It is usually supposed that Demetrius was commissioned either to replace Diotrephes at the head of the church or else to institute Gaius in that position. In fact, the ancient Christian text, the *Apostolic Constitutions* (7, 46) contains lists of bishops which include the names of Gaius and Demetrius as bishops of Pergamum and Philadelphia respectively; however, the historical accuracy of these data is in doubt.

Although it does not contain any new teachings, the letter is a valuable testimony to the way of life of the early communities, and a model of the letters of introduction and recommendation mentioned elsewhere in the New Testament (cf. Acts 18:27; 2 Cor 3:3).

THE THIRD LETTER OF JOHN

The Revised Standard Version, with notes

Greeting

¹The elder to the beloved Gaius, whom I love in the truth.

²Beloved, I pray that all may go well with you and that you may be in health; I know that it is well with your soul.

2 Jn 1

Praise of Gaius

³For I greatly rejoiced when some of the brethren arrived and testified to the truth of your life, as indeed you do follow the truth. ⁴No greater joy can I have than this, to hear that my children follow the truth.

2 Jn 4

1 Jn 3:19

1–2. Gaius was a common name in the classical world. In St Paul's life, for example, others of the same name appear (cf. Acts 19:29; 20:4; 1 Cor 1:14; Rom 16:23). We know nothing about this Gaius other than what the letter says. An ancient Christian text (*Apostolic Constitutions*, 7, 46) mentions a Gaius as bishop of Pergamum and a Demetrius (v. 12) as bishop of Philadelphia; but the historical accuracy of these data is in doubt. From what the apostle says here, Gaius does not—at least yet—seem to hold any hierarchical office; he seems to be simply a prominent Christian faithful to his responsibilities in the Church.

"Beloved Gaius": four times St John describes him as "beloved" (vv. 1, 2, 5, 11). This really shows the deep fellowship the first Christians practised—not for them cold formality—and not only were they intimately concerned for one another's spiritual welfare, they were also interested in their physical well-being. "How well the early Christians practised this ardent charity which went far beyond the limits of mere human solidarity or natural kindness. They loved one another, through the heart of Christ, with a love tender and strong. Tertullian, writing in the second century, tells us how impressed the pagans were by the behaviour of the faiithful at that time. So attractive was it both supernaturally and humanly that they often remarked: 'See how they love another' (*Apologeticum*, 39)" (St Josemaría Escrivá, *Friends of God*, 225).

3–8. With great simplicity St John says why his paternal heart feels so happy— because Gaius, as his charity shows (vv. 5–8), is such a good-living man (vv. 3–4).

He uses a typically Semitic turn of phrase to describe Gaius' upright life: "you follow the truth." In the Old Testament the patriarchs are praised for "walking with God" (cf., e.g., Gen 5:22, 24; 6:9). This image of the wayfarer took on great importance after the Exodus: the people of Israel by divine will made their way as pilgrims to the Promised Land and in the course of that journey the great event of the Covenant took place (cf. Ex 19:24). "Walking with God" means the same as "fulfilling what the Covenant requires", that is, the commandments (cf. 2 Jn 4). With the coming of Christ, who said of himself, "I am the way, and the truth, and the life" (Jn 14:6), it has become quite clear that walking in the truth means being totally attached to the person of Christ: "live in him" (Col 2:6), "walk in the light" (1 Jn 1:7), "follow the truth" (2 Jn 4), all means the same sort of thing —living in communion with Christ, being a genuine Christian in everything one thinks and does.

Tit 3:13

[5]Beloved, it is a loyal thing you do when you render any service to the brethren, especially to strangers, [6]who have testified to your love before the church. You will do well to send them on their journey as befits God's service. [7]For they have set out for his

Mt 10:40
Heb 13:2

sake and have accepted nothing from the heathen. [8]So we ought to support such men, that we may be fellow workers in the truth.

Diotrephes' misconduct

[9]I have written something to the church; but Diotrephes, who likes to put himself first, does not acknowledge my authority. [10]So if I

Gaius' charity expressed itself in welcoming and helping the preachers sent by John (in the early times of the Church itinerant missionaries helped to keep alive the faith and promote solidarity among the scattered churches). They had set out "for his sake", that is, Christ's (v. 7; cf. Acts 5:41; Phil 2:9–10; Jas 2:7). By helping (even materially), Christians become "fellow workers in the truth" (v. 8) and merit the reward promised by our Lord: "He who receives you receives me, and he who receives me receives him who sent me" (Mt 10:40).

"Fellow workers in the truth": the Second Vatican Council applies these words to lay people when explaining how their apostolate and the ministry proper to pastors complement each other. And it goes on: "Lay people have countless opportunities for exercising the apostolate of evangelization and sanctification. The very witness of a Christian life, and good works done in a supernatural spirit, are effective in drawing people to the faith and to God; and that is what the Lord has said: 'Let your light shine so brightly before men, that they may see your good works and give glory to your Father who is in heaven' (Mt 5:16).

"This witness of life, however, is not the sole element in the apostolate; the true apostle is on the look-out for opportunities to announce Christ by word, either

to unbelievers to draw them towards the faith, or to the faithful to instruct them, strengthen them and incite them to a more fervent life" (*Apostolicam actuositatem*, 6).

9–10. "I have written something to the the church": we do not know what he is referring to—possibly a letter which has not survived.

As regards Diotrephes, all we know about him is what the letter tells us. He seemed to have had a position of authority, similar to that of a bishop. His ambition led him astray: he does not recognize St John's authority and is spreading lies about him; he has refused to receive the brethren sent by the apostle (the itinerant missionaries) and even tries to prevent others doing so.

The defiant behaviour of Diotrephes reminds us, by contrast, that the attitude of someone in a position of authority in the Church should be the same as that of the Master, who "came not to be served but to serve, and to give his life as a ransom for many" (Mt 20:28). In this connexion, Vatican II reminds us that "in exercising his office of father and pastor, the bishop should be with his people as one who serves (cf. Lk 22:26–27), as a good shepherd who knows his sheep and whose sheep know him, as a true father who excels in his love and solicitude for

come, I will bring up what he is doing, prating against me with evil words. And not content with that, he refuses himself to welcome the brethren, and also stops those who want to welcome them and puts them out of the church.

Commendation of Demetrius

[11]Beloved, do not imitate evil but imitate good. He who does good is of God; he who does evil has not seen God. [12]Demetrius* has testimony from every one, and from the truth itself; I testify to him too, and you know my testimony is true.

1 Jn 3:6–7

Jn 19:25; 21:24

Conclusion and farewell

[13]I had much to write to you, but I would rather not write with pen and ink; [14]I hope to see you soon, and we will talk together face to face.

2 Jn 12

---

all, to whose divinely conferred authority all readily submit" (*Christus Dominus*, 16).

11. The apostle here provides a resume of the teaching contained in various passages of his First Letter (cf. 1 Jn 2:18–19; 3:3–10; 5:18–20): he who does right is showing that he is of God, a child of God, that he is united to Christ and abides in him; whereas he who commits sin breaks his link with God and goes over to the enemy.

"Do not imitate evil but imitate good": St John's warning is not an unnecessary one, for human nature is so weak that, despite being impressed by good example, we are more inclined to copy bad example. The Church is always putting the saints before us as models to imitate: "To look on the life of those who have faithfully followed Christ is to be inspired with a new reason for seeking the city which is to come (cf. Heb 13:14 and 11:10), while at the same time we are taught to know a most safe path by which, despite the vicissitudes of the world, and in keeping with the state of life and condition proper to each of us, we will be able to arrive at perfect union with Christ, that is, holiness. God shows to men, in a vivid way, his presence and his face in the lives of

those companions of ours in the human condition who are more perfectly transformed into the image of Christ (cf. 2 Cor 3:18). He speaks to us in them and offers us a sign of his kingdom, to which we are powerfully attracted, so great a cloud of witnesses is there given (cf. Heb 12:1) and such a witness to the truth of the Gospel" (Vatican II, *Lumen gentium*, 50).

12. The only information we have about Demetrius is contained in this verse. He may have been one of the missionaries sent by St John, and perhaps the bearer of the letter.

In addition to being recommended by all who knew him. Demetrius is testified to by "the truth itself". This may be a reference to Christ (cf. Jn 14:6) or to the Holy Spirit (the Spirit of Truth: Jn 14:17; 15:26; 1 Jn 5:6); or it may refer to Demetrius' exemplary conduct (he is one of those who "follow the truth": vv. 3–4). As at other important moments (cf., e.g., Jn 19:35; 21:24; 1 Jn 1:1–4), St John offers his own testimony.

13–15. The ending is very reminicent of that of 2 John. It is a further example of the apostle's warm affection for the faith-

¹⁵Peace be to you. The friends greet you. Greet the friends, every one of them.

---

ful in his charge: he asks Gaius to greet them "every one of them"—one by one.

"Peace be to you": this is the normal Hebrew salutation, which the apostles continued to use in their letters, giving it a Christian meaning (cf., e.g., Rom 1:7 and the note on same; 1 Pet 5:14), As he wrote these words the apostle (now an old man) would have heard the echo of our Lord's greeting on the evening of the day of the Resurrection: "Peace be with you" (Jn 20:19).

Introduction to the Letter of St Jude

THE AUTHOR

The author of this short letter introduces himself to his readers as "Jude, a servant of Jesus Christ and brother of James" (v. 1). The description "servant of Jesus Christ" is similar to that used in various New Testament epistles.[1] The term "servant" is appropriate to every Christian, but it particularly suits those who have a ministry in the Church, especially the apostles and their successors.[2]

The reference to "James" is to a prominent person highly respected by the original addressees of the letter. From information in the New Testament we know that this James was the "brother" (that is, cousin or close relative) of the Lord (cf. Gal 1:19; Mt 13:55), who along with St Peter and St John was one of the "pillars" of the Church (cf. Gal 2:9), and that he was bishop of Jerusalem (cf. Acts 12:17; 15:13; 21:18), where he was martyred in the year 62.

As in the case of the Letter of St James,[3] the question arises whether this Jude (the author of the letter, who figures among our Lord's "brethren": cf. Mt 13:55) is the apostle of the same name, or whether two different people are involved.

St Luke twice lists the apostles (cf. Lk 6:16; Acts 1:13) and both times he puts Jude second last and, to distinguish him from Judas the traitor (in Hebrew, Greek and Latin the two names are the same), he calls him, literally, "Judas of James", which can mean either son of James, or brother of James. Normally the reference would be to a person's father; however, there are exceptions: sometimes in the case of a specially important person the rest of the family is named with reference to him; since James the Less was the most famous member of his family, St Luke may have been referring to James' *brother* when he called him "Jude of James".[4]

In the other lists of apostles—in the Gospels of Matthew and Mark—he is mentioned by his surname, Thaddaeus (cf. Mt 10:4; Mk 3:18) to distinguish him from Judas Iscariot, and he comes after his brother, "James the son of Alphaeus".

Therefore, there are solid grounds for equating the author with the apostle Jude-Thaddeus but we cannot be absolutely sure about it.

1. Cf. Rom 1:1; Phil 1:1; Tit 1:1; 2 Pet 1:1; Jas 1:1. 2. Thus, one of the Pope's titles is "Servant of the servant of God". 3. Cf. "Introduction to the Letter of St James", above. 4. St Mark calls one of the holy women "Mary the mother of James" (15:40) and also "Mary [the mother] of James" (16:1).

Introduction to the Letter of St Jude

AUTHENTICITY

Some authors are of the view that this letter was written by a later disciple of St Jude. In support of this they offer evidence to do with style and vocabulary, and some turns of phrase that would suggest a later date. However, from early times Church tradition has explicitly pointed to the letter as being by the apostle St Jude. This tradition is vouched for, for example, by Origen[5] and Tertullian[6] in the first half of the third century.

CANONICITY

As well as some more or less clear allusions to the letter in the *Didaché* (second century) and St Polycarp's *Letter to the Philippians* (*c.*AD 110), there is an explicit reference in the Muratorian Fragment (*c.*180) listing the Letter of St Jude among the canonical writings of the New Testament. To the testimony of Origen and Tertullian should be added that of Clement of Alexandria, who not only quoted from the letter in his writings[7] but wrote a commentary on it.[8]

In the fourth century St Athanasius[9] and St Cyril of Alexandria,[10] to mention just two, vouch for the letter's canonicity.

The ecclesiastical writer Eusebius of Caesarea (263–330) states that most people accepted it as canonical, although there were some who thought it was not; hence his putting it among the "disputed" writings.[11] St Jerome tells us the main reasons for these doubts: "Jude has left us a short epistle, which is one of the Catholic Letters; but since he quotes the apocryphal book of Enoch it is rejected by many; yet it deserves a place in Holy Scripture because of its antiquity and the use that is made of it."[12]

Jude does (in vv. 14–15) quote the *Book of Enoch*, a text held in high regard by the Jews. But that does not mean necessarily that the sacred writer approves everything contained in that book, much less that he regards it as inspired. Not even his statement "Enoch ... prophesied" (v. 14) leads to that conclusion, for it was common at the time to refer to a well known teacher as a "prophet" (cf., e.g., Jn 1:19–28). St Paul, for that matter, quotes on one occasion a verse from a pagan poet Epimenides of Knossos, referring to him as a "prophet" (Tit 1:12).

At any event, as St Jerome made clear in the text just quoted, the Letter of St Jude enjoyed great authority from very early on and was accepted by the Church as Holy Scripture: it figures in all the lists of inspired books from the

---

5. Cf. *In Rom. comm.*, 5, 1. **6.** Cf. *De culta feminarum*, 1, 3. **7.** Cf. *Paedagogus*, 3, 8; *Stromata*, 3, 2. **8.** Cf. Eusebius of Caesarea, *Ecclesiastical History*, 6, 14. **9.** Cf. *Epist.*, 39. **10.** Cf. *Mystagogical Catechesis*, 4, 35. **11.** Cf. *Ecclesiastical History*, 3, 25, 3; 6, 13, 6; 14, 1. **12.** *Of Famous Men*, 4.

mid-fourth century onwards. Its canonicity, and that of the other books in both Testaments, was solemnly declared by the Council of Trent.

IMMEDIATE READERSHIP

We do not know exactly whom the letter was originally sent to, for the salutation uses a description applicable to Christians in general. It is fairly likely that the addressees were, for the most part, converts from Judaism. This would explain the allusions to extra-biblical Jewish traditions and apocryphal writings such as *The Assumption of Moses* (cf. v. 9) and the *Book of Enoch* (cf. vv. 14–15). Possibly the fact that no specific addressees are mentioned explains why the letter was included among the Catholic Letters from as early as the time of Origen.[13]

The fact that the letter actually mentions James (cf. v. 1) may indicate that it was sent to the same group of readers as the Letter of St James, among whom James would have been held in high regard. In the absence of any further information, this is also the only clue we have to help us date the letter. If in fact it was sent to the same readers as the Letter of James it would be reasonable to date it shortly after the death of St James, which occurred around the year 62; a similar conclusion is reached by some scholars who think it must have been written before the year 70 because it makes no reference to the destruction of Jerusalem (yet others say this silence proves nothing). However, we would not be far wrong in dating it around the year 70.

BACKGROUND AND PURPOSE

The author's purpose in writing is to exhort the faithful to protect the faith delivered to them "once and for all" (v. 3), reminding them of what the apostles already predicted about the appearance of evil men dominated by their passions (cf. 17–18).

His specific reason for writing may have been news to the effect that ungodly men of that type had already secretly wormed their way into those Christian communities (cf. v. 4).

According to the letter, their errors had more to do with morals than faith: they were people who "pervert the grace of our God into licentiousness" (v. 4) and were spreading a false interpretation of Christian freedom (an error which St Paul also exposed).[14] Sexual immorality (cf. vv. 4, 8, 11, 13, 23) and greed (cf. vv. 11, 16) are the main vices mentioned.

---

13. Cf. "General Introduction to the Catholic Letters", above.   **14.** Cf., e.g., Rom 6:1–15; 1 Cor 6:12ff; Gal 5:13ff.

At all events, this heterodox movement seems to have been in its early stages: these people are creating divisions (cf. v. 19), but they still take part in the life of the community (cf. v. 12) and there seems to be some hope of winning many of them back (cf. vv. 22–23).

The problem of false teachers and their evil influence on the faithful is also dealt with in the Second Letter of St Peter; between that letter and Jude there is a great similarity of thought and even language, especially between Jude 4–18 and 2 Peter 2:1–3:3. A comparison of the two texts suggests that the Letter of St Jude influenced 2 Peter, where some of the things said are developed further and slightly modified.[15]

PLAN AND CONTENT

The structure of the letter is fairly clear. In addition to the opening greeting (vv. 1–2), followed by the reason for writing (vv. 3–4), and a solemn doxology at the end (vv. 24–25), the body of the letter has two main parts—one exposing the false teachers (vv. 5–16) and the other exhorting the faithful (vv. 17–23).

In the first section, after showing with some biblical examples the punishment awaiting these ungodly people (vv. 5–7), their blasphemous and evil behaviour is condemned (vv. 8–13) and divine retribution is further underlined (vv. 14–16).

In the exhortation St Jude reminds them that, even in the first instruction that they gave, the apostles warned that false teachers would arise (vv. 17–19); Jude encourages them to base their life on faith, prayer, charity and hope (vv. 20–21). Finally, he tells them how they should behave towards those who have been influenced by ungodly teaching (vv. 22–23).

15. Cf. "Introduction to the Second Letter of St Peter," above, which has more to say on this.

THE LETTER OF JUDE

The Revised Standard Version, with notes

Greeting and blessing

¹Jude, a servant of Jesus Christ and brother of James,   Mt 13:55
To those who are called, beloved in God the Father and kept for Jesus Christ:
²May mercy, peace, and love be multiplied to you.   2 Pet 1:2

1–2. In line with the standard practice in the classical world (also followed in the other New Testament letters), the heading gives the name and title of the sender and the addressees (v. 1) as well as the greeting proper (v. 2).

The author of the letter is probably the apostle St Jude Thaddaeus (cf. Introduction). Although he was a relative of our Lord (cf. Mt 13:55), he does not refer to that, preferring what he regards as the better title of "servant of Jesus Christ". In the religious world of the Jews the expression "servant of God" was equivalent to "worshipper of God" (cf. note on Rom 1:1). Therefore, by introducing himself as "servant of Jesus Christ" (as some other apostles do: cf. Rom 1:1; Jas 1:1; 2 Pet 1:1) St Jude is implicitly acknowledging the divinity of Christ.

The letter is addressed to "those who are called, beloved in God the Father and kept for Jesus Christ"—three characteristics applicable to Christians in general; that was why the letter was included in the "Catholic Letters", that is, those addressed to Christians everywhere, although it would originally have been sent to a smaller group.

"Who are called": this is the literal translation: to the same Greek root belongs the word "church", which is the community of those whom God "called ... out of darkness into his marvellous light" (1 Pet 2:9), the new people of God, chosen freely by him without any merit on their part. By its regular practice of describing Christians as "called" (cf. Rom 1:7; 8:28; 1 Cor 1:24; Rev 17:4),

the New Testament underlines the gratuitous nature of the gift of faith and the Christian vocation, which has its origin not in man's will but in a divine initiative.

"Beloved in God the Father": the Old Testament also was conscious of God's loving kindness towards all his creatures (cf. Wis 11:24), especially his chosen people. The prophets were always recalling God's predilection as evidenced by the history of Israel. The supreme manifestation of the Father's eternal love is the incarnation and redemptive death of his Son Jesus Christ "so that we might live through him" (1 Jn 4:9). And God's paternal love, which made us his children (cf. Jn 3:1), never ceases to work in our favour right through our lives (cf. Rom 8:32).

"Kept for Jesus Christ": this is the most likely translation; it could also be read as "kept through Jesus Christ". God's entire plan of salvation is orientated towards Jesus, Head of the Church (cf. Col 1:18) and of the whole cosmos (cf. Eph 1:3–10). "For those whom (God) foreknew he also predestined to be conformed to the image of his Son, in order that he might be the first-born among many brethren" (Rom 8:29).

The sacred writer uses these expressions to describe what being a Christian means: a Christian's life begins with a calling from God, develops thanks to the love of God and reaches its highpoint in Jesus Christ. Undoubtedly, a Christian's vocation and perseverance derives its full meaning from the ultimate good which lies ahead of him: "The Church, to which we are all called in Christ Jesus, and in

His reason for writing

2 Pet 1:5; 2:21 ³Beloved, being very eager to write to you of our common salvation, I found it necessary to write appealing to you to contend for the faith which was once for all delivered to the saints. ⁴For admission has

---

which by the grace of God we acquire holiness, will receive its perfection only in the glory of heaven" (Vatican II, *Lumen gentium*, 48).

2. The good wishes which letters usually include in the opening greeting have a rather original ring to them here. St Jude's style is to present his ideas in sets of threes; here he describes himself as Jude/a servant of Jesus Christ/brother of James; the addressees are called/beloved in God/kept for Jesus Christ; and the blessing includes mercy/peace/love (cf. also vv. 5–8, 11, 20–21).

The three benefits included in the blessing are closely interconnected and form a summary of the graces God gives.

By mercy God loves men despite their sins. Mercy has a long and rich history in the Old Testament, as Pope John Paul II reminds us: "It is significant that in their preaching the prophets link mercy, which they often refer to because of the people's sins, with the incisive image of love on God's part. The Lord loves Israel with the love of a special choosing, much like the love of a spouse, and for this reason he pardons its sins and even its infidelity and betrayals [...]. In the preaching of the prophets *mercy signifies a special power of love*, which *prevails over the sin* and infidelity of the chosen people" (*Dives in misericordia*, 4). The redemption can be said to be the work of divine mercy.

Peace is a consequence of God's mercy. In Jewish letters peace was usually mentioned in the heading. St Paul and St Peter usually say "grace and peace" (cf. note on Rom 1:7; 1 Pet 1:2).

Love is the highest gift, which has been revealed in all its fullness in the New Testament: the love of God stirs Christians to love God and man, and is the commandment which summarizes all the rest (cf. Mt 22:34–40).

Some Fathers gave an allegorical interpretation to this greeting and those in other letters, seeing in them an implicit reference to the Blessed Trinity: according to St Augustine, mercy is attributed to the Father, peace to the Son, and love to the Holy Spirit (cf. *Unfinished Exposition on the Epistle to the Romans*, 12).

3–4. These verses explain the reason and purpose of the letter. The author is writing to the faithful about "our common salvation" (v. 3) because he has received alarming reports about the damage being done by certain false teachers with their bad doctrine and loose morals. St Jude's zeal leads him to expose these evil men (vv. 5–16) and exhort Christians to protect the faith (vv. 17–23).

3. The faith one receives must be kept intact and handed on in all its fullness. Because the faith "delivered to the saints" implies an already formed deposit of truths, some have suggested that the presence of this term means the letter should be given a later date; however, many references to this unchanging deposit are also to be found in St Paul (cf., e.g., Gal 1:6–9; 1 Cor 11:23ff; 15:1ff).

This verse reminds us of the importance of Tradition. As we know, the deposit of Christian faith and morals was entrusted to the Church "to be preserved in a continuous line of succession until

been secretly gained by some who long ago were designated for this
condemnation, ungodly persons who pervert the grace of our God
into licentiousness and deny our only Master and Lord, Jesus Christ.[a]

Gal 2:4
2 Pet 2:16

1. FALSE TEACHERS DENOUNCED

The punishment that awaits them
[5]Now I desire to remind you, though you were once for all fully
informed, that he[b] who saved a people out of the land of Egypt,

Num 14:35
1 Cor 10:5
2 Pet 1:12

the end of time. Hence the apostles, in handing on what they themselves had received, warn the faithful to maintain the traditions which they had learned either by word of mouth or by letter (cf. 2 Thess 2:15); and they warn them to fight hard for the faith that had been handed on to them once and for all (cf. Jude 3)" (Vatican II, *Dei Verbum*, 8).

Therefore, although the custody of the faith and its handing on is a basic responsibility of the Pope and the bishops of the Church, it is also an obligation which falls on all Christians, particularly those who have a teaching role—for example, parents, teachers, catechists. John Paul II says: "It is Christ alone who teaches; anyone else teaches to the extent that he is Christ's spokesman, enabling Christ to teach with his lips. Whatever the level of his responsibility in the Church, every catechist must constantly endeavour to transmit by his teaching and behaviour the teaching and life of Jesus" (*Catechesi tradendae*, 6).

4. "Admission has been secretly gained": the Greek verb meaning "to enter from outside" conveys very well the way these false teachers went about it; they were probably travelling preachers, who went from one community to the next. St Jude accuses them of two faults—one moral

and practical, that of turning grace into licentiousness; the other doctrinal, that of denying Jesus Christ. On the latter point he has very little else to say (cf. v. 8), presumably because his letter is mainly pastoral in character.

"Pervert the grace of God into licentiousness": the deviations he goes on to condemn have their origin in this perversion of values. Christ with his grace has obtained our freedom; however, this truth was quite often taken as a pretext for toning down the need to fight against sin (cf. Rom 6:1, 15; Gal 5:13; 1 Pet 2:16; 2 Pet 2:19). To understand the true nature of freedom better, we need to look at Jesus Christ who, being God, emptied himself and became obedient unto death on a cross (cf. Phil 2:6–8 and notes on same). "Thus we come to appreciate that freedom is used properly when it is directed towards the good; and that it is misused when men are forgetful and turn away from the Love of loves [...]. Freedom finds its true meaning when it is put to the service of the truth which redeems, when it is spent in seeking God's infinite Love which liberates us from all forms of slavery" (St Josemaría Escrivá, *Friends of God*, 26 and 27).

5–7. The writer makes use of three famous biblical examples as a warning to

a. Or *the only Master and our Lord Jesus Christ* b. Ancient authorities read *Jesus* or *the Lord* or *God*

Gen 6:1–2
2 Pet 2:4–9 afterward destroyed those who did not believe. ⁶And the angels that did not keep their own position but left their proper dwelling have been kept by him in eternal chains in the nether gloom until

---

false teachers—the unbelieving and complaining Israelites in the wilderness (v. 5); the angels who in their pride rebelled against God and were cast into hell (v. 6); the people of Sodom and Gomorrah, whose cities were destroyed in punishment for their sins of lust (v. 7).

At the same time, he seems to be alluding to the three main sins of the heretics he is denouncing—unbelief, pride and lust (cf. also vv. 14–16).

In 2 Peter reference is also made to the punishment of the rebellious angels and of Sodom and Gomorrah (cf. 2 Pet 2:4–10 and notes on same).

5. "The Lord" [RSV alternate reading]. In other Greek manuscripts it says "Jesus", thereby expressly attributing to Christ the liberation of Israel from Egypt, and interpreting the Old Testament in the light of the New, which is its fullness (cf. 1 Cor 10:1–12). The reading "The Lord" allows one to take it as referring either to God the Father or to Christ.

In the book of Numbers (chap. 14) we are told how the people of Israel, once they had been set free from the slavery of Egypt, rebelled against God, complaining about the trials of the journey and mistrustful of God's help. To punish their unbelief God decreed that that entire generation (except for those who had remained faithful) would die during the forty-year sojourn in the desert and never enter the promised land (cf. Num 14:20ff).

St Jude applies the lessons of that event to the situation of Christians: through Baptism they have been set free from the slavery of sin; their sights are on the promised land of heaven. However, as long as they are making their way, they must persevere in the faith "delivered once for all" (v. 3) and lead lives in line with it.

"Though you were once for all fully informed": this translation follows the great majority of the papyri and early Greek manuscripts and so is different from that of the New Vulgate, which, by changing the order of the words, applies the "once for all" to the rescue from Egypt ("the Lord—after saving the people once for all").

6. God created angels as the most sublime of creatures to form his heavenly court and to help him in the government of the cosmos, especially as protectors of and messengers to man. From the beginning they were given the gift of grace, but because they were intelligent beings it was necessary that they should respond freely to God's gift. Scripture tells us that some of them rebelled against God (cf. Rev 12:7–9) and were thrown into hell.

Some apocryphal books (for example, the *Book of Enoch*) gathered together legendary accounts of the sin of the fallen angels (cf. note on v. 7). St Jude, however, simply says that angels did sin, and were immediately punished and that that, as in the case of all who are condemned, will become plain for all to see at the Last Judgment. The Church teaches that it was pride that caused the angels' rebellion against God; "although (the angels) were all endowed with celestial gifts, very many, having rebelled against God, their Father and Creator, were hurled from those high mansions of bliss, and shut up in the darkest dungeon of earth, there to suffer for eternity the

the judgment of the great day;* [7]just as Sodom and Gomorrah and the surrounding cities, which likewise acted immorally and indulged in unnatural lust, serve as an example by undergoing a punishment of eternal fire.

Gen 19:4–25
Mt 10:15
2 Pet 2:6–10

Their immorality

[8]Yet in like manner these men in their dreamings defile the flesh, reject authority, and revile the glorious ones.[c] [9]But when the

2 Pet 2:10

---

punishment of their pride" (*St Pius V Catechism*, 1, 2, 17).

7. The inhabitants of Sodom and Gomorrah were particularly depraved (cf. Gen 18:20ff): their sins—including unnatural vice (sodomy)—were proverbial (Jer 23:14; Ezek 16:48–50). The whole region was destroyed (cf. Gen 19:24–25) and its cities have always been cited as the classic example of the severity of God's punishment of evildoers (cf. Jer 49:18; 50:40; Amos 4:11).

These cities were located on the shore of the Dead Sea, where "evidence of their wickedness still remains: a continually smoking wasteland, plants bearing fruit that does not ripen" (Wis 10:7). Jesus also referred to Sodom and Gomorrah as symbols of divine punishment (cf. Mt 10:15; 11:13; Lk 10:12; 17:29).

"Which ... acted immorally": probably a reference to the angels, alluding to the mythical account in the *Book of Enoch* and other apocrypha, which thought that the sin of the angels had been one of impurity; this opinion was common among the Jews. The sacred writer is not saying that these accounts are true; he is simply using things in the popular imagination to show the gravity of sins and the severity of the punishment they attract.

"Undergoing a punishment of eternal fire": these words make it quite clear that God's decision as Judge is irrevocable; this passage is quoted in the *Creed of the People of God*, 12 to describe the suffering of the damned in hell: "Those who have responded to the love and compassion of God will go into eternal life. Those who have refused them to the end will be consigned to the fire that is never extinguished."

The existence of hell as a place of eternal punishment is constant in Christian teaching. God's purpose in revealing this truth was not to strike terror into us but to encourage us to be converted and to persevere in right living. It has led many people to return to the right path.

"There is a hell. Not a very original statement, you think. I will repeat it to you, then: there is a hell! Echo it for me, at the right moment, in the ear of one friend, and of another, and another" (St Josemaría Escrivá, *The Way*, 749).

8–10. The sacred writer wants to expose the arrogance of the false teachers, whose personal conduct is like that of the people just mentioned (vv. 5–7). They are led not by the truth but by dreams (cf. v. 8), like the false prophets of old (cf. e.g. Deut 13:1–5).

Their corrupt behaviour is summed up in three sins (v. 8), whose exact nature is difficult to identify: "defiling the flesh" with sins of impurity, making themselves like the people of Sodom and Gomorrah (cf. vv. 4 and 7); "rejecting authority" (literally, "rejecting lordship", probably

c. Greek *glories*

Dan 10:13; 12:1
Zech 3:2
2 Pet 2:11
2 Pet 2:12

Gen 4:8
2 Pet 2:15
Num 16:22

Ezek 34:8
Prov 25:14

archangel Michael, contending with the devil, disputed about the body of Moses, he did not presume to pronounce a reviling judgment upon him, but said, "The Lord rebuke you."* [10]But these men revile whatever they do not understand, and by those things that they know by instinct as irrational animals do, they are destroyed. [11]Woe to them! For they walk in the way of Cain, and abandon themselves for the sake of gain to Balaam's error, and perish in Korah's rebellion. [12]These are blemishes[d] on your love

in the sense that their licentious behaviour amounted in practice to rejecting the lordship of Christ: v. 4); it may also refer to the Church, whose authority they despised.

"Reviling the glorious ones", that is, the angels. It is not clear, however, whether this refers only to the good angels or to angelic nature in general (including therefore demons). Nor do we know what kind of blaspheming is being referred to. Perhaps the depraved customs spoken about by St Irenaeus (cf. *Against Heresies*, 1, 31) and St Epiphanius (cf. *Adversus haereses Panarium*, 38) began around this time: towards the beginning of the second century some Gnostic heretics went as far as to invoke the angels as patrons of their licentious behaviour.

To illustrate the wickedness of these insults to the angels, St Jude points out that not even the Archangel St Michael dared to curse the devil; he simply exclaimed, "The Lord rebuke you." St Jude attributes these words to him when they were arguing over "the body of Moses" (he assumes his readers are familiar with the story, which was to be found in the apocryphal *Assumption of Moses* and in other Jewish writings, to the effect that St Michael and the devil disputed over the body of Moses). The sacred writer does not make these speculations his own (there is no mention of them in the Bible: cf. Deut 34:5–6); he simply uses them to make a moral point.

d. Or *reefs*

The archangel's prudence only serves to highlight these people's arrogance.

11. With three further biblical examples he shows how evil the deceivers are. Cain is depicted in the Bible as the model of unbelief and fratricide (cf. Gen 4:3ff; Heb 11:14; 1 Jn 3:12). Balaam, a famous soothsayer (Num 22–24), was the epitome of greed and seduction, having led the Israelites into idolatry and fornication (cf. Num 31:16; 2 Pet 2:15; Rev 2:4).

Korah and his followers rebelled against Moses and Aaron and were punished by Yahweh who made the earth open and swallow them (Num 16).

The evildoers denounced by St Jude were leading Christians astray in a similar way—encouraging apostasy and licentiousness and creating discord (v. 19).

12–13. Using similes from nature, Jude now provides a clear description of the false teachers which stresses their arrogance and hypocrisy; they are attractive superficially, but all emptiness within.

They take part in the Christians' fraternal meals or love feasts (*ágapes*: cf. note on 1 Cor 11:17–22), where they freely indulge their greed and spread their false ideas. They are "blemishes", stains in the proper sense or in a moral sense; that is how the New Vulgate translates the term used here. It can also mean "scandal", coming from the original Greek meaning a "reef", a rock lying

feasts, as they boldly carouse together, looking after themselves; 2 Pet 2:13, 17
waterless clouds, carried along by winds; fruitless trees in late
autumn, twice dead, uprooted; [13]wild waves of the sea, casting up Is 57:20
the foam of their own shame; wandering stars for whom the nether
gloom of darkness has been reserved for ever.

The judgment of God

[14]It was of these also that Enoch in the seventh generation from Gen 5:18–24
Adam prophesied, saying, "Behold, the Lord came with his holy

---

just under the water and therefore a danger to navigation. "Looking after themselves"; that is, insolent and ambitious; possibly also a reference to their not respecting Church authority (cf. vv. 8, 16).

Pointing to the sterility and falsehood of their lives, St Jude calls them "waterless clouds" (deceiving those who expect rain), and "fruitless trees of late autumn", trees which should have been laden with fruit and instead produce nothing. They are "twice dead": perhaps a reference to their abandonment of the faith, which leaves them worse off than they were before Baptism (cf. 2 Pet 2:20–22; "uprooted": "Every plant which my heavenly Father has not planted", our Lord had said, "will be rooted up" (Mt 15:13).

And so, just as the waves of the sea deposit filth and debris on the shore, these people are casting the bad example of their impure lives before the faithful. Appearing as stars which reflect light for a while, they turn out to be "wandering stars" which go nowhere.

"The nether gloom of darkness": a reference to the darkest of dark places, where punishment awaits the ungodly (cf. note on v. 7).

14–16. The letter contains various allusions to the *Book of Enoch*, and now it quotes directly from it. This apocryphal text, written many years before Jesus Christ, has come down to us mainly in

Ethiopian and Coptic versions; it belongs to the category of "apocalyptic writing", which contains many legendary accounts linked to obscure Old Testament passages. Like almost all apocryphal books, the author is unknown and it is attributed (to give it authority) to a prominent Old Testament figure: Enoch appears in Genesis as the seventh in line from Adam, and is a man praised for his goodness (cf. Gen 5:22–24; Sir 44:16; 49:14; Heb 11:5). These apocryphal writings had considerable popularity as spiritual literature and undoubtedly did much good despite their inaccuracies; but they were never regarded by the people of Israel or by the Church as inspired.

"Behold, the Lord came with his holy myriads": without going into what these words mean in the *Book of Enoch*, it is clear that in this letter the Lord is Christ, who will come as Judge of all, accompanied by the angels (cf. Dan 7:10; Heb 12:22), as he himself foretold (cf. Mt 25:31). In the language of apocalyptic writing, which is also used by the prophets, future events are spoken of as if they had already occurred.

Although God's judgment will affect everyone, this passage speaks above all of the condemnation that awaits the wicked—specifically, the false teachers the letter is denouncing. That is why it actually repeats the main charges against them—rebellion against lawful church

myriads, [15] to execute judgment on all, and to convict all the ungodly of all their deeds of ungodliness which they have committed in such an ungodly way, and of all the harsh things
2 Pet 2:10, 18 which ungodly sinners have spoken against him." [16]These are
Lev 19:15 grumblers, malcontents, following their own passions, loud-mouthed boasters, flattering people to gain advantage.

2. EXHORTATION

False teachers were predicted

2 Pet 3:2 [17]But you must remember, beloved, the predictions of the apostles of our Lord Jesus Christ; [18]they said to you, "In the last time there

---

authority, unbelief, lust, pride and greed (vv. 4, 8, 10, 11).

Reflection on the eternal truths is a good antidote against sin: "For it often happens", Fray Luis of Granada teaches, "that when the sinner realizes the torment which lies ahead of him, even though he may not love God for his own sake, he begins to give up his evildoing and desires and tries to follow another way, and little by little with heaven's help he comes to love and serve the Lord whole-heartedly and willingly. For divine mercy is so great that it is extended to man in all kinds of ways and by many different routes" (*Compendium of Christian Doctrine*, 8).

17–23. Having denounced the false teachers (vv. 5–16), St Jude now turns to the faithful to remind them about apos-tolic teaching on future heresy (cf. vv. 17–19) and to exhort them to practise the Christian virtues (vv. 20–21). The letter ends with some practical pieces of advice about how to behave towards those who go astray (vv. 22–23).

17–19. In their initial oral teaching, the apostles who founded the various Christian communities warned of the danger of false teachers within the Church itself (cf. Acts 20:29f; 1 Tim 4:1–3; 2 Tim 3:1–5). These warnings can be traced back to what Christ himself said: "False Christs and false prophets will arise and show great signs and wonders, so as to lead astray, if possible, even the elect" (Mt 24:24).

The way the writer refers to "the apostles of our Lord Jesus Christ" does not mean that he was not one of them. He could be referring simply to the fact that some of them had already died. The other point about this verse is the importance it gives to Tradition (cf. note on v. 3).

"In the last time" (v. 18): in the prophets this expression refers to the messianic era (cf., e.g., Is 2:2; Mic 4:1), which brings to an end the long period of waiting for the promised Redeemer and marks the start of the Kingdom of God, which will last forever (cf. Dan 7:14, 27; Lk 1:33). The fullness of time (cf. Gal 4:4) began with the coming of Christ and will reach its zenith with his return in glory for the Last Judgment. In the New Testament perspective, therefore, "the last time" covers the entire period of the Christian era; it is the era of the Church. This earthly phase of the Kingdom of God is characterized, by, among other

will be scoffers, following their own ungodly passions." [19]It is these who set up divisions, worldly people, devoid of the Spirit.

1 Tim 4:1
2 Pet 3:3
1 Cor 2:14

Faith, hope and charity
[20]But you, beloved, build yourselves up on your most holy faith; pray in the Holy Spirit; [21]keep yourselves in the love of God; wait for the mercy of our Lord Jesus Christ unto eternal life.

Col 2:7
1 Thess 5:11

Attitude towards waverers
[22]And convince some, who doubt; [23]save some, by snatching them

Amos 4:11
Rev 3:4

---

things, the presence of the "good" and the "bad" side by side (cf. Mt 13:47–48), the cockle sown among the wheat (cf. Mt 13:24ff).

"Worldly people": *psychikoi*, literally, "animal" or "natural" men. As in some texts of St Paul (cf. 1 Cor 2:14; 15:44–46), these are the opposite of "spiritual" men, that is, Christians who have the Holy Spirit and are docile to him (cf. Rom 5:5; 8:14). On the other hand, those who are "devoid of the Spirit", who is the source of supernatural life, form judgments and make decisions under the sole guidance of human nature wounded by original sin. Theirs is a merely earthly wisdom (cf. Jas 3:15), a wisdom of the flesh (cf. 1 Cor 3:3).

20–21. The Christian life can be summed up as living the three theological virtues (faith, hope and charity, accompanied by prayer), through the action of each of the three divine Persons—the love of God the Father, the mercy of our Lord Jesus Christ, and fellowship with the Holy Spirit.

The spiritual building is founded on faith, that is, on the truths revealed by God for our salvation and delivered once for all to the Church (cf. v. 3). Therefore it is a "most holy" faith—of divine origin, worthy of the highest respect, and unchangeable. Prayer is essential for penetrating deeper and deeper into the unfathomable riches of the faith. The Christian prays "in the Holy

Spirit" because, as St Paul teaches, "you have received the spirit of sonship. When we cry, 'Abba, Father!' ..." (Rom 8:15); and "the Spirit helps us in our weakness; for we do not know how to pray as we ought, but the Spirit himself intercedes for us with sighs too deep for words" (Rom 8:26). To the love of God (the source of divine filiation in the Holy Spirit) the Christian should respond by striving to abide in that love and constantly increase it. Trust in God's help and in his mercy build up our hope of ultimately seeing the Lord face to face.

The Second Vatican Council reminds us that the faithfulness of a Christian's life depends on active communion with Christ: "A life like this calls for a continuous exercise of faith, hope and charity. Only the light of faith and meditation on the Word of God can enable us to find God everywhere and always [...]. Those with such a faith live in the hope of the revelation of the sons of God, keeping in mind the cross and resurrection of the Lord [...]. With the love that comes from God's prompting, they do good to all, especially to their brothers in the faith (cf. Gal 6:10)" (*Apostolicam actuositatem*, 4).

22–23. The apostle now gives some practical advice on how to behave towards those who have been affected by false ideas.

out of the fire; on some have mercy with fear, hating even the garment spotted by the flesh.[e]

1 Thess 5:23
Phil 1:10
2 Pet 3:14

Rom 16:27

Final doxology

[24]Now to him who is able to keep you from falling and to present you without blemish before the presence of his glory with rejoicing, [25]to the only God, our Saviour through Jesus Christ our Lord, be glory, majesty, dominion, and authority, before all time and now and for ever. Amen.

The Greek text can be read in various ways. According to some codexes and the Vulgate, it is referring to three categories of people—waverers; those who have already been harmed by error but can still be recovered; and those who persist in heresy. That is how the RSV translates it. Other codexes, followed by the New Vulgate, first give a counsel valid for dealings with everyone affected by error and then go on to distinguish two groups—those who can still be recovered and those who seem to be beyond help.

Christians should always show kindness to those who break with sound teaching. In this way they will attract many back to the faith; but there will be others with whom they will not succeed; in their case, particularly if their lifestyle is depraved, it will be necessary to be prudent (to hate "even the garment spotted by the flesh"), in order to avoid contagion; but one should still treat them affectionately and pray for them. "It is a characteristic of the perfect", St Augustine teaches, "not to hate anything in sinners other than their sins; and to love those people themselves" (*Contra Adimantum*, 17, 5).

24–25. The letter does not end with the usual greetings but with a solemn doxology or hymn of praise addressed to God the Father through Jesus Christ. It may have come from a liturgical hymn.

"Only God": this does not exclude the divinity of the Son and the Holy Spirit; it is simply confessing that there is only one God (cf. Jn 17:3).

God reveals his power particularly in the work of our salvation. We constantly need his grace if we are to avoid sin in this life and one day obtain the glory of heaven. Jesus Christ is the Mediator both of our salvation and of our praise of God. From the beginning the Church has had the custom of addressing liturgical prayer to the Father through Jesus Christ.

---

e. The Greek text in this sentence is uncertain at several points

New Vulgate Text

EPISTOLA IACOBI

[1] [1]Iacobus, Dei et Domini Iesu Christi servus, duodecim tribubus, quae sunt in dispersione, salutem. [2]Omne gaudium existimate, fratres mei, cum in tentationibus variis incideritis, [3]scientes quod probatio fidei vestrae patientiam operatur; [4]patientia autem opus perfectum habeat, ut sitis perfecti et integri, in nullo deficientes. [5]Si quis autem vestrum indiget sapientia, postulet a Deo, qui dat omnibus affluenter et non improperat, et dabitur ei. [6]Postulet autem in fide nihil haesitans; qui enim haesitat, similis est fluctui maris, qui a vento movetur et circumfertur. [7]Non ergo aestimet homo ille quod accipiat aliquid a Domino, [8]vir duplex animo, inconstans in omnibus viis suis. [9]Glorietur autem frater humilis in exaltatione sua, [10]dives autem in humilitate sua, quoniam sicut flos feni transibit. [11]Exortus est enim sol cum ardore et arefecit fenum, et flos eius decidit, et decor vultus eius deperiit; ita et dives in itineribus suis marcescet. [12]Beatus vir, qui suffert tentationem, quia, cum probatus fuerit, accipiet coronam vitae, quam repromisit Deus diligentibus se. [13]Nemo, cum tentatur, dicat: «A Deo tentor»; Deus enim non tentatur malis, ipse autem neminem tentat. [14]Unusquisque vero tentatur a concupiscentia sua abstractus et illectus; [15]dein concupiscentia, cum conceperit, parit peccatum, peccatum vero, cum consummatum fuerit, generat mortem. [16]Nolite errare, fratres mei dilectissimi. [17]Omne datum optimum et omne donum perfectum de sursum est, descendens a Patre luminum, apud quem non est transmutatio nec vicissitudinis obumbratio. [18]Voluntarie genuit nos verbo veritatis, ut simus primitiae quaedam creaturae eius. [19]Scitis, fratres mei dilecti. Sit autem omnis homo velox ad audiendum, tardus autem ad loquendum et tardus ad iram; [20]ira enim viri iustitiam Dei non operatur. [21]Propter quod abicientes omnem immunditiam et abundantiam malitiae in mansuetudine suscipite insitum verbum, quod potest salvare animas vestras. [22]Estote autem factores verbi et non auditores tantum fallentes vosmetipsos. [23]Quia si quis auditor est verbi et non factor, hic comparabitur viro consideranti vultum nativitatis suae in speculo; [24]consideravit enim se et abiit, et statim oblitus est qualis fuerit. [25]Qui autem perspexerit in lege perfecta libertatis et permanserit, non auditor obliviosus factus sed factor operis, hic beatus in facto suo erit. [26]Si quis putat se religiosum esse non freno circumducens linguam suam sed seducens cor suum, huius vana est religio. [27]Religio munda et immaculata apud Deum et Patrem haec est: visitare pupillos et viduas in tribulatione eorum, immaculatum se custodire ab hoc saeculo. **[2]** [1]Fratres mei, nolite in personarum acceptione habere fidem Domini nostri Iesu Christi gloriae. [2]Etenim si introierit in synagogam vestram vir aureum anulum habens in veste candida, introierit autem et pauper in sordido habitu, [3]et intendatis in eum, qui indutus est veste praeclara, et dixeritis: «Tu sede hic bene», pauperi autem dicatis: «Tu sta illic aut sede sub scabello meo», [4]nonne iudicatis apud vosmetipsos et facti estis iudices cogitationum iniquarum? [5]Audite, fratres mei dilectissimi. Nonne Deus elegit, qui pauperes sunt mundo, divites in fide et heredes regni, quod repromisit diligentibus se? [6]Vos autem exhonorastis pauperem. Nonne divites opprimunt vos et ipsi trahunt vos ad iudicia? [7]Nonne ipsi blasphemant bonum nomen, quod invocatum est super vos? [8]Si tamen legem perficitis regalem secundum Scripturam: «*Diliges proximum tuum sicut teipsum*», bene facitis; [9]si autem personas accipitis, peccatum operamini, redarguti a lege quasi transgressores. [10]Quicumque autem totam legem servaverit, offendat autem in uno, factus est omnium reus. [11]Qui enim dixit: «*Non moechaberis*», dixit et: «*Non occides*»; quod si non moecharis, occidis autem, factus es transgressor legis. [12]Sic loquimini et sic facite sicut per legem libertatis iudicandi. [13]Iudicium enim sine misericordia illi, qui non fecit misericordiam; superexsultat misericordia iudicio. [14]Quid proderit, fratres mei, si fidem quis dicat se habere, opera autem non habeat? Numquid poterit fides salvare eum? [15]Si frater aut soror nudi sunt et indigent victu cotidiano, [16]dicat autem aliquis de vobis illis: «Ite in pace, calefacimini et saturamini», non dederitis autem eis, quae necessaria sunt corporis, quid proderit? [17]Sic et fides, si non habeat opera, mortua est in semetipsa. [18]Sed dicet quis: «Tu fidem habes, et ego opera habeo». Ostende mihi fidem tuam sine operibus, et ego tibi ostendam ex operibus meis fidem. [19]Tu credis quoniam unus est Deus? Bene facis; et daemones credunt et contremiscunt! [20]Vis autem scire, o homo inanis, quoniam fides sine operibus otiosa est? [21]Abraham pater noster nonne ex operibus iustificatus est offerens Isaac filium suum super altare?

²²Vides quoniam fides cooperabatur operibus illius, et ex operibus fides consummata est, ²³et suppleta est Scriptura dicens: *«Credidit Abraham Deo, et reputatum est illi ad iustitiam»*, et amicus Dei appellatus est. ²⁴Videtis quoniam ex operibus iustificatur homo et non ex fide tantum. ²⁵Similiter autem et Rahab meretrix nonne ex operibus iustificata est suscipiens nuntios et alia via eiciens? ²⁶Sicut enim corpus sine spiritu emortuum est, ita et fides sine operibus mortua est. **[3]** ¹Nolite plures magistri fieri, fratres mei, scientes quoniam maius iudicium accipiemus. ²In multis enim offendimus omnes. Si quis in verbo non offendit, hic perfectus est vir, potens etiam freno circumducere totum corpus. ³Si autem equorum frenos in ora mittimus ad oboediendum nobis, et omne corpus illorum circumferimus. ⁴Ecce et naves, cum tam magnae sint et a ventis validis minentur, circumferuntur a minimo gubernaculo, ubi impetus dirigentis voluerit; ⁵ita et lingua modicum quidem membrum est et magna exsultat. Ecce quantus ignis quam magnam silvam incendit! ⁶Et lingua ignis est, universitas iniquitatis; lingua constituitur in membris nostris, quae maculat totum corpus et inflammat rotam nativitatis et inflammatur a gehenna. ⁷Omnis enim natura et bestiarum et volucrum et serpentium et etiam cetorum domatur et domita est a natura humana; ⁸linguam autem nullus hominum domare potest, inquietum malum, plena veneno mortifero. ⁹In ipsa benedicimus Dominum et Patrem et in ipsa maledicimus homines, qui ad similitudinem Dei facti sunt; ¹⁰ex ipso ore procedit benedictio et maledictio. Non oportet, fratres mei, haec ita fieri. ¹¹Numquid fons de eodem foramine emanat dulcem et amaram aquam? ¹²Numquid potest, fratres mei, ficus olivas facere aut vitis ficus? Neque salsa dulcem potest facere aquam. ¹³Quis sapiens et disciplinatus inter vos? Ostendat ex bona conversatione operationem suam in mansuetudine sapientiae. ¹⁴Quod si zelum amarum habetis et contentiones in cordibus vestris, nolite gloriari et mendaces esse adversus veritatem. ¹⁵Non est ista sapientia desursum descendens, sed terrena, animalis, diabolica; ¹⁶ubi enim zelus et contentio, ibi inconstantia et omne opus pravum. ¹⁷Quae autem desursum est sapientia primum quidem pudica est, deinde pacifica, modesta, suadibilis, plena misericordia et fructibus bonis, non iudicans, sine simulatione; ¹⁸fructus autem iustitiae in pace seminatur facientibus pacem. **[4]** ¹Unde bella et unde lites in vobis? Nonne hinc, ex concupiscentiis vestris, quae militant in membris vestris? ²Concupiscitis et non habetis; occiditis et zelatis et non potestis adipisci; litigatis et belligeratis. Non habetis, propter quod non postulatis; ³petitis et non accipitis, eo quod male petitis, ut in concupiscentiis vestris insumatis. ⁴Adulteri, nescitis quia amicitia huius mundi inimica est Dei? Quicumque ergo voluerit amicus esse saeculi huius, inimicus Dei constituitur. ⁵Aut putatis quia inaniter Scriptura dicat: *«Ad invidiam concupiscit Spiritus, qui inhabitat in nobis?»*. ⁶Maiorem autem dat gratiam; propter quod dicit: *«Deus superbis resistit, / humilibus autem dat gratiam»*. ⁷Subicimini igitur Deo; resistite autem Diabolo, et fugiet a vobis. ⁸Appropiate Deo, et appropinquabit vobis. Emundate manus, peccatores, et purificate corda, duplices animo. ⁹Miseri estote et lugete et plorate; risus vester in luctum convertatur et gaudium in maerorem. ¹⁰Humiliamini in conspectu Domini, et exaltabit vos. ¹¹Nolite detrahere alterutrum, fratres; qui detrahit fratri aut qui iudicat fratrem suum, detrahit legi et iudicat legem; si autem iudicas legem, non es factor legis sed iudex. ¹²Unus est legislator et iudex, qui potest salvare et perdere; tu autem quis es, qui iudicas proximum? ¹³Age nunc, qui dicitis: «Hodie aut crastino ibimus in illam civitatem et faciemus quidem ibi annum et mercabimur et lucrum faciemus», ¹⁴qui ignoratis, quae erit in crastinum vita vestra! Vapor enim estis ad modicum parens, deinceps exterminatur; ¹⁵pro eo ut dicatis: «Si Dominus voluerit, et vivemus et faciemus hoc aut illud». ¹⁶Nunc autem gloriamini in superbiis vestris; omnis gloriatio talis maligna est. ¹⁷Scienti igitur bonum facere et non facienti, peccatum est illi! **[5]** ¹Age nunc, divites, plorate ululantes in miseriis, quae advenient vobis. ²Divitiae vestrae putrefactae sunt, et vestimenta vestra a tineis comesta sunt, ³aurum et argentum vestrum aeruginavit, et aerugo eorum in testimonium vobis erit et manducabit carnes vestras sicut ignis: thesaurizastis in novissimis diebus. ⁴Ecce merces operariorum, qui messuerunt regiones vestras, quae fraudata est a vobis, clamat, et clamores eorum, qui messuerunt, in aures Domini Sabaoth introierunt. ⁵Epulati estis super terram et in luxuriis fuistis, enutristis corda vestra in die occisionis. ⁶Addixistis, occidistis iustum. Non resistit vobis. ⁷Patientes igitur estote, fratres, usque ad adventum Domini. Ecce agricola exspectat pretiosum fructum terrae, patienter ferens, donec accipiat *imbrem temporaneum et serotinum*. ⁸Patientes estote et vos, confirmate corda vestra, quoniam adventus Domini appropinquavit. ⁹Nolite ingemiscere, fratres, in alterutrum, ut non iudicemini; ecce iudex ante ianuam assistit. ¹⁰Exemplum accipite, fratres, laboris et patientiae prophetas, qui locuti sunt in nomine Domini. ¹¹Ecce beatificamus eos, qui sustinuerunt; sufferentiam Iob audistis et finem Domini vidistis, quoniam *misericors est Dominus et miserator*. ¹²Ante omnia autem, fratres mei, nolite iurare, neque per caelum neque per terram, neque aliud quodcumque iuramentum; sit autem vestrum «Est» est, et «Non» non, uti non sub iudicio decidatis. ¹³Tristatur aliquis vestrum? Oret. Aequo animo est? Psallat. ¹⁴Infirmatur quis in vobis? Advocet presbyteros ecclesiae, et orent super eum, unguentes eum oleo in nomine Domini.

[15]Et oratio fidei salvabit infirmum, et allevabit eum Dominus; et si peccata operatus fuerit, dimittentur ei. [16]Confitemini ergo alterutrum peccata et orate pro invicem, ut sanemini. Multum enim valet deprecatio iusti operans. [17]Elias homo erat similis nobis passibilis et oratione oravit, ut non plueret, et non pluit super terram annos tres et menses sex; [18]et rursum oravit, et caelum dedit pluviam, et terra germinavit fructum suum. [19]Fratres mei, si quis ex vobis erraverit a veritate et converterit quis eum, [20]scire debet quoniam, qui converti fecerit peccatorem ab errore viae eius, salvabit animam suam a morte et operiet multitudinem peccatorum.

EPISTOLA PRIMA PETRI

[1] [1]Petrus apostolus Iesu Christi electis advenis dispersionis Ponti, Galatiae, Cappadociae, Asiae et Bithyniae, [2]secundum praescientiam Dei Patris, in sanctificatione Spiritus, in oboedientiam et aspersionem sanguinis Iesu Christi: gratia vobis et pax multiplicetur. [3]Benedictus Deus et Pater Domini nostri Iesu Christi, qui secundum magnam misericordiam suam regeneravit nos in spem vivam per resurrectionem Iesu Christi ex mortuis, [4]in hereditatem incorruptibilem et incontaminatam et immarcescibilem, conservatam in caelis propter vos, [5]qui in virtute Dei custodimini per fidem in salutem paratam revelari in tempore novissimo. [6]In quo exsultatis, modicum nunc si oportet contristati in variis tentationibus, [7]ut probatio vestrae fidei multo pretiosior auro, quod perit, per ignem quidem probato, inveniatur in laudem et gloriam et honorem in revelatione Iesu Christi. [8]Quem cum non videritis, diligitis; in quem nunc non videntes, credentes autem, exsultatis laetitia inenarrabili et glorificata, [9]reportantes finem fidei vestrae salutem animarum. [10]De qua salute exquisierunt atque scrutati sunt prophetae, qui de futura in vos gratia prophetaverunt, [11]scrutantes in quod vel quale tempus significaret, qui erat in eis Spiritus Christi, praenuntians eas, quae in Christo sunt, passiones et posteriores glorias; [12]quibus revelatum est quia non sibi ipsis, vobis autem ministrabant ea, quae nunc nuntiata sunt vobis per eos, qui evangelizaverunt vos, Spiritu Sancto misso de caelo, in quae desiderant angeli prospicere. [13]Propter quod succincti lumbos mentis vestrae, sobrii, perfecte sperate in eam, quae offertur vobis, gratiam in revelatione Iesu Christi. [14]Quasi filii oboedientiae, non configurati prioribus in ignorantia vestra desideriis, [15]sed secundum eum, qui vocavit vos, sanctum, et ipsi sancti in omni conversatione sitis, [16]quoniam scriptum est: «*Sancti eritis, quia ego sanctus sum*». [17]Et si Patrem invocatis eum, qui sine acceptione personarum iudicat secundum uniuscuiusque opus, in timore incolatus vestri tempore conversamini, [18]scientes quod non corruptibilibus argento vel auro redempti estis de vana vestra conversatione a patribus tradita, [19]sed pretioso sanguine quasi Agni incontaminati et immaculati Christi, [20]praecogniti quidem ante constitutionem mundi, manifestati autem novissimis temporibus propter vos, [21]qui per ipsum fideles estis in Deum, qui suscitavit eum a mortuis et dedit ei gloriam, ut fides vestra et spes esset in Deum. [22]Animas vestras castificantes in oboedientia veritatis ad fraternitatis amorem non fictum, ex corde invicem diligite attentius, [23]renati non ex semine corruptibili sed incorruptibili per verbum Dei vivum et permanens; [24]quia *omnis caro ut fenum, / et omnis gloria eius tamquam flos feni. / Exaruit fenum, et flos decidit; /* [25]*verbum autem Domini manet in aeternum*. Hoc est autem verbum, quod evangelizatum est in vos. [2][1]Deponentes igitur omnem malitiam et omnem dolum et simulationes et invidias et omnes detractiones, [2]sicut modo geniti infantes, rationale sine dolo lac concupiscite, ut in eo crescatis in salutem, [3]si *gustastis quoniam dulcis Dominus*. [4]Ad quem accedentes, lapidem vivum, ab hominibus quidem reprobatum, coram Deo autem electum, pretiosum, [5]et ipsi tamquam lapides vivi aedificamini domus spiritalis in sacerdotium sanctum offerre spiritales hostias acceptabiles Deo per Iesum Christum. [6]Propter quod continet Scriptura: «*Ecce pono in Sion lapidem angularem, electum, pretiosum; / et, qui credit in eo, non confundetur*». [7]Vobis igitur honor credentibus; non credentibus autem «*Lapis, quem reprobaverunt aedificantes, / hic factus est in caput anguli*» [8]et «*lapis offensionis et petra scandali*»; qui offendunt verbo non credentes, in quod et positi sunt. / [9]Vos autem *genus electum, regale sacerdotium, gens sancta, populus in acquisitionem, ut virtutes annuntietis* eius, qui de tenebris vos vocavit in admirabile lumen suum; [10]qui aliquando *non populus*, nunc autem *populus Dei; qui non consecuti misericordiam*, nunc autem *misericordiam consecuti*. [11]Carissimi, obsecro tamquam advenas et peregrinos abstinere vos a carnalibus desideriis, quae militant adversus animam; [12]conversationem vestram inter gentes habentes bonam, ut in eo, quod detrectant de vobis tamquam de malefactoribus, ex bonis operibus considerantes glorificent Deum in die visitationis. [13]Subiecti estote omni humanae creaturae propter Dominum: sive regi quasi praecellenti [14]sive ducibus tamquam ab eo missis ad vindictam malefactorum, laudem vero bonorum; [15]quia sic est

voluntas Dei, ut benefacientes obmutescere faciatis imprudentium hominum ignorantiam, [16]quasi liberi, et non quasi velamen habentes malitiae libertatem, sed sicut servi Dei. [17]Omnes honorate, fraternitatem diligite, Deum timete, regem honorificate. [18]Servi, subditi estote in omni timore dominis, non tantum bonis et modestis sed etiam pravis. [19]Haec est enim gratia, si propter conscientiam Dei sustinet quis tristitias, patiens iniuste. [20]Quae enim gloria est, si peccantes et colaphizati sustinetis? Sed si benefacientes et patientes sustinetis, haec est gratia apud Deum. [21]In hoc enim vocati estis, quia / et Christus passus est pro vobis, / vobis relinquens exemplum, / ut sequamini vestigia eius: / [22]qui *peccatum non fecit, / nec inventus est dolus in ore ipsius;* / [23]qui cum malediceretur, non remaledicebat; / cum pateretur, non comminabatur, / commendabat autem iuste iudicanti; / [24]qui *peccata* nostra *ipse pertulit* / in corpore suo super lignum, / ut peccatis mortui iustitiae viveremus; / cuius *livore sanati estis.* / [25]Eratis enim *sicut oves errantes,* sed conversi estis nunc ad pastorem et episcopum animarum vestrarum.   **[3]** [1]Similiter mulieres subditae sint suis viris, ut et si qui non credunt verbo, per mulierum conversationem sine verbo lucrifiant, [2]considerantes castam in timore conversationem vestram; [3]quarum sit non extrinsecus capillaturae aut circumdationis auri aut indumenti vestimentorum cultus, [4]sed qui absconditus cordis est homo in incorruptibilitate mitis et quieti spiritus, qui est in conspectu Dei locuples. [5]Sic enim aliquando et sanctae mulieres sperantes in Deo ornabant se subiectae propriis viris, [6]sicut Sara oboediebat Abrahae dominum eum vocans; cuius estis filiae benefacientes et non timentes ullam perturbationem. [7]Viri similiter cohabitantes secundum scientiam quasi infirmiori vaso muliebri impertientes honorem, tamquam et coheredibus gratiae vitae, uti ne impediantur orationes vestrae. [8]In fine autem omnes unanimes, compatientes, fraternitatis amatores, misericordes, humiles, [9]non reddentes malum pro malo vel maledictum pro maledicto, sed e contrario benedicentes, quia in hoc vocati estis, ut benedictionem hereditate accipiatis. [10]«Qui enim *vult vitam diligere / et videre dies bonos, / coerceat linguam suam a malo, / et labia eius ne loquantur dolum;* / [11]*declinet autem a malo et faciat bonum, / inquirat pacem et persequatur eam.* / [12]*Quia oculi Domini super iustos, / et aures eius in preces eorum; / vultus autem Domini super facientes mala».* [13]Et quis est qui vobis noceat, si boni aemulatores fueritis? [14]Sed et si patimini propter iustitiam, beati! *Timorem autem eorum ne timueritis et non conturbemini,* [15]*Dominum* autem Christum *sanctificate* in cordibus vestris, parati semper ad defensionem omni poscenti vos rationem de ea, quae in vobis est spe, [16]sed cum mansuetudine et timore, conscientiam habentes bonam, ut in quo de vobis detrectatur, confundantur, qui calumniantur vestram bonam in Christo conversationem. [17]Melius est enim benefacientes, si velit voluntas Dei, pati quam malefacientes. [18]Quia et Christus semel pro peccatis passus est, iustus pro iniustis, ut vos adduceret ad Deum, mortificatus quidem carne, vivificatus autem Spiritu; [19]in quo et his, qui in carcere erant, spiritibus adveniens praedicavit, [20]qui increduli fuerant aliquando, quando exspectabat Dei patientia in diebus Noe, cum fabricaretur arca, in qua pauci, id est octo animae, salvae factae sunt per aquam. [21]Cuius antitypum, baptisma, et vos nunc salvos facit, non carnis depositio sordium sed conscientiae bonae rogatio in Deum, per resurrectionem Iesu Christi, [22]qui est in dextera Dei, profectus in caelum, subiectis sibi angelis et potestatibus et virtutibus.   **[4]** [1]Christo igitur passo in carne, et vos eadem cogitatione armamini, quia, qui passus est carne, desiit a peccato, [2]ut iam non hominum concupiscentiis sed voluntate Dei quod reliquum est in carne vivat temporis. [3]Sufficit enim praeteritum tempus ad voluntatem gentium consummandam, vobis, qui ambulastis in luxuriis, concupiscentiis, vinolentiis, comissationibus, potationibus et illicitis idolorum cultibus. [4]In quo mirantur non concurrentibus vobis in eandem luxuriae effusionem, blasphemantes; [5]qui reddent rationem ei, qui paratus est iudicare vivos et mortuos. [6]Propter hoc enim et mortuis evangelizatum est, ut iudicentur quidem secundum homines carne, vivant autem secundum Deum Spiritu. [7]Omnium autem finis appropinquavit. Estote itaque prudentes et vigilate in orationibus. [8]Ante omnia mutuam in vosmetipsos caritatem continuam habentes, quia caritas operit multitudinem peccatorum; [9]hospitales invicem sine murmuratione; [10]unusquisque, sicut accepit donationem, in alterutrum illam administrantes sicut boni dispensatores multiformis gratiae Dei. [11]Si quis loquitur, quasi sermones Dei; si quis ministrat, tamquam ex virtute, quam largitur Deus, ut in omnibus glorificetur Deus per Iesum Christum: cui est gloria et imperium in saecula saeculorum. Amen. [12]Carissimi, nolite mirari in fervore, qui ad tentationem vobis fit, quasi novi aliquid vobis contingat, [13]sed, quemadmodum communicatis Christi passionibus, gaudete, ut et in revelatione gloriae eius gaudeatis exsultantes. [14]Si exprobramini in nomine Christi, beati, quoniam Spiritus gloriae et Dei super vos requiescit. [15]Nemo enim vestrum patiatur quasi homicida aut fur aut maleficus aut alienorum speculator; [16]si autem ut christianus, non erubescat, glorificet autem Deum in isto nomine. [17]Quoniam tempus est, ut incipiat iudicium a domo Dei; si autem primum a nobis, qui finis eorum, qui non credunt Dei evangelio? [18]«Et si *iustus vix salvatur, / impius et peccator ubi parebit?».* [19]Itaque et hi, qui patiuntur secundum voluntatem Dei, fideli Creatori commendent animas suas in benefacto.

[5] [1]Seniores ergo, qui in vobis sunt, obsecro, consenior et testis Christi passionum, qui et eius, quae in futuro revelanda est, gloriae communicator: [2]Pascite, qui est in vobis, gregem Dei, providentes non coacto sed spontanee secundum Deum, neque turpis lucri gratia sed voluntarie, [3]neque ut dominantes in cleris sed formae facti gregis. [4]Et cum apparuerit Princeps pastorum, percipietis immarcescibilem gloriae coronam. [5]Similiter, adulescentes, subditi estote senioribus. Omnes autem invicem humilitatem induite, quia *Deus superbis resistit, / humilibus autem dat gratiam.* [6]Humiliamini igitur sub potenti manu Dei, ut vos exaltet in tempore, [7]omnem sollicitudinem vestram proicientes in eum, quoniam ipsi cura est de vobis. [8]Sobrii estote, vigilate. Adversarius vester Diabolus tamquam leo rugiens circuit quaerens quem devoret. [9]Cui resistite fortes fide, scientes eadem passionum ei, quae in mundo est, vestrae fraternitati fieri. [10]Deus autem omnis gratiae, qui vocavit vos in aeternam suam gloriam in Christo Iesu, modicum passos ipse perficiet, confirmabit, solidabit, fundabit. [11]Ipsi imperium in saecula saeculorum. Amen. [12]Per Silvanum vobis fidelem fratrem, ut arbitror, breviter scripsi, obsecrans et contestans hanc esse veram gratiam Dei; in qua state. [13]Salutat vos, quae est in Babylone, coelecta et Marcus filius meus. [14]Salutate invicem in osculo caritatis. Pax vobis omnibus, qui estis in Christo.

EPISTOLA SECUNDA PETRI

[1] [1]Simon Petrus servus et apostolus Iesu Christi his, qui coaequalem nobis sortiti sunt fidem in iustitia Dei nostri et salvatoris Iesus Christi: [2]gratia vobis et pax multiplicetur in cognitione Dei et Iesu Domini nostri. [3]Quomodo omnia nobis divinae virtutis suae ad vitam et pietatem donatae per cognitionem eius, qui vocavit nos propria gloria et virtute, [4]per quae pretiosa et maxima nobis promissa donata sunt, ut per haec efficiamini divinae consortes naturae, fugientes eam, quae in mundo est in concupiscentia, corruptionem; [5]et propter hoc ipsum curam omnem subinferentes ministrate in fide vestra virtutem, in virtute autem scientiam, [6]in scientia autem continentiam, in continentia autem patientiam, in patientia autem pietatem, [7]in pietate autem amorem fraternitatis, in amore autem fraternitatis caritatem. [8]Haec enim vobis, cum adsint et abundent, non vacuos nec sine fructu vos constituunt in Domini nostri Iesu Christi cognitionem; [9]cui enim non praesto sunt haec, caecus est et nihil procul cernens, oblivionem accipiens purgationis veterum suorum delictorum. [10]Quapropter, fratres, magis satagite, ut firmam vestram vocationem et electionem faciatis. Haec enim facientes non offendetis aliquando; [11]sic enim abundanter ministrabitur vobis introitus in aeternum regnum Domini nostri et salvatoris Iesu Christi. [12]Propter quod incipiam vos semper commonere de his, et quidem scientes et confirmatos in praesenti veritate. [13]Iustum autem arbitror, quamdiu sum in hoc tabernaculo, suscitare vos in commonitione, [14]certus quod velox est depositio tabernaculi mei, secundum quod et Dominus noster Iesus Christus significavit mihi; [15]dabo autem operam et frequenter habere vos post obitum meum, ut horum memoriam faciatis. [16]Non enim captiosas fabulas secuti notam fecimus vobis Domini nostri Iesu Christi virtutem et adventum, sed speculatores facti illius magnitudinis. [17]Accipiens enim a Deo Patre honorem et gloriam, voce prolata ad eum huiuscemodi a magnifica gloria: «Filius meus, dilectus meus hic est, in quo ego mihi complacui»; [18]et hanc vocem nos audivimus de caelo prolatam, cum essemus cum ipso in monte sancto. [19]Et habemus firmiorem propheticum sermonem, cui bene facitis attendentes quasi lucernae lucenti in caliginoso loco, donec dies illucescat, et lucifer oriatur in cordibus vestries, [20]hoc primum intellegentes quod omnis prophetia Scripturae propria interpretatione non fit; [21]non enim voluntate humana prolata est prophetia aliquando, sed a Spiritu Sancto ducti locuti sunt a Deo homines.
[2] [1]Fuerunt vero et pseudoprophetae in populo, sicut et in vobis erunt magistri mendaces, qui introducent sectas perditionis et eum, qui emit eos, Dominatorem negantes superducent sibi celerem perditionem. [2]Et multi sequentur eorum luxurias, propter quos via veritatis blasphemabitur; [3]et in avaritia fictis verbis de vobis negotiabuntur. Quibus iudicium iam olim non cessat, et perditio eorum non dormitat. [4]Si enim Deus angelis peccantibus non pepercit, sed rudentibus inferni detractos in tartarum tradidit in iudicium reservatos; [5]et originali mundo non pepercit, sed octavum Noe iustitiae praeconem custodivit diluvium mundo impiorum inducens; [6]et civitates Sodomae et Gomorrae in cinerem redigens eversione damnavit, exemplum ponens eorum, quae sunt impiis futura; [7]et iustum Lot oppressum a nefandorum luxuria conversationis eruit: [8]aspectu enim et auditu iustus habitans apud eos, de die in diem animam iustam iniquis operibus cruciabat. [9]Novit Dominus pios de tentatione eripere, iniquos vero in diem iudicii puniendos reservare, [10]maxime autem eos, qui post carnem in concupiscentia immunditiae ambulant dominationemque contemnunt. Audaces, superbi, glorias non metuunt blasphemantes, [11]ubi angeli fortitudine et virtute cum sint maiores, non portant adversum illas coram

Domino iudicium blasphemiae. [12]Hi vero velut irrationabilia animalia naturaliter genita in captionem et in corruptionem, in his, quae ignorant, blasphemantes, in corruptione sua et corrumpentur [13]inviti percipientes mercedem iniustitiae; voluptatem existimantes diei delicias, coinquinationes et maculae deliciis affluentes, in voluptatibus suis luxuriantes vobiscum, [14]oculos habentes plenos adulterae et incessabiles delicti, pellicientes animas instabiles, cor exercitatum avaritiae habentes, maledictionis filii, [15]derelinquentes rectam viam erraverunt, secuti viam Balaam ex Bosor, qui mercedem iniquitatis amavit, [16]correptionem vero habuit suae praevaricationis; subiugale mutum in hominis voce loquens prohibuit prophetae insipientiam. [17]Hi sunt fontes sine aqua et nebulae turbine exagitatae, quibus caligo tenebrarum reservatur. [18]Superba enim vanitatis loquentes pelliciunt in concupiscentiis carnis luxuriis illos, qui paululum effugiunt eos, qui in errore conversantur, [19]libertatem illis promittentes, cum ipsi servi sint corruptionis; a quo enim quis superatus est, huius servus est. [20]Si enim refugientes coinquinationes mundi in cognitione Domini nostri et Salvatoris Iesu Christi his rursus implicati superantur, facta sunt eis posteriora deteriora prioribus. [21]Melius enim erat illis non cognoscere viam iustitiae quam post agnitionem retrorsum converti ab eo, quod illis traditum est, sancto mandato. [22]Contigit enim eis illud veri proverbii: «*Canis reversus ad suum vomitum,* / et sus lota in volutabro luti».   [3] [1]Hanc vobis, carissimi, iam secundam scribo epistulam, in quibus excito vestram in commonitione sinceram mentem, [2]ut memores sitis eorum, quae praedicta sunt verborum a sanctis prophetis, et ab apostolis traditi vobis praecepti Domini et Salvatoris; [3]hoc primum scientes quod venient in novissimis diebus in illusione illudentes, iuxta proprias concupiscentias suas ambulantes, [4]dicentes: «Ubi est promissio adventus eius?». Ex quo enim patres dormierunt, omnia sic perseverant ab initio creaturae. [5]Latet enim eos hoc volentes quod caeli erant prius et terra de aqua et per aquam consistens Dei verbo, [6]per quae ille tunc mundus aqua inundatus periit; [7]caeli autem, qui nunc sunt, et terra eodem verbo reposti sunt igni, servati in diem iudicii et perditionis impiorum hominum. [8]Unum vero hoc non lateat vos, carissimi, quia unus dies apud Dominum sicut mille anni, et mille anni sicut dies unus. [9]Non tardat Dominus promissionem, sicut quidam tarditatem existimant, sed patienter agit in vos nolens aliquos perire, sed omnes ad paenitentiam reverti. [10]Adveniet autem dies Domini ut fur, in qua caeli magno impetu transient, elementa vero calore solventur, et terra et opera, quae in ea invenientur. [11]Cum haec omnia ita dissolvenda sint, quales oportet esse vos in sanctis conversationibus et pietatibus [12]exspectantes et properantes adventum diei Dei, propter quam caeli ardentes solventur, et elementa ignis ardore tabescent. [13]*Novos* vero *caelos et terram novam* secundum promissum ipsius exspectamus, in quibus iustitia habitat. [14]Propter quod, carissimi, haec exspectantes satagite immaculati et inviolati ei inveniri in pace [15]et Domini nostri longanimitatem salutem arbitramini, sicut et carissimus frater noster Paulus secundum datam sibi sapientiam scripsit vobis, [16]sicut et in omnibus epistulis loquens in eis de his, in quibus sunt quaedam difficilia intellectu, quae indocti et instabiles depravant sicut et ceteras Scripturas ad suam ipsorum perditionem. [17]Vos igitur, dilecti, praescientes custodite, ne iniquorum errore simul abducti excidatis a propria firmitate; [18]crescite vero in gratia et in cognitione Domini nostri et Salvatoris Iesu Christi. Ipsi gloria et nunc et in diem aeternitatis. Amen.

EPISTOLA PRIMA IOANNIS

[1] [1]Quod fuit ab initio, quod audivimus, quod vidimus oculis nostris, quod perspeximus, et manus nostrae contrectaverunt de verbo vitae [2]—et vita apparuit, et vidimus et testamur et annuntiamus vobis vitam aeternam, quae erat coram Patre et apparuit nobis—[3]quod vidimus et audivimus, annuntiamus et vobis, ut et vos communionem habeatis nobiscum. Communio autem nostra est cum Patre et cum Filio eius Iesu Christo. [4]Et haec scribimus nos, ut gaudium nostrum sit plenum. [5]Et haec est annuntiatio, quam audivimus ab eo et annuntiamus vobis, quoniam Deus lux est, et tenebrae in eo non sunt ullae. [6]Si dixerimus quoniam communionem habemus cum eo et in tenebris ambulamus, mentimur et non facimus veritatem; [7]si autem in luce ambulemus, sicut ipse est in luce, communionem habemus ad invicem, et sanguis Iesu Filii eius mundat nos ab omni peccato. [8]Si dixerimus quoniam peccatum non habemus, nosmetipsos seducimus, et veritas in nobis non est. [9]Si confiteamur peccata nostra, fidelis est et iustus, ut remittat nobis peccata et emundet nos ab omni iniustitia. [10]Si dixerimus quoniam non peccavimus, mendacem facimus eum, et verbum eius non est in nobis.   [2] [1]Filioli mei, haec scribo vobis, ut non peccetis. Sed si quis peccaverit, advocatum habemus ad Patrem, Iesum Christum iustum; [2]et ipse est propitiatio pro peccatis nostris, non pro nostris autem tantum sed etiam pro totius mundi. [3]Et in hoc cognoscimus quoniam novimus eum: si mandata eius servemus. [4]Qui dicit: «Novi eum», et

mandata eius non servat, mendax est, et in isto veritas non est; [5]qui autem servat verbum eius, vere in hoc caritas Dei consummata est. In hoc cognoscimus quoniam in ipso sumus. [6]Qui dicit se in ipso manere, debet, sicut ille ambulavit, et ipse ambulare. [7]Carissimi, non mandatum novum scribo vobis, sed mandatum vetus, quod habuistis ab initio: mandatum vetus est verbum, quod audistis. [8]Verumtamen mandatum novum scribo vobis, quod est verum in ipso et in vobis, quoniam tenebrae transeunt, et lumen verum iam lucet. [9]Qui dicit se in luce esse et fratrem suum odit, in tenebris est usque adhuc. [10]Qui diligit fratrem suum, in lumine manet, et scandalum ei non est; [11]qui autem odit fratrem suum, in tenebris est et in tenebris ambulat et nescit quo vadat, quoniam tenebrae obcaecaverunt oculos eius. [12]Scribo vobis, filioli: Remissa sunt vobis peccata propter nomen eius. [13]Scribo vobis, patres: Nostis eum, qui ab initio est. Scribo vobis, adulescentes: Vicistis Malignum. [14]Scripsi vobis, parvuli: Nostis Patrem. Scripsi vobis, patres: Nostis eum, qui ab initio est. Scripsi vobis, adulescentes: Fortes estis, et verbum Dei in vobis manet, et vicistis Malignum. [15]Nolite diligere mundum neque ea, quae in mundo sunt. Si quis diligit mundum, non est caritas Patris in eo; [16]quoniam omne, quod est in mundo, concupiscentia carnis et concupiscentia oculorum et iactantia divitiarum, non est ex Patre, sed ex mundo est. [17]Et mundus transit et concupiscentia eius; qui autem facit voluntatem Dei, manet in aeternum. [18]Filioli, novissima hora est; et sicut audistis quia antichristus venit, ita nunc antichristi multi adsunt, unde cognoscimus quoniam novissima hora est. [19]Ex nobis prodierunt, sed non erant ex nobis, nam si fuissent ex nobis, permansissent nobiscum; sed ut manifestaretur quoniam illi omnes non sunt ex nobis. [20]Sed vos unctionem habetis a Sancto et scitis omnes. [21]Non scripsi vobis quasi nescientibus veritatem sed quasi scientibus eam, et quoniam omne mendacium ex veritate non est. [22]Quis est mendax, nisi is qui negat quoniam Iesus est Christus? Hic est antichristus, qui negat Patrem et Filium. [23]Omnis, qui negat Filium, nec Patrem habet; qui confitetur Filium, et Patrem habet. [24]Vos, quod audistis ab initio, in vobis permaneat; si in vobis permanserit, quod ab initio audistis, et vos in Filio et in Patre manebitis. [25]Et haec est repromissio, quam ipse pollicitus est nobis: vitam aeternam. [26]Haec scripsi vobis de eis, qui seducunt vos. [27]Et vos unctionem, quam accepistis ab eo, manet in vobis, et non necesse habetis, ut aliquis doceat vos; sed sicut unctio ipsius docet vos de omnibus, et verum est et non est mendacium, et, sicut docuit vos, manetis in eo. [28]Et nunc, filioli, manete in eo, ut, cum apparuerit, habeamus fiduciam et non confundamur ab eo in adventu eius. [29]Si scitis quoniam iustus est, scitote quoniam et omnis, qui facit iustitiam, ex ipso natus est.   **[3]** [1]Videte qualem caritatem dedit nobis Pater, ut filii Dei nominemur, et sumus! Propter hoc mundus non cognoscit nos, quia non cognovit eum. [2]Carissimi, nunc filii Dei sumus, et nondum manifestatum est quid erimus; scimus quoniam, cum ipse apparuerit, similes ei erimus, quoniam videbimus eum, sicuti est. [3]Et omnis, qui habet spem hanc in eo, purificat se, sicut ille purus est. [4]Omnis, qui facit peccatum, et iniquitatem facit, quia peccatum est iniquitas. [5]Et scitis quoniam ille apparuit, ut peccata tolleret, et peccatum in eo non est. [6]Omnis, qui in eo manet, non peccat; omnis, qui peccat, non vidit eum nec novit eum. [7]Filioli, nemo vos seducat. Qui facit iustitiam, iustus est, sicut ille iustus est; [8]qui facit peccatum, ex Diabolo est, quoniam a principio Diabolus peccat. Propter hoc apparuit Filius Dei, ut dissolvat opera Diaboli. [9]Omnis, qui natus est ex Deo, peccatum non facit, quoniam semen ipsius in eo manet; et non potest peccare, quoniam ex Deo natus est. [10]In hoc manifesti sunt filii Dei et filii Diaboli: omnis, qui non facit iustitiam, non est ex Deo, et qui non diligit fratrem suum. [11]Quoniam haec est annuntiatio, quam audistis ab initio, ut diligamus alterutrum. [12]Non sicut Cain: ex Maligno erat et occidit fratrem suum. Et propter quid occidit eum? Quoniam opera eius maligna erant, fratris autem eius iusta. [13]Nolite mirari, fratres, si odit vos mundus. [14]Nos scimus quoniam transivimus de morte in vitam, quoniam diligimus fratres; qui non diligit, manet in morte. [15]Omnis, qui odit fratrem suum, homicida est, et scitis quoniam omnis homicida non habet vitam aeternam in semetipso manentem. [16]In hoc novimus caritatem quoniam ille pro nobis animam suam posuit; et nos debemus pro fratribus animas ponere. [17]Qui habuerit substantiam mundi et viderit fratrem suum necesse habere et clauserit viscera sua ab eo, quomodo caritas Dei manet in eo? [18]Filioli, non diligamus verbo nec lingua sed in opere et veritate. [19]In hoc cognoscemus quoniam ex veritate sumus, et in conspectu eius placabimus corda nostra, [20]quoniam si reprehenderit nos cor, maior est Deus corde nostro et cognoscit omnia. [21]Carissimi, si cor nostrum non reprehenderit nos, fiduciam habemus ad Deum [22]et, quodcumque petierimus, accipimus ab eo, quoniam mandata eius custodimus et ea, quae sunt placita coram eo, facimus. [23]Et hoc est mandatum eius, ut credamus nomini Filii eius Iesu Christi et diligamus alterutrum, sicut dedit mandatum nobis. [24]Et, qui servat mandata eius, in ipso manet, et ipse in eo; et in hoc cognoscimus quoniam manet in nobis, ex Spiritu, quem nobis dedit.   **[4]** [1]Carissimi, nolite omni spiritui credere, sed probate spiritus si ex Deo sint, quoniam multi pseudoprophetae prodierunt in mundum. [2]In hoc cognoscitis Spiritum Dei: omnis spiritus, qui confitetur Iesum Christum in carne venisse, ex Deo est. [3]Et omnis spiritus, qui non confitetur Iesum, ex Deo non est; et hoc est antichristi, quod audistis quoniam venit, et nunc iam in mundo est. [4]Vos ex Deo estis, filioli, et vicistis eos, quoniam maior est, qui in vobis est quam qui in mundo. [5]Ipsi ex mundo sunt; ideo ex mundo loquuntur, et mundus eos audit. [6]Nos ex Deo sumus. Qui cognoscit Deum, audit nos; qui non est ex Deo, non audit nos. Ex hoc cognoscimus Spiritum veritatis et spiritum erroris. [7]Carissimi, diligamus invicem, quoniam caritas ex Deo est, et omnis, qui diligit, ex Deo natus est et cognoscit Deum. [8]Qui non diligit, non cognovit Deum, quoniam Deus caritas est. [9]In hoc apparuit caritas Dei in nobis, quoniam Filium suum unigenitum misit Deus in mundum, ut vivamus per eum. [10]In hoc est caritas, non quasi nos dilexerimus Deum, sed quoniam ipse dilexit nos et misit Filium suum propitiationem pro peccatis nostris. [11]Carissimi, si sic Deus dilexit nos, et nos debemus alterutrum diligere. [12]Deum nemo vidit umquam; si diligamus invicem, Deus in nobis manet, et caritas eius in nobis consummata est. [13]In hoc cognoscimus quoniam in ipso manemus, et ipse in nobis, quoniam de Spiritu suo dedit nobis. [14]Et nos vidimus et testificamur quoniam Pater misit Filium salvatorem mundi. [15]Quisque confessus fuerit: «Iesus est Filius Dei», Deus in ipso manet, et ipse in Deo. [16]Et nos, qui credidimus, novimus caritatem, quam habet Deus in nobis. Deus caritas est, et, qui manet in caritate, in Deo manet, et Deus in eo manet. [17]In hoc consummata est caritas nobiscum, ut fiduciam habeamus in die iudicii, quia sicut ille est, et nos sumus in hoc mundo. [18]Timor non est in caritate, sed perfecta caritas foras mittit timorem, quoniam timor poenam habet; qui autem timet, non est consummatus in caritate. [19]Nos diligimus, quoniam ipse prior dilexit nos. [20]Si quis dixerit: «Diligo Deum», et fratrem suum oderit, mendax est; qui enim non diligit fratrem suum, quem videt, Deum, quem non videt, non potest diligere. [21]Et hoc mandatum habemus ab eo, ut, qui diligit Deum, diligat et fratrem suum. **[5]** [1]Omnis, qui credit quoniam Iesus est Christus, ex Deo natus est; et omnis, qui diligit Deum qui genuit, diligit et eum qui natus est ex eo. [2]In hoc cognoscimus quoniam diligimus natos Dei, cum Deum diligamus et mandata eius faciamus. [3]Haec est enim caritas Dei, ut mandata eius servemus; et mandata eius gravia non sunt, [4]quoniam omne, quod natum est ex Deo, vincit mundum; et haec est victoria, quae vicit mundum: fides nostra. [5]Quis est qui vincit mundum, nisi qui credit quoniam Iesus est Filius Dei? [6]Hic est qui venit per aquam et sanguinem, Iesus Christus; non in aqua solum sed in aqua et in sanguine. Et Spiritus est, qui testificatur, quoniam Spiritus est veritas. [7]Quia tres sunt qui testificantur: [8]Spiritus et aqua et sanguis; et hi tres in unum sunt. [9]Si testimonium hominum accipimus, testimonium Dei maius est, quoniam hoc est testimonium Dei, quia testificatus est de Filio suo. [10]Qui credit in Filium Dei, habet testimonium in se. Qui non credit Deo, mendacem facit eum, quoniam non credidit in testimonium, quod testificatus est Deus de Filio suo. [11]Et hoc est testimonium, quoniam vitam aeternam dedit nobis Deus, et haec vita in Filio eius est. [12]Qui habet Filium, habet vitam; qui non habet Filium Dei, vitam non habet. [13]Haec scripsi vobis, ut sciatis quoniam vitam habetis aeternam, qui creditis in nomen Filii Dei. [14]Et haec est fiducia, quam habemus ad eum, quia si quid petierimus secundum voluntatem eius, audit nos. [15]Et si scimus quoniam audit nos, quidquid petierimus, scimus quoniam habemus petitiones, quas postulavimus ab eo. [16]Si quis videt fratrem suum peccare peccatum non ad mortem, petet, et dabit ei Deus vitam, peccantibus non ad mortem. Est peccatum ad mortem; non pro illo dico, ut roget. [17]Omnis iniustitia peccatum est, et est peccatum non ad mortem. [18]Scimus quoniam omnis, qui natus est ex Deo, non peccat, sed ille qui genitus est ex Deo, conservat eum, et Malignus non tangit eum. [19]Scimus quoniam ex Deo sumus, et mundus totus in Maligno positus est. [20]Et scimus quoniam Filius Dei venit et dedit nobis sensum, ut cognoscamus eum, qui verus est; et sumus in eo, qui verus est, in Filio eius Iesu Christo. Hic est qui verus est, Deus et vita aeterna. [21]Filioli, custodite vos a simulacris!

EPISTOLA SECUNDA IOANNIS

[1]Presbyter electae dominae et filiis eius, quos ego diligo in veritate, et non ego solus, sed et omnes, qui noverunt veritatem, [2]propter veritatem, quae permanet in nobis et nobiscum erit in sempiternum. [3]Erit nobiscum gratia, misericordia, pax a Deo Patre et a Iesu Christo, Filio Patris, in veritate et caritate. [4]Gavisus sum valde quoniam inveni de filiis tuis ambulantes in veritate, sicut mandatum accepimus a Patre. [5]Et nunc rogo te, domina, non tamquam mandatum novum scribens tibi, sed quod habuimus ab initio, ut diligamus alterutrum. [6]Et haec est caritas, ut ambulemus secundum mandata eius; hoc mandatum est, quemadmodum audistis ab initio, ut in eo ambuletis. [7]Quoniam multi seductores prodierunt in mundum, qui non confitentur Iesum Christum venientem in carne; hic est seductor et antichristus. [8]Videte vosmetipsos, ne perdatis, quae operati estis, sed ut mercedem plenam accipiatis. [9]Omnis, qui ultra procedit et non manet in doctrina Christi, Deum non habet; qui permanet in doctrina,

hic et Patrem et Filium habet. [10]Si quis venit ad vos et hanc doctrinam non affert, nolite accipere eum in domum nec «Ave» ei dixeritis; [11]qui enim dicit illi: «Ave», communicat operibus illius malignis. [12]Plura habens vobis scribere nolui per chartam et atramentum, spero enim me futurum apud vos et os ad os loqui, ut gaudium nostrum plenum sit. [13]Salutant te filii sororis tuae electae.

EPISTOLA TERTIA IOANNIS

[1]Presbyter Gaio carissimo, quem ego diligo in veritate. [2]Carissime, in omnibus exopto prospere te agere et valere, sicut prospere agit anima tua. [3]Nam gavisus sum valde venientibus fratribus et testimonium perhibentibus veritati tuae, quomodo tu in veritate ambules. [4]Maius horum non habeo gaudium, quam ut audiam filios meos in veritate ambulare. [5]Carissime, fideliter facis, quidquid operaris in fratres et hoc in peregrinos, [6]qui testimonium reddiderunt caritati tuae in conspectu ecclesiae. Bene facies subveniens illis in via digne Deo; [7]pro nomine enim profecti sunt, nihil accipientes a gentilibus. [8]Nos ergo debemus sublevare huiusmodi, ut cooperatores simus veritatis. [9]Scripsi aliquid ecclesiae; sed is qui amat primatum gerere in eis, Diotrephes, non recipit nos. [10]Propter hoc, si venero, commonebo eius opera, quae facit verbis malignis garriens in nos; et quasi non ei ista sufficiant, nec ipse suscipit fratres et eos, qui cupiunt, prohibet et de ecclesia eicit. [11]Carissime, noli imitari malum, sed quod bonum est. Qui benefacit, ex Deo est; qui malefacit, non vidit Deum. [12]Demetrio testimonium redditur ab omnibus et ab ipsa veritate; sed et nos testimonium perhibemus, et scis quoniam testimonium nostrum verum est. [13]Multa habui scribere tibi, sed nolo per atramentum et calamum scribere tibi; [14]spero autem protinus te videre, et os ad os loquemur. [15]Pax tibi. Salutant te amici. Saluta amicos nominatim.

EPISTOLA IUDAE

[1]Iudas Iesu Christi servus, frater autem Iacobi, his qui sunt vocati, in Deo Patre dilecti et Christo Iesu conservati: [2]misericordia vobis et pax et caritas adimpleatur. [3]Carissimi, omnem sollicitudinem faciens scribendi vobis de communi nostra salute necesse habui scribere vobis, deprecans certare pro semel tradita sanctis fide. [4]Subintroierunt enim quidam homines, qui olim praescripti sunt in hoc iudicium, impii, Dei nostri gratiam transferentes in luxuriam et solum Dominatorem et Dominum nostrum Iesum Christum negantes. [5]Commonere autem vos volo, scientes vos omnia, quoniam Dominus semel populum de terra Aegypti salvans, secundo eos, qui non crediderunt, perdidit; [6]angelos vero, qui non servaverunt suum principatum, sed dereliquerunt suum domicilium, in iudicium magni diei vinculis aeternis sub caligine reservavit. [7]Sicut Sodoma et Gomorra et finitimae civitates, simili modo exfornicatae et abeuntes post carnem alteram, factae sunt exemplum, ignis aeterni poenam sustinentes. [8]Similiter vero et hi somniantes carnem quidem maculant, dominationem autem spernunt, glorias autem blasphemant. [9]Cum Michael archangelus cum Diabolo disputans altercaretur de Moysis corpore, non est ausus iudicium inferre blasphemiae, sed dixit: «Increpet te Dominus!». [10]Hi autem, quaecumque quidem ignorant, blasphemant, quaecumque autem naturaliter tamquam muta animalia norunt, in his corrumpuntur. [11]Vae illis, quia via Cain abierunt et errore Balaam mercede effusi sunt et contradictione Core perierunt! [12]Hi sunt in agapis vestris maculae convivantes sine timore, semetipsos pascentes, nubes sine aqua, quae a ventis circumferuntur, arbores autumnales infructuosae bis mortuae, eradicatae, [13]fluctus feri maris despumantes suas confusiones, sidera errantia, quibus procella tenebrarum in aeternum servata est. [14]Prophetavit autem et his septimus ab Adam Henoch dicens: «Ecce venit Dominus in sanctis milibus suis [15]facere iudicium contra omnes et arguere omnem animam de omnibus operibus impietatis eorum, quibus impie egerunt, et de omnibus duris, quae locuti sunt contra eum peccatores impii». [16]Hi sunt murmuratores, querelosi, secundum concupiscentias suas ambulantes, et os illorum loquitur superba, mirantes personas quaestus causa. [17]Vos autem, carissimi, memores estote verborum, quae praedicta sunt ab apostolis Domini nostri Iesu Christi, [18]quoniam dicebant vobis: «In novissimo tempore venient illusores, secundum suas concupiscentias ambulantes impietatum». [19]Hi sunt qui segregant, animales, Spiritum non habentes. [20]Vos autem, carissimi, superaedificantes vosmetipsos sanctissimae vestrae fidei, in Spiritu Sancto orantes, [21]ipsos vos in dilectione Dei servate, exspectantes

misericordiam Domini nostri Iesu Christi in vitam aeternam. [22]Et his quidem miseremini disputantibus, [23]illos vero salvate de igne, rapientes, aliis autem miseremini in timore, odientes et eam, quae carnalis est, maculatam tunicam. [24]Ei autem, qui potest vos conservare sine peccato et constituere ante conspectum gloriae suae immaculatos in exsultatione, [25]soli Deo salvatori nostro per Iesum Christum Dominum nostrum gloria, magnificentia, imperium et potestas ante omne saeculum et nunc et in omnia saecula. Amen.

Explanatory Notes

Asterisks in the text of the New Testament refer to these "Explanatory Notes" in the RSVCE.

THE LETTER OF JAMES

1:1, *twelve tribes*: i.e., Jewish Christians outside Palestine.

1:22: This is the main theme of the letter.

2:1–7: These are hard words, but no harder than those of Jesus.

2:10: In keeping the Law, we must keep *the whole Law*. We cannot pick and choose.

2:14: Good works are necessary besides faith.

5:3: The "treasure" they have laid up is described in the following verses.

5:13–15: This passage is the scriptural basis for the sacrament of Anointing of the Sick.

THE FIRST LETTER OF PETER

1:1: See note on Jas 1:1. Baptism is the main theme of this letter, which may in fact, have been a baptismal address.

1:11, *Spirit of Christ*: Christ, as the eternally existing Word, is envisaged as inspiring the prophets of old.

3:1–6: Peter's teaching on the behaviour and status of women corresponds to that of Paul, though without Paul's forthrightness.

4:1, *ceased from sin*: Peter means that a continual acceptance of suffering is incompatible with a proneness to sin.

5:13, *Babylon*: Rome was as full of iniquity as ancient Babylon; cf. Rev 17:9.

THE SECOND LETTER OF PETER

1:4, *partakers of the divine nature*: A strong expression to describe the transformation of human nature by divine grace.

1:16–18: A reference to the transfiguration.

2:3: Much of the material of this chapter appears to be from the Letter of Jude.

3:16: *this* seems to refer to the theme of the end of the world and the Second Coming of Christ, about which Paul had written in his letters to the Thessalonians.

THE FIRST LETTER OF JOHN

1:1–7: Note the likeness with John's Gospel 1:1–18.

1:3, *fellowship*: A Johannine theme.

1:5, *light . . . darkness*: Another familiar theme in John's Gospel.

2:3: cf. the words of Jesus, "If you love me, you will keep my commandments" (Jn 14:15).

2:18, *the last hour*: John exhorts his readers to hold fast, as though the end were at hand.

3:6, *sins*: i.e., remains in sin, or has a habit of sin.

4:1, *test the spirits*: i.e., examine those who claim to have special gifts from the Holy Spirit; cf.1 Cor 14:32.

5:8, *There are three witnesses*: After these words, the Vulgate adds the following: "in heaven, the Father, the Word, and the Holy Ghost. And these three are one. And these are three that give testimony on

Explanatory Notes

earth." This passage, known as the Comma Johanneum or "The Three Heavenly Witnesses," is first found in the Latin (fourth century), and does not appear in any Greek New Testament manuscript before the sixteenth century. It is probably a marginal gloss which found its way into the text.

THE SECOND LETTER OF JOHN

1, *The elder*: Perhaps the head of the group or "college" of elders that presided over each Christian community. John was head not only of the Ephesus community but of all the communities in the province of Asia.
   the elect lady: Probably not an individual lady but a particular church or community in Asia.
13, *children*: i.e., the Christians of Ephesus.

THE THIRD LETTER OF JOHN

12, *Demetrius*: Evidently a leading Christian, recommended to Gaius.

THE LETTER OF JUDE

6: It is not clear to what Jude refers. Perhaps Gen 6:2 or the apocryphal Enoch, chapters 6–15.
9: Apparently a reference to another apocryphal work, the Assumption of Moses.

Headings added to the Biblical Text

JAMES

Greeting 1:1

1. OPENING INSTRUCTIONS
The value of suffering 1:2
The source of temptation 1:13
Doers of the word, not hearers only 1:19
Impartiality 2:1

2. FAITH AND GOOD WORKS
Faith without good works is dead 2:14
Examples from the Bible 2:20

3. PRACTICAL APPLICATIONS
Controlling one's tongue 3:1
True and false wisdom 3:13
The source of discord 4:1
Trust in divine providence 4:13
A warning to the rich 5:1

4. FINAL COUNSELS
A call for constancy 5:7
On oath-taking 5:12
The value of prayer. The sacrament of the Anointing of
    the Sick 5:13
Concern for one another 5:19

1 PETER

Greeting 1:1
Praise and thanksgiving to God 1:3

1. A CALL TO HOLINESS
Christians are called to be saints 1:13
The blood of Christ has ransomed us 1:17
Brotherly love 1:22
Like newborn babies 2:1
The priesthood that all believers share 2:4

2. THE OBLIGATIONS OF CHRISTIANS
Setting an example for pagans 2:11
Obedience to civil authority 2:13
Duties towards masters. Christ's example 2:18

Exemplary family life 3:1
Love of the brethren 3:8

3. THE CHRISTIAN'S ATTITUDE TO SUFFERING
Undeserved suffering is a blessing 3:13
Christ's suffering and glorification 3:18
The Christian has broken with sin 4:1
A call for charity 4:7
The Christian meaning of suffering 4:12

4. FINAL EXHORTATIONS
To priests 5:1
To all the faithful 5:5
Words of farewell 5:12

2 PETER

Greeting 1:1

1. A CALL TO FIDELITY
Divine largesse 1:3
Christian virtues 1:5
Spiritual testimony 1:12
The Transfiguration, an earnest of the Second Coming 1:16
Prophecy and the Second Coming 1:19

2. FALSE TEACHERS DENOUNCED
The harm done by false teachers 2:1

The punishment that awaits them 2:4
Their arrogance and immorality 2:10
Apostasy, a grave sin 2:20

3. THE SECOND COMING OF CHRIST
The teaching of Tradition 3:1
Mistaken notions 3:3
True teaching about the End 3:5
Moral lessons to be drawn 3:11
Final exhortation and doxology 3:17

Headings added to the Biblical Text

1 JOHN

Prologue 1:1

1. UNION WITH GOD
God is light 1:5
Walking in the light. Rejecting sin 1:6
Keeping the commandments 2:3
The apostle's confidence in the faithful 2:12
Detachment from the world 2:15
Not listening to heretics 2:18

2. LIVING AS GOD'S CHILDREN
We are children of God 3:1

A child of God does not sin 3:3
Loving one another 3:11

3. FAITH IN CHRIST. BROTHERLY LOVE
Faith in Christ, not in false prophets 4:1
God is love. Brotherly love, the mark of Christians 4:7
Everyone who believes in Jesus overcomes the world 5:1
Testimony borne to Christ 5:6

4. CONCLUSION
Prayer for sinners 5:14
The Christian's confidence as a child of God 5:18

2 JOHN

Greeting 1
The law of love 4

Precautions against heretics 7
Conclusion and greetings 12

3 JOHN

Greeting 1
Praise of Gaius 3
Diotrephes' misconduct 9

Commendation of Demetrius 11
Conclusion and farewell 13

JUDE

Greeting and blessing 1
His reason for writing 3

1. FALSE TEACHERS DENOUNCED
The punishment that awaits them 5
Their immorality 8
The judgment of God 14

2. EXHORTATION
False teachers were predicted 17
Faith, hope and charity 20
Attitude towards waverers 22
Final doxology 24

Sources quoted in the Navarre Bible
New Testament Commentary

1. DOCUMENTS OF THE CHURCH AND OF POPES

Benedict XII
Const. *Benedictus Deus*, 29 January 1336
Benedict XV
Enc. *Humani generis redemptionem*, 15 June 1917
Enc. *Spiritus Paraclitus*, 1 September 1920
Clement of Rome, St
Letter to the Corinthians
Constantinople, First Council of
Nicene-Constantinopolitan Creed
Constantinople, Third Council of
Definitio de duabus
in Christo voluntatibus et operationibus
Florence, Council of
Decree *Pro Jacobitis*
Laetentur coeli
Decree *Pro Armeniis*
John Paul II
Addresses and homilies
Apos. Exhort. *Catechesi tradendae*, 16 October
1979
Apos. Exhort. *Familiaris consortio*, 22 November
1981
Apos. Exhort. *Reconciliatio et paenitentia*, 2
December 1984
Apos. Letter. *Salvifici doloris*, 11 February 1984
Bull, *Aperite portas*, 6 January 1983
Enc. *Redemptor hominis*, 4 March 1979
Enc. *Dives in misericordia*, 30 November 1980
Enc. *Dominum et Vivificantem*, 30 May 1986
Enc. *Laborem exercens*, 14 September 1981
Letter to all priests, 8 April 1979
Letter to all bishops, 24 February 1980
Gelasius I
Ne forte
Gregory the Great, St
Epistula ad Theodorum medicum contra
Fabianum
Exposition on the Seven Penitential
Ne forte
In Evangelia homiliae
In Ezechielem homiliae
Moralia in Job

Regulae pastoralis liber
Innocent III
Letter *Eius exemplo*, 18 December 1208
John XXIII
Pacem in terris, 11 April 1963
Enc. *Ad Petri cathedram*, 29 June 1959
Lateran Council (649)
Canons
Leo the Great, St
Homilies and sermons
Licet per nostros
Promisisse mem=meni
Leo IX
Creed
Leo XIII
Enc. *Aeterni Patris*, 4 August 1879
Enc. *Immortale Dei*, 1 November 1885
Enc. *Libertas praestantissimum*, 20 June 1888
Enc. *Sapientiae christianae*, 18 January 1890
Enc. *Rerum novarum*, 15 May 1891
Enc. *Providentissimus Deus*, 18 November 1893
Enc. *Divinum illud munus*, 9 May 1897
Lateran, Fourth Council of (1215)
De fide catholica
Lyons, Second Council of (1274)
Doctrina de gratia
Profession of faith of Michael Palaeologue
Orange, Second Council of (529)
De gratia
Paul IV
Const. *Cum quorumdam*, 7 August 1555
Paul VI
Enc. *Ecclesiam suam*, 6 August 1964
Enc. *Mysterium fidei*, 9 September 1965
Apos. Exhort. *Marialis cultus*, 2 February 1967
Apos. Letter *Petrum et Paulum*, 27 February 1967
Enc. *Populorum progressio*, 26 March 1967
Enc. *Sacerdotalis coelibatus*, 24 June 1967
Creed of the People of God: Solemn Profession
of Faith, 30 June 1968
Apos. Letter *Octagesima adveniens*, 14 June
1971

Sources quoted in the Commentary

Apos. Exhort. *Gaudete in Domino*, 9 May 1975
Apos. Exhort. *Evangelii nuntiandi*, 8 Dec. 1975
Homilies and addresses
Pius V, St
*Catechism of the Council of Trent for Parish
    Priests* or *Pius V Catechism*
Pius IX, Bl.
Bull *Ineffabilis Deus*, 8 December 1854
Syllabus of Errors
Pius X, St
Enc. *E supreme apostolatus*, 4 October 1903
Enc. *Ad Diem illum*, 2 February 1904
Enc. *Acerbo nimis*, 15 April 1905
Catechism of Christian Doctrine, 15 July 1905
Decree *Lamentabili*, 3 July 1907
Enc. *Haerent animo*, 4 August 1908
Pius XI
Enc. *Quas primas*, 11 December 1925
Enc. *Divini illius magistri*, 31 December 1929
Enc. *Mens nostra*, 20 December 1929
Enc. *Casti connubii*, 31 December 1930
Enc. *Quadragesimo anno*, 15 May 1931
Enc. *Ad catholici sacerdotii*, 20 December 1935
Pius XII
Enc. *Mystici Corporis*, 29 June 1943
Enc. *Mediator Dei*, 20 November 1947
Enc. *Divino afflante Spiritu*, 30 September 1943
Enc. *Humani generis*, 12 August 1950
Apost. Const. *Menti nostrae*, 23 September 1950
Enc. *Sacra virginitas*, 25 March 1954
Enc. *Ad caeli Reginam*, 11 October 1954
Homilies and addresses
Quierzy, Council of (833)
*Doctrina de libero arbitrio hominis et de
    praedestinatione*
Trent, Council of (1545–1563)
De sacris imaginibus

De Purgatorio
De reformatione
De sacramento ordinis
De libris sacris
De peccato originale
De SS. Eucharistia
De iustificatione
De SS. Missae sacrificio
De sacramento matrimonio
Doctrina de peccato originali
Doctrina de sacramento extremae unctionis
Doctrina de sacramento paenitentiae
Toledo, Ninth Council of (655)
De Redemptione
Toledo, Eleventh Council of (675)
De Trinitate Creed
Valence, Third Council of (855)
De praedestinatione
Vatican, First Council of the (1869–1870)
Dogm. Const. *Dei Filius*
Dogm. Const. *Pastor aeternus*
Vatican, Second Council of the
    (1963–1965)
Const. *Sacrosanctum Concilium*
Decree *Christus Dominus*
Decl. *Dignitatis humanae*
Decl. *Gravissimum educationis*
Decl. *Nostrae aetate*
Decree *Optatam totius*
Decree *Ad gentes*
Decree *Apostolicam actuositatem*
Decree *Perfectae caritatis*
Decree *Presbyterorum ordinis*
Decree *Unitatis redintegratio*
Dogm. Const. *Dei Verbum*
Dogm. Const. *Lumen gentium*
Past. Const. *Gaudium et spes*

Liturgical Texts

Roman Missal: Missale Romanum, editio typica altera (Vatican City, 1975)
The Divine Office (London, Sydney, Dublin, 1974)

Other Church Documents

Code of Canon Law
Codex Iuris Canonici (Vatican City, 1983)
Congregation for the Doctrine of the Faith
Declaration concerning Sexual Ethics,
    December 1975
Instruction on Infant Baptism, 20 October 1980
Inter insigniores, 15 October 1976
*Letter on certain questions concerning
    Eschatology*, 17 May 1979

Libertatis conscientia, 22 March 1986
Sacerdotium ministeriale, 6 August 1983
Libertatis nuntius, 6 August 1984
Mysterium Filii Dei, 21 February 1972
Pontifical Biblical Commission
Replies
New Vulgate
*Nova Vulgata Bibliorum Sacrorum editio typica
    altera* (Vatican City, 1986)

Sources quoted in the Commentary

2. THE FATHERS, ECCLESIASTICAL WRITERS AND OTHER AUTHORS

Alphonsus Mary Liguori, St
Christmas Novena
The Love of Our Lord Jesus Christ reduced to
practice
Meditations for Advent
Thoughts on the Passion
Shorter Sermons
Sunday Sermons
Treasury of Teaching Material
Ambrose, St
De sacramentis
De mysteriis
De officiis ministrorum
Exameron
Expositio Evangelii secundum Lucam
Expositio in Ps 118
Treatise on the Mysteries
Anastasius of Sinai, St
Sermon on the Holy Synaxis
Anon.
Apostolic Constitutions
Didache, or *Teaching of the Twelve Apostles*
Letter to Diognetus
Shepherd of Hermas
Anselm, St
Prayers and Meditations
Aphraates
Demonstratio
Athanasius, St
Adversus Antigonum
De decretis nicaenae synodi
De Incarnatio contra arianos
Historia arianorum
Oratio I contra arianos
Oratio II contra arianos
Oratio contra gentes
Augustine, St
The City of God
Confessions
Contra Adimantum Manichaei discipulum
De Actis cum Felice Manicheo
De agone christiano
De bono matrimonii
De bono viduitatis
De catechizandis rudibus
De civitate Dei
De coniugiis adulterinis
De consensu Evangelistarum
De correptione et gratia
De doctrina christiana
De dono perseverantiae
De fide et operibus

De fide et symbolo
De Genesi ad litteram
De gratia et libero arbitrio
De natura et gratia
De praedestinatione sanctorum
De sermo Domini in monte
De spiritu et littera
De Trinitate
De verbis Domini sermones
Enarrationes in Psalmos
Enchiridion
Expositio epistulae ad Galatas
In I Epist. Ioann. ad Parthos
In Ioannis Evangelium tractatus
Letters
Quaestiones in Heptateuchum
Sermo ad Cassariensis Ecclesiae plebem
Sermo de Nativitate Domini
Sermons
Basil, St
De Spiritu Sancto
Homilia in Julittam martyrem
In Psalmos homiliae
Bede, St
Explanatio Apocalypsis
In Ioannis Evangelium expositio
In Lucae Evangelium expositio
In Marci Evangelium expositio
In primam Epistolam Petri
In primam Epistolam S. Ioanis
Sermo super Qui audientes gavisi sunt
Super Acta Apostolorum expositio
Super divi Iacobi Epistolam
Bernal, Salvador
Monsignor Josemaría Escrivá de Balaguer,
  Dublin, 1977
Bernard, St
Book of Consideration
De Beata Virgine
De fallacia et brevitate vitae
De laudibus novae militiae
Divine amoris
Meditationes piissimae de cognitionis humanae
  conditionis
Sermons on Psalm 90
Sermon on Song of Songs
Sermons
Bonaventure, St
In IV Libri sententiarum
Speculum Beatae Virgine
Borromeo, St Charles
Homilies

Sources quoted in the Commentary

Catherine of Siena, St
Dialogue
Cano, Melchor
De locis
Cassian, John
Collationes
De institutis coenobiorum
Clement of Alexandria
Catechesis III, De Baptismo
Commentary on Luke
Quis dives salvetur?
Stromata
Cyprian, St
De bono patientiae
De dominica oratione
De mortalitate
De opere et eleemosynis
De unitate Ecclesiae
De zelo et livore
Epist. ad Fortunatum
Quod idola dii non sint
Cyril of Alexandria, St
Commentarium in Lucam
Explanation of Hebrews
Homilia XXVIII in Mattheum
Cyril of Jerusalem, St
Catecheses
Mystagogical Catechesis
Diadochus of Photike
Chapters on Spiritual Perfection
Ephrem, St
Armenian Commentary on Acts
Commentarium in Epistolam ad Haebreos
Eusebius of Caesarea
Ecclesiastical History
Francis de Sales, St
Introduction to the Devout Life
Treatise on the Love of God
Francis of Assisi, St
Little Flowers
Reflections on Christ's Wounds
Fulgentius of Ruspe
Contra Fabianum libri decem
De fide ad Petrum
Gregory Nazianzen, St
Orationes theologicae
Sermons
Gregory of Nyssa, St
De instituto christiano
De perfecta christiana forma
On the Life of Moses
Oratio catechetica magna
Oratio I in beatitudinibus
Oratio I in Christi resurrectionem

Hippolytus, St
De consummatione saeculi
Ignatius of Antioch, St
Letter to Polycarp
Letters to various churches
Ignatius, Loyola, St
Spiritual Exercises
Irenaeus, St
Against Heresies
Proof of Apostolic Preaching
Jerome, St
Ad Nepotianum
Adversus Helvidium
Comm. in Ionam
Commentary on Galatians
Commentary on St Mark's Gospel
Contra Luciferianos
Dialogus contra pelagianos
Expositio in Evangelium secundum Lucam
Homilies to neophytes on Psalm 41
Letters
On Famous Men
John of Avila, St
Audi, filia
Lecciones sobre Gálatas
Sermons
John Chrysostom, St
Ante exilium homilia
Adversus Iudaeos
Baptismal Catechesis
De coemeterio et de cruce
De incomprehensibile Dei natura
De sacerdotio
De virginitate
Fifth homily on Anna
Hom. De Cruce et latrone
Homilies on St Matthew's Gospel, St John's
    Gospel, Acts of the Apostles, Romans,
    Ephesians, 1 and 2 Corinthians, Colossians,
    1 and 2 Timothy, 1 and 2 Thessalonians,
    Philippians, Philemon, Hebrews
II Hom. De proditione Iudae
Paraeneses ad Theodorum lapsum
Second homily in praise of St Paul
Sermon recorded by Metaphrastus
John of the Cross, St
A Prayer of the Soul enkindled by Love
Ascent of Mount Carmel
Dark Night of the Soul
Spiritual Canticle
John Damascene, St
De fide orthodoxa
John Mary Vianney, St
Sermons

Sources quoted in the Commentary

Josemaría Escrivá, St
Christ Is Passing By
Conversations
The Forge
Friends of God
Furrow
Holy Rosary
In Love with the Church
The Way
The Way of the Cross
Josephus, Flavius
Against Apion
Jewish Antiquities
The Jewish War
Justin Martyr, St
Dialogue with Tryphon
First and Second Apologies
à Kempis, Thomas
The Imitation of Christ
Luis de Granada, Fray
Book of Prayer and Meditation
Guide for Sinners
Introduccíon al símbolo de la fe
Life of Jesus Christ
Sermon on Public Sins
Suma de la vida cristiana
Luis de León, Fray
Exposición del Libro de Job
Minucius Felix
Octavius
Newman, J.H.
Biglietto Speech
Discourses to Mixed Congregations
Historical Sketches
Origen
Contra Celsum
Homilies on Genesis
Homilies on St John
In Exodum homiliae
Homiliae in Iesu nave
In Leviticum homiliae
In Matth. comm.
In Rom. comm.
Philo of Alexandria
De sacrificio Abel
Photius
Ad Amphilochium
Polycarp, St
Letter to the Philippians
del Portillo, A.
On Priesthood, Chicago, 1974
Primasius
Commentariorum super Apocalypsim B. Ioannis
  libri quinque
Prosper of Aquitaine, St
De vita contemplativa

Pseudo-Dionysius
De divinis nominibus
Pseudo-Macarius
Homilies
Severian of Gabala
Commentary on 1 Thessalonians
Teresa of Avila, St
Book of Foundations
Exclamations of the Soul to God
Interior Castle
Life
Poems
Way of Perfection
Tertullian
Against Marcion
Apologeticum
De baptismo
De oratione
Theodore the Studite, St
Oratio in adorationis crucis
Theodoret of Cyrrhus
Interpretatio Ep. ad Haebreos
Theophylact
Enarratio in Evangelium Marci
Thérèse de Lisieux, St
The Autobiography of a Saint
Thomas Aquinas, St
Adoro te devote
Commentary on St John = Super Evangelium S.
  Ioannis lectura
Commentaries on St Matthew's Gospel, Romans,
  1 and 2 Corinthians, Galatians, Ephesians,
  Colossians, Philippians, 1 and 2 Timothy,
  1 and 2 Thessalonians, Titus, Hebrews
De veritate
Expositio quorumdam propositionum ex Epistola
  ad Romanos
On the Lord's Prayer
On the two commandments of Love and the ten
  commandments of the Law
Summa contra gentiles
Summa theologiae
Super Symbolum Apostolorum
Thomas More, St
De tristitia Christi
Victorinus of Pettau
Commentary on the Apocalypse
Vincent Ferrer, St
Treatise on the Spiritual Life
Vincent of Lerins, St
Commonitorium
Zosimus, St
Epist. Enc. "Tractoria" ad Ecclesias Orientales

217